CONNECTING PEOPLE WITH TECHNOLOGY

Issues in Professional Communication

Edited by
George F. Hayhoe and Helen M. Grady
Mercer University School of Engineering

Baywood's Technical Communications Series
Series Editor: CHARLES H. SIDES

Baywood Publishing Company, Inc.
AMITYVILLE, NEW YORK

Baywood Publishing Company, Inc.
26 Austin Avenue
P.O. Box 337
Amityville, NY 11701
(800) 638-7819
E-mail: baywood@baywood.com
Web site: baywood.com

Library of Congress Catalog Number: 2008013541
ISBN: 978-0-89503-375-8

Library of Congress Cataloging-in-Publication Data

Connecting people with technology : issues in professional communication / edited by George F. Hayhoe and Helen M. Grady.
        p. cm. -- (Baywood's technical communications series)
    Includes bibliographical references and index.
    ISBN 978-0-89503-375-8 (hbk. : alk. paper) 1. Communication of technical information. I. Hayhoe, George F. II. Grady Helen M., 1953-

    T10.5.C63 2008
    601'.4--dc22

                                                          2008013541

Table of Contents

PART III: HEALTH AND SAFETY: INFORMING SOCIETY OF RISKS AND DANGERS

PART IV. BIOTECHNOLOGY: REPORTING ITS POTENTIAL AND ITS PROBLEMS

PART V. CORPORATE ENVIRONMENT: IMPROVING COMMUNICATION

Introduction

George F. Hayhoe and Helen M. Grady

HOW THIS COLLECTION EVOLVED

Technical and professional communicators today face a host of challenges, and information about these challenges and ways that we can respond to them is published in a diverse array of sources. This book explores a number of these important areas where technology impacts society and suggests ways that human communication can facilitate the use of that technology.

We perceived the need for this collection after our experience serving as program chair and proceedings chair for the 2005 IEEE International Professional Communication Conference (IPCC 2005) in Limerick, Ireland. We believed that an anthology that would make available essays on the cutting-edge topics presented at that conference by acknowledged experts in their fields would have great value to both practitioners in industry and students preparing for careers in technical and professional communication. We asked the authors of some of the best papers at that conference to revise and update their manuscripts for inclusion in this anthology.

WHY WE SELECTED THE TOPICS

We chose five topic areas based on their importance to our profession: usability, globalization, health and safety, biotechnology, and corporate communication.

Usability has become a foundational discipline in technical and professional communication that grows out of our rhetorical roots, which emphasize purpose and audience. As our appreciation of audience has grown beyond engineers and scientists to lay users of technology, our appreciation of the diversity of those audiences in terms of age, geography, and other factors has similarly expanded. Just as importantly, our focus on usability has established and strengthened connections between technical and professional communication and human/computer interface design, cognitive psychology, instructional design, and other disciplines.

We are also coming to grips with what Thomas Friedman calls the "flat world." This flat world paradigm influences how we communicate with members of other cultures and speakers of other languages. And because most of the flatteners either are technologies themselves or are technology-driven, technical and professional communicators need to leverage these technologies to serve global audiences.

Similarly, we are inundated with information about world crises involving health and safety issues. These crises are driven by the effects of terrorism, the aging population, HIV/AIDS, and both human-made and natural disasters. These issues are becoming more visible because they are literally matters of life and death. Furthermore, they are of special concern to audiences whom technical and professional communicators have little experience in targeting—the shapers of public policy, seniors, adolescents, and those impacted by disaster. Our awareness of these nontraditional audiences and the need to communicate effectively with them results from communication channels such as cable network news and the Internet. As these nontraditional audiences become increasingly visible, technical and professional communicators need to develop skills to communicate effectively with them.

Biotechnology is another arena that has provided new roles for technical and professional communicators. We are only beginning to understand how to communicate the science accurately without either deceiving or panicking our audience. We need to develop a more sophisticated understanding of how communication can shape reactions to biotechnology developments. Confronting this complex network of issues, we're challenged to fashion both our message and the audience's perceptions ethically.

Finally, today's corporate environment is being shaped by technology and the global nature of business. Technical and professional communicators can play a role in capturing and managing knowledge, in using technology effectively in the virtual workplace, and in understanding how language shapes organizational culture.

These five topics were well represented among the presentations at IPCC 2005. The authors we invited to contribute to this volume were often acknowledged experts on these issues, many of whom had written monographs targeting these issues. We believe that their insights presented at Limerick are worthy of a wider audience, and thus we have prepared this collection of essays that they have revised and updated from the original versions published in the conference proceedings.

WHAT YOU'LL FIND IN THESE PAGES

Usability

In "Making Connections: Teaming Up to Connect Users, Developers, and Usability Experts," Carol Barnum and her colleagues tell the story of a collaboration of stakeholders in redesigning a product to make it more accessible to less technical users. They demonstrate the potential of usability testing as part of a user-centered design process that can actually change an organization's attitudes as it improves the product for customers.

Whitney Quesenbery's "Usability Standards: Connecting Practice Around the World" explores whether choices of usability methods, techniques, and processes depend on context and country. Her examination of national and international standards and guidelines considers how effective they have been in fostering good usability practice and creating international consensus on practice.

To demonstrate how usability studies can leverage technology, seven researchers at the University of Washington analyzed the logs of remote users' Web-browsing behaviors. Their research into how users navigate through complex information, reported in "Conducting an Automated Experiment over the Internet to Assess Navigation Design for a Medical Web Site Containing Multi-Page Articles," is significant because it sampled large numbers of users in a natural environment rather than a usability lab.

Seniors are a new and growing user group for a variety of technical products, and they often experience more problems than other users. Thus, Floor van Horen and colleagues' "Manuals for the Elderly: Text Characteristics That Help or Hinder Older Users" contributes significantly to our understanding of how to make instructions more helpful to this crucial audience.

Globalization

In Reinhard Schäler's "Communication as a Key to Global Business," a summary of his keynote address at IPCC 2005, he argues that communication is the tie that binds our global community. It must be conducted in such a way that its content is accessible to all and respectful of local languages and cultures. Schäler maintains that localization is the key enabler for making connections in the digital world and provides arguments based on mainstream localization practice for those wondering whether they should localize their digital content.

Marie-Louise Flacke also believes that localization is essential. In "The Hidden Costs of Cross-cultural Documentation," she asserts that going beyond translation and providing an effective localization for each target country is the key to successful global marketing. Project managers who neglect cultural, legal, and geographic aspects of a target country might damage the company's image and increase localization costs. She advocates including local experts in the localization team and setting up a direct connection between management and country specialists as a way to achieve cost-effective localization.

Further information on how to minimize translation costs is provided by Margaretha Eriksson in "How to Save Time and Money by Connecting the Writing Process to the Update and Translation Process." She discusses how translation memories, which allow the re-use of phrases that have already been translated, can save both time and money in the translation process. Eriksson offers technical communicators a number of practical tips for incorporating translation memory in the document translation cycle.

In "Technical Communication and Cross-cultural Miscommunication: User Culture and the Outsourcing of Writing," Joseph Jeyaraj discusses another aspect of globalization, which results when individuals in one culture may not only be maintaining business processes and designing new products for those in another, but also producing the documentation for those products and business processes. He argues that when documentation and processes are outsourced, cultural miscommunication often arises because writing is a culturally situated activity, and offers suggestions for making writing more culturally situated.

Finally, in "Presenting in English to International Audiences: A Critical Survey of Published Advice and Actual Practice," Thomas Orr and his colleagues discuss how English has become the *lingua franca* of presentations to international audiences. As a result, speakers as well as listeners may be required to function in English, with limited abilities in the language. This chapter summarizes a study comparing and contrasting advice form books and journal articles on oral presentations, published in English and Japanese, with actual presentations given by nonnative English speakers. General guidelines for making successful oral presentations to international audiences are included.

Health and Safety

Expert testimony at governmental hearings shapes the perceptions of both policymakers and the general public. In "Public Professional Communication in the Anti-terror Age: A Discourse Analysis," Catherine Smith demonstrates that when the topic is terrorism, it can be vitally important to recognize the functions of perspective in public discourse to communicate skepticism of or disagreement with prevailing views in helping to formulate policy. Helping prepare this very specialized audience for testimony by giving them the tools that they need to analyze public policy discourse is an important new role for teachers and trainers in the field of technical and professional communication.

Whether the disaster results from tsunamis or famine, from ethnic cleansing or religious persecution, effective information and communication systems play a vital role in saving lives and relieving suffering. In "Challenges to Effective Information and Communication Systems in Humanitarian Relief Organizations," Christina Maiers and colleagues explore the major issues and challenges inherent in developing an effective system within nongovernmental organizations providing humanitarian relief that involve not only information technology but also people, practices, policies, and organizational environments.

Michaël Steehouder's "Using Role Sets to Engage and Persuade Visitors to Web Sites That Promote Safe Sex" addresses communication with adolescents about the dangers of unsafe sex. Promoting safe sexual behavior is difficult because of the face-threatening nature of such messages. Steehouder argues that creating appropriate author and reader roles can be an effective way of overcoming this problem.

Finally, in "Physicians and Patients: How Professionals Build Relationships Through Rapport Management," Kim Sydow Campbell analyses doctor-patient interaction, a very important type of professional communication. Drawing on concepts of rapport management from sociolinguistics, she demonstrates that success or failure in establishing good rapport is often based on the verbal communication techniques employed by physicians.

Biotechnology

In "Connecting Popular Culture and Science: The Case of Biotechnology," Susan Allender-Hagedorn and Cheryl Ruggiero analyze the influence of biotechnology on popular culture, such as films and cartoons, and then consider how texts from popular culture appeal to biotechnologists in the scientific marketplace via advertisements that draw on popular films, television shows, and music. Their approach, intended to broaden the appreciation of scientific audience, will be of interest to those who work for companies that manufacture scientific equipment or supplies, that purchase such commodities, or that need to communicate with peer organizations or with the public about research results.

Steven Katz's "Biotechnology and Global Miscommunication with the Public: Rhetorical Assumptions, Stylistic Acts, Ethical Implications" analyzes the assumptions embedded in the language used in reports by the Canadian Biotechnology Advisory Board. He effectively demonstrates that the language used reflects values and assumptions that negatively affect the public, and that the risk model of communication that is commonly used with the public about biotechnology is both rhetorically and ethically flawed.

The last chapter in this section, Dale Sullivan's "The Need for Technical Communicators as Facilitators of Negotiation in Controversial Technology Transfer Cases" examines Monsanto's attempt to release transgenic wheat in the upper midwestern United States and the failure of efforts to accommodate public concern. He explores the potential for technical communicators to facilitate negotiations between stakeholders.

Corporate Environment

Technical and professional communicators often work in complex and technologically sophisticated organizations. The six chapters in this section of the anthology describe various aspects of communicating in such organizations. First, Paul Dombrowski's "Technical Language: Learning from the *Columbia* and *Challenger* Reports" analyzes the consequences of taking technical language as more definite, unequivocal, and agreed-upon than it really is through his study of the communication processes that occurred during the *Columbia* and *Challenger* space shuttle tragedies. His analysis of these tragedies highlights how the vagaries of language use and organizational culture help shape technical discourse.

Judith Strother and Svafa Grönfeldt's "The Theoretical Foundations of Service Leadership: A New Paradigm" provides an example of the challenge of developing a new paradigm and communicating it to the international business community. Service leadership is just such a paradigm, which incorporates a multidisciplinary approach to embedding empowered leadership within a service organization's culture. They discuss how effective communication is essential to helping an organization achieve a high level of service quality and customer satisfaction.

Communication is also essential between members of multidisciplinary teams involved in product development. In "Managing Collaboration: Adding Communication and Documentation Environment to a Product Development Cycle," Laura Batson and Susan Feinberg describe a communication and documentation model used to produce e-learning computer games. Their model provides a process for managing a project with a high turnover rate of multidisciplinary specialists.

Team members or co-workers who are not co-located and who may come from various national and cultural backgrounds face another set of communication challenges. Kirk St.Amant examines five of the problematic communication areas related to international virtual offices (IVOs) and provides technical communicators with strategies for working efficiently in this international environment in "Virtual Office Communication Protocols: A System for Managing International Virtual Teams."

Knowledge management has been touted as one of the key differentiators in developing, sustaining, and improving technology-dependent businesses. David Harvey and Robert Holdsworth identify and discuss several knowledge management challenges for aerospace companies and the need for such companies to have a clear understanding of what can be achieved (and at what cost) through knowledge management initiatives in their chapter "Knowledge Management in the Aerospace Industry."

Knowledge management is also key for organizations that are focused on maintaining the environment and the health of individuals. In the last chapter, "Using Their Digital Notes: Three Cases to Make Tacit Knowledge Visible in a Web-based Surrounding," Liesbeth Rentinck discusses how the National Institute for Health and Environment in the Netherlands is using an XML database extracted directly from the work of scientists to enable the sharing of implicit and tacit knowledge in that organization.

Where the Conversation Goes from Here

We hope that this anthology will provide insights into emerging facets of technical and professional communication practice. These facets, defined by the intersection of technology and people, result in new opportunities for technical and professional communicators to address new audiences and new subject domains. We believe that by connecting people and technology, technical and professional communicators will play a critical role in contributing to the success of businesses and improving the quality of human life.

PART I

Usability:
Making Technology Fit Its Users

CHAPTER 1

Making Connections: Teaming Up to Connect Users, Developers, and Usability Experts

Carol Barnum, David Dayton,
Kevin Gillis, and Joe O'Connor

IPSWITCH AND ITS
PRODUCT DEVELOPMENT PROCESS

Ipswitch, Inc. is a private software company established in 1991 and based in Lexington, Massachusetts, with research and development in Augusta and Atlanta, Georgia, and a sales office in Amsterdam, the Netherlands. The company, which specializes in client and server products for Internet file transfer, network monitoring, and messaging, has established a strong presence in the small and medium businesses market. By late 2003 it had developed three mature product lines, each at version 8, without the benefit of formal usability testing.

Although informal, internal usability testing had been done on a few occasions, it was not until R&D planned for a major release of the WS_FTP Pro product that formal usability testing was put on the agenda for the first time. Ipswitch began to search in earnest for an external vendor to provide the usability testing.

IPSWITCH'S COLLABORATION WITH THE
USABILITY CENTER AT SOUTHERN POLYTECHNIC

The Usability Center at Southern Polytechnic (http://usability.spsu.edu), one of three vendors receiving RFPs for the work, impressed the Ipswitch visiting team because of its prior software product experience, its full-solution collaborative process, and its state-of-the-art facility, especially its large and comfortable

user groups / user profiles

executive viewing room. Location was also a plus, as the Ipswitch R&D group was in Augusta, Georgia, a two-hour drive from The Usability Center, and one product group was located nearby in suburban Atlanta. Ipswitch wanted a vendor that could manage the project, but would also work as a team with the product experts. They also wanted as many employees as possible to participate and observe the testing firsthand. Southern Polytechnic's process and facilities met these goals.

The product to be tested was the pending major release of WS_FTP Pro, the industry leader and most-used commercial FTP client, which was being redesigned to have a new look and feel to address the criticisms that the user interface was difficult for new users and that it was "dated." The product team did not have direct or detailed feedback from users and was left to guess at what changes would help the situation. Thus, usability testing for WS_FTP Pro was deemed essential. The users would be the judge!

When Ipswitch approached The Usability Center about conducting a single test of the WS_FTP Pro product, they were wary about testing early prototypes, thinking that they needed the product further along in development to be able to gauge the issues for users. In the initial meeting, the usability experts asked the question: What will Ipswitch do with the findings from a late-stage usability test of its product? The response: Except for the quick fixes that could be handled right away, Ipswitch would use the information for the next release.

Southern Polytechnic suggested: Why not do an earlier test in some prototype phase, then iterate the design and test again to see whether Ipswitch got it right? Ipswitch was uncertain about this approach, but Southern Polytechnic convinced them of its viability. Thus, it was agreed in late November 2003 that the first of two tests of WS_FTP would take place in January 2004, focusing on two user groups: the professional (business) user and a new "home" user, a novice to FTP.

Members from The Usability Center and Ipswitch's development groups formed a team. With Carol Barnum leading the collaborative effort to plan the test, the team defined the specific user profile for each group, created the tasks and built the scenarios, designed the pretest, posttask, and posttest questionnaires, and planned the approach to analyzing the results. The Extended University, which administers The Usability Center, took charge of recruiting to match the specific user profile for each group.

Three key components led to a successful collaboration:

1. Development of the user profiles, scenarios, and questionnaires was a joint effort, with Southern Polytechnic providing the usability expertise, and Ipswitch providing the product knowledge.
2. The logging was also a key component of the testing process, as the log forms the basis for a detailed analysis of the findings from each user. Using the rich qualitative process established by The Usability Center, David Dayton logged each user's interactions along with any relevant comments or questions from team members in the control room. As a bottom-up approach was used to collate the findings, the team's review of the logs was critical to achieving a consensus in detecting and naming the issues experienced by users, as well as

categories / *findings*

highlighting the positive experiences. The first round of testing produced more than 100 findings, grouped into fewer than 10 categories, including mental model, learnability, terminology, interface, feedback, and so forth. These categories then became the standard for later tests.

More than 30 different employees observed one or two days of testing from the executive viewing room, including the company president, Roger Greene, and vice president of research and development, Mary Beth Westmoreland, whose commitment to the testing had been firm and enthusiastic. So much discussion ensued among the developers and other observers during the test sessions that it was decided to kick off the findings meetings in the executive viewing room with each person's observations about the most important (or surprising) thing they observed. After that, the core team from Ipswitch and The Usability Center went into the detailed analysis session, which took several hours. Videotapes were handed off to the company and reviewed again by the president, plus others who had not attended; a report was submitted a week later, documenting the process, the user groups, the scenarios, and the findings.

3. A significant challenge was to incorporate the findings into the next iteration of the product. The usability team focused on findings, and deliberately stayed away from solutions. Ben Henderson, development manager at Ipswitch, participated in every step of the usability test. He then created a matrix that mapped the findings to the product's design documents and led the product design team through an iterative process to address each of the findings.

ROUND 1: MAJOR FINDINGS

The usability testing brought forth much more than the broad comments R&D had heard about the dated, too technical interface. As the users worked through tasks in the test scenarios, it became clear to the observers that there were issues with mental model, navigation and system feedback, and work flow.

The Missing Mental Model

The connection wizard is the first set of screens that the user sees on completing installation. Its purpose is to get users connected to an FTP server so they can transfer files. Reactions from most of the new users revealed that the connection wizard did not fit their mental model of what the software was supposed to do. The terminology, task sequence, and feedback left them confused about what it meant to set up a "site" and the difference between the site name and the site address (see Figure 1). When users did understand the connection concept, they failed to note that they were also saving the information as a site (like a favorite) that they could quickly connect to again.

The solution was to clarify the presentation in the connection wizard (see Figure 2) and to provide a getting-started tour that introduces key concepts.

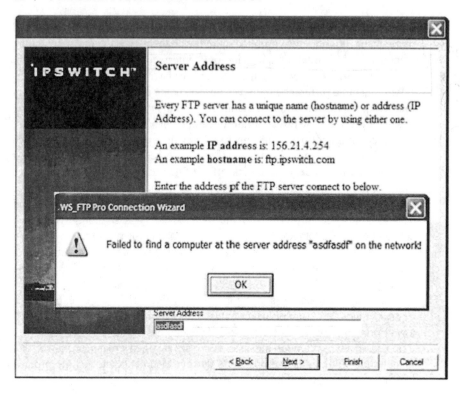

Figure 1. Before testing: Connection Wizard failed to anticipate
new users' mental model.
© 2008 by Ipswitch, Inc. used with permission.

Navigation and Feedback Issues

While mental model issues were a sticking point for novice users, advanced users experienced problems with navigation and feedback. The prototype used multiple windows to show the directory/file lists for two or more FTP connections, in conformance with Microsoft's Multiple Document Interface (MDI).

Nevertheless, the WS_FTP Pro users, all of whom had 7+ years of IT experience, had difficulty navigating the windows in the MDI format (see Figure 3). Some tried to view all windows at once by tiling them, but then had to scroll in the smaller windows. Another resized windows and overlapped them, then lost track of which window represented which FTP connection. Another copied from one window, then clicked around until he found the other connection. All expressed frustration as they experienced these navigation problems, muttering comments such as "Where is the site?," "Now how do I get these to the other site?," and "I wish I could drag these to the site" (actually, the user could, but it did not look possible).

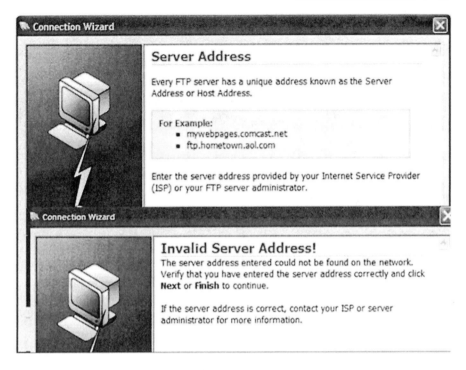

Figure 2. After testing: Connection Wizard helps new users
understand "server address."
© 2008 by Ipswitch, Inc. used with permission.

The solution for the Pro version of the product was to use tabs to represent each FTP connection and the local file system (see Figure 4).

Overly Complex Work Flow

An innovative feature of the FTP product for advanced users was the ability to encrypt an FTP connection and encrypt files using OpenPGP (pretty good privacy), an encryption method based on standards set by the OpenPGP Working Group of the Internet Engineering Task Force. Most of the advanced users were new to PGP but had worked with other encryption methods, and yet none of them successfully completed the tasks in the PGP scenario. Actions and comments indicated that even when the task was understood, the user could not make sense of the many paths available in the PGP dialogs. The workflow to accomplish the task was not understood. User comments included "PeeGeePee" (as if to say, "I've never seen this acronym before"); "What's the difference between 'trust' and 'sign'?"; and "This [application] should step me through the process; I understand PGP, but can't figure out this interface." The solution for this roadblock to usability was to develop a PGP setup wizard that walks the user through the process.

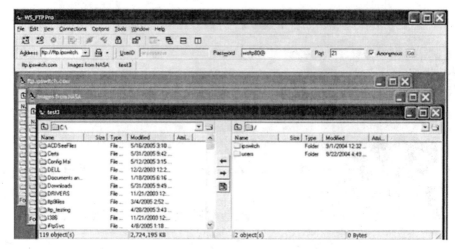

Figure 3. Before testing: Multiple FTP connections frustrated users.
© 2008 by Ipswitch, Inc. used with permission.

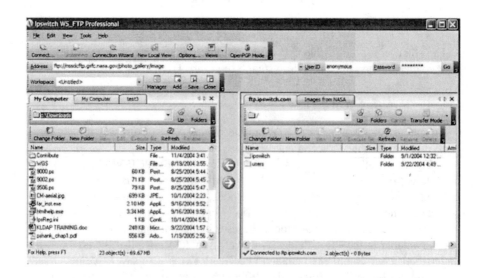

Figure 4. After testing: Tabbed interface for multiple FTP
connections proved easier to use.
© 2008 by Ipswitch, Inc. used with permission.

ROUND 2: RETEST THE REDESIGN

The major discovery from the first round of testing was that even highly technical users needed and asked for help in the form of wizards or getting started guides for aspects of the product that were unfamiliar to them, such as the innovative tool for encrypting files with PGP. This became clear to the product team only after they observed these users and heard them talk about their frustrations and desires.

Several months after the prototype test, the redesign was tested with both the home (novice) and technical (advanced) user groups. Here's what we observed from these users:

- The startup wizard made the first time experience a positive one.
- The getting started guide provided the mental model for the process and approach to the interface.
- Tabs made the interface intuitive and easy to navigate (replacing the initial MDI design).
- The PGP setup wizard made a confusing concept and process clear.

CULTURAL CHANGE AT IPSWITCH

The first test of the Ipswitch WS_FTP product was described as an "eye opener" by many of the observers. The product team, upon seeing users work with the product, immediately recognized how different the user's view was from their own view. Throughout the testing, ideas for improvements percolated among the team in the observation room. The product team embraced the findings from usability testing and went to work on plans for the redesign of selected features.

Since that first successful test, Ipswitch and The Usability Center at Southern Polytechnic have teamed up to test other products, including WS_FTP Server and WhatsUp Professional. What's more, a cultural change began to take place at Ipswitch, with usability testing helping to move the company toward a user-centered design process. In particular, usability became part of the product development cycle through incorporation into the product requirements document, the seminal document that guides major software releases. Also, "usability" is now a bug category in Ipswitch's defect tracking system. And "mental model" has become an often-heard expression in discussions of products at Ipswitch product planning meetings.

SOME RESULTS FROM AN INTERNAL SURVEY

We believed that the product improvements resulting from companywide involvement in usability testing produced changes in attitudes toward usability testing among developers and other employees of Ipswitch. To investigate that perception, we administered an online survey, and 96 Ipswitch employees responded—about a 64% response rate. In a nutshell, the results revealed that Ipswitch employees held a strongly positive view of usability testing, and among those who knew about the testing conducted at Southern Polytechnic, most were overwhelmingly positive about it.

Likert-scale opinion items in the survey were adapted from a survey of software developers reported by Frick, Boling, Kim, Oswald, Sugar, and Zazelenchuk (2001). The degree to which opinions were positive toward usability testing varied across the Likert-scale attitude statements (see Table 1). The ranked scores on those items suggested that concerns about perceived tradeoffs of usability testing—additional work, time, and costs—weakened the strength of pro-usability attitudes.

Both the Likert-scale items and especially the open-ended responses revealed that several developers were skeptical about the ultimate value of usability testing. The number of respondents with negative attitudes, however, was more than matched by respondents who were positive about usability testing and wanted Ipswitch to do much more to incorporate usability into product development.

Eight to One, Positive to Negative

Question 11 on the survey asked all respondents to "sum up your opinions about the effects of usability testing on product development and product quality at Ipswitch." About three-fourths of the respondents (76) wrote something in response. We categorized their messages as follows:

11 Didn't know enough to give an opinion
 2 No opinion
 2 Strongly negative
 5 Mildly negative
23 Generally positive statements
24 Strongly positive statements
 9 Positive and wanted stronger usability effort

In sum, positive usability-testing statements outnumbered negative statements 8 to 1. Table 2 presents sample responses from some of the categories listed above.

The survey asked respondents who had observed usability testing, either at Southern Polytechnic or before being hired at Ipswitch, this question: "Did observing usability tests change your opinions at all about usability testing?" Three of 13 respondents (23%) who had observed usability tests before hiring on at Ipswitch and who had not observed tests at Southern Polytechnic said that observing usability tests had changed their opinions about usability testing. To the same question, 8 of 20 respondents (40%) who had observed usability testing for the first time at The Usability Center said that the experience had changed their opinions.

Getting the Word Out—Inside the Company

Because so many people from Ipswitch observed the usability testing at Southern Polytechnic, we were surprised that the extent of Ipswitch's usability testing efforts at The Usability Center and the impact of the test results on product design were unknown to 13 of the survey's respondents, including two senior software developers, a member of upper management, and two members of the marketing team. In addition, about one-third of the 68 respondents (24) who had not observed

Table 1. Rank Order of Initial Nine Likert-Scale Items by
Strength of Pro-Usability Attitudes

Question 10 opinion statements in descending order of mean score on 1-5 scale with 5 = most positive	Positives minus Negatives[a]	Neutral and "No Opinion" answers	Mean ($n = 94$)
Usability testing by Ipswitch . . .			
should be used more often	+70	22	4.46
has made development teams more concerned about usability	+70	33	4.36
has not been worth the effort	+61	25	4.27
has improved ease-of-use of products tested	+65	22	4.19
has improved usefulness of products tested	+57	33	4.07
has made development teams more customer-centered	+47	31	3.82
has hurt cost-effectiveness[b]	+30	54	3.79
has showed down product development[b]	+7	47	3.20
has made extra work for developers[b]	−6	45	3.03

[a]The number of answers on the side of the Likert scale reflecting a positive-toward-usability-testing attitude minus the number of answers on the side of the Likert scale reflecting a negative-toward-usability-testing attitude.

[b]Negative statements about usability testing; responses to these were reverse coded so that a higher score reflects a pro-usability-testing attitude. For these items, then, a higher score indicates more disagreement than agreement with a *negative* statement about usability testing.

or taken part in usability testing at Southern Polytechnic indicated that they knew only that usability testing had taken place; they didn't know much more than that.

One repercussion of our survey was to make Ipswitch employees more aware of and knowledgeable about usability testing and its impact. One lesson learned by Ipswitch was that it needed to make sure employees, customers, and potential customers learned the story of its successful collaboration with The Usability Center at Southern Polytechnic.

SUCCESS METRICS

Internal satisfaction with usability testing and the incorporation of a user-centered design process is a positive outcome of usability testing. But if it doesn't improve the bottom line, it won't last. Thus, success metrics are critical to understanding usability testing's real value.

Like many software companies, Ipswitch offers a 30-day free evaluation of its products. Therefore, the major metric for success is based on conversion rates (the percentage of free-demo users who purchase the product). For WS_FTP Home, the first new Ipswitch product to be usability tested before release, the conversion rate in its first half-year on the market was about 45% more than Ipswitch typically achieved for WS_FTP Professional and WS_FTP Server.

Table 2. Examples of Responses Summing Up Opinions
about Usability Testing

Strongly negative	I think in some cases (WS_FTP) the Usability review went too far. Too many advanced features were hidden, making the product more difficult to use by a knowledgeable person.
Mildly negative	The jury is out on this. I will wait for more feedback. I think that there was some functionality left out of the [WhatsUp Pro] product, because of the testing. The functionality missing is more of a troubleshooting, power-user functions that a casual user wouldn't be interested in.
Generally positive	I have seen WS_FTP and the WhatsUp line UIs [user interfaces] improve.
Strongly positive	Can't believe we survived so long without it! This has been a worthwhile initiative and welcome change to the product development process. I think the key was that both Development (especially product development and information development) and Product Manager embraced and wanted to move forward with user-centered testing.
Positive, wants more	While I hold a high opinion on the effects of usability testing, I have concerns that it may be relegated to a post-production process and not an approach in design.

Ipswitch's WS_FTP Server product also benefited from design changes due to usability testing in 2004, and the conversion rate for the year was up 33%, though some of that improvement was due to marketing changes that reduced the number of novices downloading WS_FTP Server when they really wanted to download and evaluate WS_FTP Pro or Home.

Another typical metric for usability effectiveness is a reduction in tech support calls. For the WS_FTP products in 2004, the number of users and overall revenue grew, but the skill level dropped because of the many new home users. Nevertheless, the number of technical support calls stayed constant despite changes predicting greater demand for technical support: more complex features in WS_FTP Pro and greater restrictions on technical support availability when Ipswitch ended free e-mail support and required Pro 9 users to pay extra for 12 months of support. The result, as expected, was that customers paying for support were more likely to use the support they had already paid for.

Before it turned to formal usability testing, Ipswitch had set out to broaden the appeal of its products. Our survey showed that the prevailing opinion within the company was that usability testing had been a huge step in the right direction, and most in the company believed that the benefits of usability testing extended to products designed for all levels of users, from novice to advanced.

CONCLUSION

It's relatively easy to conduct a usability test, whether internally or with a vendor. It's challenging but highly beneficial to make changes to the product with the information from the test. What's more difficult to accomplish is a change in process and perspective, one that moves from speculation about users to confirmation of user preferences and approaches, which is then built into design from the ground up.

We believe that this was accomplished as a result of collaboration between essential stakeholders at Ipswitch and The Usability Center at Southern Polytechnic. The collaboration involved in planning, testing, and analyzing usability findings led to education and learning within Ipswitch and to a new emphasis on usability in product design. The collaboration led to an improved understanding and appreciation of the needs of customers, both current and prospective. And the collaboration led to an increased desire to learn more about users through contextual inquiry and other user-research methods.

REFERENCE

Frick, T., Boling, E., Kim, K. J., Oswald, D., Sugar, W., & Zazelenchuk, T. (2001). Software developers' attitudes toward user-centered design, 2000. In *Proceedings of AECT 2001 Conference* (pp. 140-146). Association for Educational Communications and Technology, Atlanta, Georgia.
http://education.indiana.edu/~frick/aect2001/theodorefrick_softwaredevelopersattitudes.doc

CHAPTER 2

Usability Standards: Connecting Practice Around the World

Whitney Quesenbery

Design and usability standards are difficult to create and hard to enforce. Although many groups have tried to create general design standards or patterns, the diversity of industry and content has made it difficult to create strong standards to embody usability knowledge and practice.

We will look at three popular usability standards and two governmental programs, and consider how effective they have been in both fostering good usability practice and in creating an international consensus on practice.

THREE USABILITY STANDARDS

There are several standards that have been influential in shaping international understanding of usability and user-centered design, and in formalizing ad hoc practices. Three of them take very different approaches to standardization. By looking at what they attempted to standardize and how well they have been adopted by industry, we can see some of the strengths and weaknesses of standards as an influence on industry practice. The three standards we will examine are

- ISO 13407:1999—*Human-centred Design Process for Interactive Systems*
- ISO 25062:2006—*Common Industry Format (CIF) for Usability Test Reports*
- WAI—*The W3C Web Accessibility Initiative*

A User-Centered Design Process

User-centered design is the common name for a process for designing the user interface for software and other products. The term *user-centered design* is widely used in industry although there is no formal definition beyond some general shared values. It is often described as a way to accomplish usability (Wikipedia, 2006). The Usability Professionals' Association (2006) Web site says, "User-centered design (UCD) is an approach to design that grounds the process in information about the people who will use the product. UCD processes focus on users through the planning, design and development of a product."

In 1999 an International Organization for Standardization (ISO) standard, ISO 13407:1999, *Human-centred Design Processes for Interactive Systems*, was approved (ISO, 1999); it embodies the general industry approach to UCD. It is a short generic description of the process that can be applied to any system or product.

The standard describes four principles of human-centred design (User Focus, 2006):

1. Active involvement of customers (or those who speak for them)
2. Appropriate allocation of function (making sure human skill is used properly)
3. Iteration of design solutions (therefore, allow time in project planning)
4. Multidisciplinary design (but beware overly large design teams)

The core of the standard is the description of five activities, four of which interlock and form the basis for an iterative approach to the requirements-design test cycle (see Figure 1).

The activities in ISO 13407 are iterative, repeating the cycle until the program meets usability and business goals.

1. Acknowledge the need for user-centered design and plan for it.
2. Understand and specify the context of use.
3. Specify user requirements.
4. Produce design solutions.
5. Evaluate designs against requirements.

Acceptance of ISO 13407

A brief examination of presentations on user-centered design at industry conferences easily shows the influence of this standard. Whether it is mentioned by name or whether the process described simply mirrors the one in the standard, it is clear that the industry has embraced at least the principles and broad outline of this standard. The standard has also found acceptance in government documents. The Quality Framework for U.K. Government Web sites (E-Government Unit, 2003), published by the office of the E-Envoy, says that "Underpinning this is an increasing focus on human centred design issues, supported by the standards ISO13407 and ISO TR 18529."

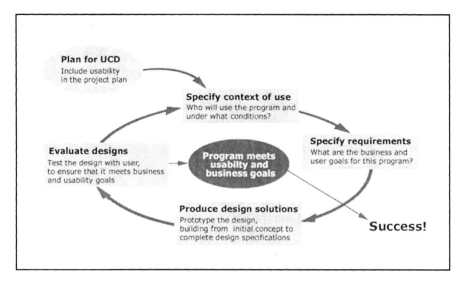

Figure 1. The user-centered design cycle activities described in ISO 13407 can be seen as a cycle that can be completed only when the evaluation of a product shows that it meets the requirements.

This general acceptance leads to the obvious question of the value of such an elastic standard. The very vagueness of this standard may be in its favor. Corporate usability processes can claim to be derived from it, with little fear of contradiction. Government documents can cite it without introducing the substantial burden of detailed requirements. It also has value in building a consensus around an approach that incorporates usability into a design and development process. It allows for experimentation and innovation around the common core understanding in an emerging discipline. Despite the fact that this standard is simply a high-level description of an approach, the approach itself is novel for many organizations. By being loosely descriptive, it enables organizations to take steps toward a UCD process under its umbrella.

Common Industry Format (CIF) for Usability Reports

A project at the U.S. National Institute for Standards and Technology (NIST, 2006) took a different approach. The Industry Usability Reporting (IUSR) project was started in order to explore ways that software purchasers could compare the usability of competitive products.

As with ISO 13407, one of the goals was to encourage better usability practice. Project members felt that "one way to encourage software developers to integrate usability engineering into their development process is for purchasers to require evidence of product usability" (Butler, Wichansky, Laskowski, Morse, & Scholtz, 2003).

With no agreed-upon usability metrics or standard conformance tests, the project focused instead on reporting. The CIF (ISO, 2006) is a template for reporting on the results of summative usability testing. By insisting on a standard presentation of test data (and therefore a test that would produce that data), the project was able to create a way to compare two products, even in the largely qualitative world of usability testing. The CIF template is a standardized table of contents for any report, with some guidance on what information should be included in each section.

- Title page: Product tested, dates of the test and report, people who led the test
- Executive summary
- Introduction: Product description, test objectives, test method, test participants
- Test context: Tasks and scenarios, test facility, participant's computing environment
- Experimental design: Test procedure
- Usability metrics: Efficiency metrics, effectiveness metrics, satisfaction metrics
- Results: Data analysis, performance results
- Appendices: Participant questionnaires, participant instructions, release notes

Acceptance of the CIF

The project team has done an admirable job of communicating the content and value of the CIF through a large number of industry publications (all listed on the project site), and it seems to have gained general acceptance in the industry. Unfortunately, however, the template seems to be used only infrequently, in part because so few companies do the summative usability testing for which it was intended. This standard also may codify a common understanding among practitioners rather than dictating details of practice.

Web Accessibility Initiative

The World Wide Web Consortium (W3C, 2006b) "develops interoperable technologies to lead the Web to its full potential" and "is a forum for information, commerce, communication, and collective understanding." It issues specifications and recommendations through a public consensus process. Most of the W3C guidelines are technical specifications, such as those for HTML, CSS, and other languages.

One of the W3C projects is the Web Accessibility Initiative (WAI) (W3C, 2006a). The WAI addresses not just technical requirements but a social goal, as stated in this quote from Tim Berners-Lee, W3C director and inventor of the World Wide Web: "The power of the Web is in its universality. Access by everyone regardless of disability is an essential aspect." The WAI sets guidelines for authoring Web sites that are accessible to people with disabilities and those using assistive devices. Their core work is the Web Content Authoring Guidelines 1.0 (WCAG) (W3C, 1999). The WCAG defines three levels, called Priorities, of design and coding practice, each with higher levels of difficulty. The WAI also publishes a collection of advice, tools, and other informational material to help Web authors create accessible Web sites.

The pocket reference card "Quick Tips to Make Accessible Web Sites" (W3C, 2001) is widely distributed and mentioned in many industry publications. It lists the ten top guidelines for creating an accessible site.

Legal Regulations Using the WCAG

The work of the WAI has been used as the basis for legislation in the United States, the United Kingdom, and European Union as well as other countries. In the United States, the Access Board (Architectural and Transportation Barriers Compliance Board) used the core provisions of the WCAG 1.0 as the basis for federal regulations known as "Section 508" (Access Board, 2000).

Acceptance of the WCAG

Because its work concerns the Web, activities of the W3C usually garner wide attention. That fact alone would give it more visibility than other usability standards, but the relationship of the WCAG to many national legal regulations gives it a special prominence. In addition, there is a microindustry that has sprung up to provide training, technical support, and tools to help companies and government agencies comply with the regulations.

Unfortunately, there is only limited compliance, despite the enthusiasm with which the WCAG has been embraced. Almost five years after the Recommendation was accepted, few sites achieve more than Priority Level 1 compliance. Despite— or perhaps because of—this wide attention, the WCAG has also been the center of some controversy. The two biggest complaints are

- The WCAG guidelines are not specific and prescriptive enough. They some-times call for Web sites to meet goals, but do not explain what they must to do meet these goals.
- The WCAG guidelines are too onerous and cause hardships for Web developers.

TWO GOVERNMENTAL PROGRAMS

Governments around the world have taken an interest in usability as more and more government services have moved online. Corporations may, to some extent, choose their users and can decide to aim their usability efforts at their most important customers. Governments have a mandate to make their information and services available to all citizens and are often overseen by public and private watchdog agencies. This has made governments particularly sensitive to usability issues (although this does not always speed up implementation). Governmental programs are also convenient to study because they are usually in the public domain and available for all to review.

We will look at two examples, each taking a different approach to ensuring usability in government Web sites:

- The U.S.-based "Research-based Web Design and Usability Guidelines" (Usability.gov, 2006)
- The U.K.-based "Quality Framework for UK Government Website Design" (E-Government Unit, 2003)

Research-Based Guidelines

The "Research-based Web Design and Usability Guidelines" (Usability.gov, 2006) are an excellent example of a "bottom up" approach. These guidelines are offered as a set of best practices, addressing specific common problems or design elements in Web sites and thus provide building blocks out of which a usable site could be created.

This program was created by the usabilty.gov group, originally housed at the National Cancer Institute and now a joint program of the Department of Health and Human Services and the General Services Administration. Because of its connection to a scientific research community, this project took an unusual approach to determining the content of these guidelines: following a peer-reviewed process. A panel of experts evaluated a list of more than 500 candidate guidelines for their relative importance. This process was used to reduce the set of guidelines and to clarify the remaining ones. Then a second panel of experts classified each on strength of evidence in both academic research and general design practice. Guidelines that had no support from either research or practice were dropped.

In the end, 187 guidelines were accepted for publication. They are presented with the aggregate score for both "Strength of Evidence" and "Relative Importance" and are divided into 17 groups that range from the general (Content Organization) to the specific (Links).

Acceptance of the Research-Based Guidelines

It is hard to assess the acceptance of these guidelines. They are offered as advice, but with no other force behind them. They have, however, generated some acceptance on the strength of the work that went into creating them.

The Quality Framework

The "Quality Framework for UK Government Website Design" takes a more "top down" approach. Rather than offer specific design advice, it offers guidance on an overall process for creating a high-quality, usable, and accessible Web site.

Like the "Research-Based Guidelines," the "Quality Framework" draws on a wide range of industry expertise to "clarify what relevant usability and design criteria should be used when planning a government website or judging how good it is" (E-Government Unit, 2003). In this approach, it is closer to the ISO 13407 standard, on which it is partially based.

The Framework is organized into six short sections, plus an annex with an extensive list of references and tools:

1. Incorporating users' needs into the design process
2. Human-centred design
3. Working with Web designers
4. Getting content right
5. Getting services right
6. Conclusion: useful, usable, used

These guidelines do not include much specific advice on the design or content of Web pages, though it does refer to the broader reference, the "Illustrated Handbook for Web Management Teams," which includes technical and process guidance for the overall Web site.

Acceptance of the Framework

When the Framework was first released, it was not universally accepted. In a widely publicized article, Louise Ferguson (2003) quoted many in the U.K. usability community who criticized it as unuseful, unusable, and destined to be unused, "a good idea in principle, but poorly executed." Their assessment may be correct, as a Google search for the Framework has few hits besides the document itself and the articles criticizing it. If there is a lesson here, it is that positive uptake among usability thought leaders is critical for a standard to gain acceptance.

THE VALUE OF STANDARDS

The standards and guidelines that have been discussed in this chapter are just a few of the many that exist or are being developed. But what is the value of all this work? Standards are just empty documents unless they are used in practice, so it is worth considering the impact they might have in relation to the work and time they take to create. Have they helped to improve the usability of information technology products and Web sites? Have they helped create an international understanding for shared practice?

Can Standards Improve Usability?

The answer to this question has to be a qualified "perhaps."

Most usability standards activities have as one of their goals to increase the level of usability of the products or Web sites they affect. The CIF, for example, states that one of their goals is to "Encourage software supplier and purchaser organizations to work together to understand user needs and tasks" (ISO, 2006). These sorts of goals are noble statements, but the standards themselves are usually more limited in scope. This fact makes it possible to meet the standard, while not achieving the underlying goal. This problem is especially true for documentation or process standards. For example, the CIF does not require that there be a positive outcome to the usability test, simply that it be documented in a standard way.

Furthermore, design or technical standards can allow a situation in which products that meet the letter of the standards fail to meet the broader goals underlying them. A recent case in point is a U.K. Disability Rights Commission (2004) report that said not only were sites not meeting the standards, but that

> This report demonstrates that most websites are inaccessible to many disabled people and fail to satisfy even the most basic standards for accessibility recommended by the World Wide Web Consortium.

It went on to claim that even compliance did not always provide good accessibility, and that use of the Web itself is just part of a larger social problem in assisting people with disabilities.

> It is also clear that compliance with the technical guidelines and the use of automated tests are only the first steps toward accessibility: there can be no substitute for involving disabled people themselves in design and testing, and for ensuring that disabled users have the best advice and information available about how to use assistive technology, as well as the access features provided by web browsers and computer operating systems.

Killam and Autry (2004) made a similar point in a talk on design standards. After examining several types of standards they conclude that, "design guidelines . . . are all valuable, but are best for teaching and learning—not for doing. Designers should know them before starting a design." Their point is that the standards should reflect best common practice, which should be well-known by designers. They also point out that "process standards are more important, as well as dedicated, skilled people."

The government regulations have been used as the basis for successful legal challenges. The Australian Olympic Committee, for example, lost a court suit alleging that their site failed to provide access for people with disabilities (Maguire v The Sydney Organizing Committee of the Olympic Games, 2000). Although this ruling punishes lack of compliance rather than promoting good usability or accessibility *in a specific Web site,* the incentive to improve compliance with both the letter and the spirit is obvious.

Can Standards Promote Shared Practice?

The answer to this question is more positive. All three of the standards examined here have strong international support.

- ISO 13407 is an international standard and is used as the basis for user-centered design practice around the world.
- The CIF moved quickly from a project to an international standard and has been reported in papers in several countries.
- The WCAG has been used as the basis for both international Web design and legal regulations in many countries.

There is especially strong anecdotal evidence that ISO 13407 represents a truly international view of practice, as the same diagrams and list of activities have been spotted in conference presentations and on company Web sites around the world. What is not clear is whether the standard created this consensus or describes this shared understanding. Either way, it is valuable.

REFERENCES

Access Board (Architectural and Transportation Barriers Compliance Board). (2000). *Section 508 Electronic and information technology*, 36 CFR Par 1194. http://www.access-board.gov/508.htm

Butler, K., Wichansky, A., Laskowski, S., Morse, E., & Scholtz, J. (2003, September). *The Common Industry Format: A way for vendors and customers to talk about software usability.* Presentation at Computer-Human Interaction Conference, Bath, UK.

E-Government Unit, Cabinet Office. (2003). *Quality framework for UK Government website design.* http://www.cabinetoffice.gov.uk/e-government/resources/quality-framework.asp

Ferguson, L. (2003, August 19). eGov feature on e-Envoy framework causes questions (and fur?) to fly. *Usability News.* http://www.usabilitynews.com/news/article1248.asp

International Organization for Standardization (ISO). (1999). ISO 13407:1999. *Human-centred Design Processes for Interactive Systems.*

International Organization for Standardization (ISO). (2006). ISO/IEC 25062:2006. *Common Industry Format for usability test reports.*

Killam, W., & Autry, M. (2004, May). *Are design standards any use for designing systems?* Presentation at the 51st Annual STC Conference, Baltimore, Maryland.

Maguire v The Sydney Organizing Committee of the Olympic Games. (2000). *Decision of the Australian Human Rights and Equal Opportunity Commission*, Sydney Australia, August 24, 2000. http://www.hreoc.gov.au/disability_rights/decisions/comdec/2000/DD000120.htm

National Institute of Standards and Technology (NIST). (2006). *Industry usability reporting.* http://www.nist.gov/iusr/

U.K. Disabilities Rights Commission. (2004). *Formal investigation: The web: Access and inclusion for disabled people.* http://www.drc-gb.org/publicationsandreports/report.asp

Usability Professionals' Association. (2006). What is user centered design? *Resources: About usability.* http://www.usabilityprofessionals.org/usability_resources/about_usability/what_is_ucd.html

Usability.gov. (2006). *Research-based web design and usability guidelines.* http://www.usability.gov/pdfs/guidelines.html

User Focus. (2006). Resources. *ISO 13407.* http://www.userfocus.co.uk/resources/iso9241 /iso13407.html

W3C. (1999). *Web content accessibility guidelines 1.0. May 5, 1999.* http://www.w3.org/TR/WCAG10/

W3C. (2001) *Quick tips to make accessible Web sites.* http://www.w3.org/WAI/References/QuickTips/

W3C. (2006a). *Web accessibility initiative.* http://www.w3.org/WAI/

W3C. (2006b). *The World Wide Web Consortium.* http://www.w3c.org

Wikipedia. (2006). Usability. http://en.wikipedia.org/wiki/Usability

CHAPTER 3

Conducting an Automated Experiment Over the Internet to Assess Navigation Design for a Medical Web Site Containing Multipage Articles

Elisabeth Cuddihy, Carolyn Wei,
Alexandra L. Bartell, Jennifer Barrick, Brandon Maust,
Seth S. Leopold, and Jan H. Spyridakis

The Web has become a major resource for people seeking information about health, education, and government services. Many Web sites that convey information on these topics have been carefully crafted with rubrics intended to enhance site usability. However, a majority of design guidelines are based on best practices, small-scale lab studies, and designers' instincts rather than large-scale empirical studies conducted in natural settings (Spyridakis, Wei, Barrick, Cuddihy, & Maust, 2005).

Our research group has been conducting remote Internet-based experiments to test the effectiveness of Web design guidelines. We have examined issues such as heading frequency (Schultz & Spyridakis, 2004), local navigational link wording (Mobrand & Spyridakis, 2007), hyperlink wording (Wei, Evans, Eliot, Barrick, Maust, & Spyridakis, 2005), and credibility features (Freeman & Spyridakis, 2004). Our experiments have been conducted on the intended populations for a Web site and at times with university students. Conducting Web design research remotely through the Internet allows researchers to sample large numbers of naturally occurring users as they interact with actual sites, making it possible to study users' natural Web behavior. We argue that the use of large-scale, rigorous empirical studies conducted "in the wild" validates the effectiveness of Web design guidelines and enhances the certainty with which designers can apply them.

HEALTH WEB SITES AND USABILITY

In 2006, 10 million Americans daily turned "to the web for health information—about as many as those who pay bills online, read blogs or look up a phone number or address" (Pew Internet and American Life, 2006). The usability of online health information is critical, yet it has not been extensively examined in the e-health field (Croft & Peterson, 2002; Elkin et al., 2002; Eysenbach & Köhler, 2002; Fetters, Ivankova, Ruffin, Creswell, & Power, 2004; Fuller & Hinegardner, 2001; McCray et al., 2000; Seidler-Patterson & Patterson, 2001).

Some recent empirical studies have examined navigation and usability on health-related Web sites through Internet-based testing. Mobrand and Spyridakis (2007) conducted an Internet-based study that tested how various types of local navigational cues affected user comprehension, perceptions, and browsing behavior on a Web site for osteoarthritis. Similarly, Schultz and Spyridakis (2004) conducted an Internet-based study of the effect of heading frequency on users' comprehension and perceptions of sites about osteoarthritis or rheumatoid arthritis.

The study reported here continues in a similar vein by investigating how intra-article navigation affects readers' browsing behavior, perceptions, and comprehension of lengthy articles about orthopedic surgery on an informational site. The findings should provide insight about how people who seek health information navigate and process information on medical sites, as well as augment the growing research on empirically-based Web design guidelines.

NAVIGATION AND COMPREHENSION OF LENGTHY WEB-BASED ARTICLES

The presentation of lengthy articles as multiple Web pages presents a number of challenges that are less problematic or nonexistent when such information is presented in print. One difficulty is that readers cannot assess lengthy Web articles at a glance without scrolling or clicking through multiple pages. In print, a reader can see an entire page at once and gauge organizational structure by scanning headings or attending to the number of pages. Web-based articles, however, often obscure important structural information. Their pages may appear to be of an indeterminate length, forcing users to scroll without any sense of page or article length.

 Further, while headings are employed to help readers understand content and structure, they cannot scan all the headings on a long page at once. Similarly, the Web parallel of a reader quickly thumbing through a printed book or article to get the lay of the land requires a time investment of searching, clicking links, and waiting for pages to load.

Web design guidelines suggest that long Web pages should have a table of contents to help users understand what a page contains (Koyani, Bailey, & Nall, 2004), a claim supported by other researchers (Bieber, 1997; Farkas & Farkas, 2000; Haas & Grams, 1998; Spyridakis, 2000). It is logical to assert that a more complex case—a multipage Web article—would also benefit from a table of contents in order to make up for the lack of cues that would otherwise be available in print.

Articles that are presented as Web pages are typically done so within a site's design template. A site may have one or more templates that organize global site elements such as sitewide search boxes, top-level navigation, utility links (e.g., "Home," "Site Map," "Contact Us"), and branding logos; such templates may also provide a space for content that will vary from page to page. Articles, including their internal navigation features, are treated as a kind of content that must fit within the content area of the template.

However, when an article is broken into multiple pages, one must question how to best display internal navigation or a table of contents so readers can better comprehend the article's structure and contents, and access its sections. An example of a site that offers internal navigation within articles is *Wired Webmonkey* (http://webmonkey.wired.com). It provides a numbered table of contents on the left of each article page, which explicitly signals that it provides article-specific internal navigation by using the word "Pages" and numbering the links.

Web sites need to clearly differentiate different navigational elements, such as global and intra-article navigation. Users quickly learn to anticipate the location of global elements, particularly when such elements are near the top of pages, and they move their mouse toward important links before moving their eyes (Bernard, 2001, 2002; Koyani et al., 2004). In contrast, if visually similar designs and locations are used for global Web site navigation and internal article navigation, it is likely that users will confuse the two or fail to notice that intra-article navigation has been made available. Because the Web supports many different structures serving different purposes, users can become disoriented or experience cognitive overload (Yu & Roh, 2002), and a menu that does not provide adequate structural cues may make users feel like they are "lost in space" (Yu & Roh, 2002; Dieberger, 1997).

UNIVERSITY OF WASHINGTON ORTHOPAEDIC SURGERY AND SPORTS MEDICINE WEB SITE

The study reported here uses an article drawn from the Web site of the Department of Orthopaedic Surgery and Sports Medicine (http://www.orthop.uwmedicine.org) at the University of Washington. The site delivers information about the department as well as articles about orthopedic conditions. These articles are typically eight pages, and each page is usually much longer than one screen. The site's article template displays a Table of Contents in a left-hand navigation bar that replaces the global navigation menu that appears on other content pages. The layout and design of this intra-article navigation bar (see Figure 1, right) are nearly identical to the global navigation bar that exists outside the article pages (see Figure 1, left). The intra-article navigation bar lists the articles' first-level headings (e.g., Summary, Review of the condition, Considering surgery, Preparing for surgery) and links to separate pages structured with additional subheadings.

Users navigate between pages of an article by clicking on the intra-article navigation menu or by clicking the "Next Page" or "Previous Page" links at the top and bottom of each content page. From within an article, beyond the utility links to the home page and site map, the only global reference providing links to the rest of

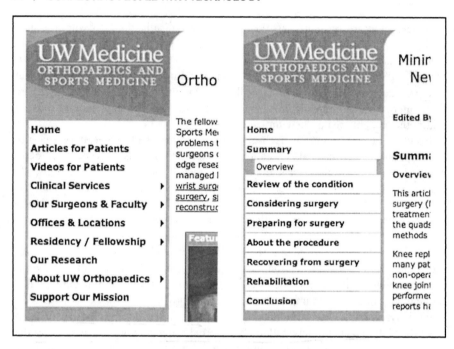

Figure 1. The left image shows the Web site's global navigation bar
and the right image shows its intra-article navigation bar.
Both use nearly identical structural and graphical styles.
Reproduced with the permission of the Department of Orthopaedic Surgery
and Sports Medicine, University of Washington.

the site is a short breadcrumb trail to the Home page or a menu of other patient
information articles (see Figure 2).

HYPOTHESES

We predicted that users would have better comprehension with lengthy, multipage
articles on highly technical topics if the Web site explicitly displayed article structure and differentiated that display from the global navigation structure. On the
UW Orthopaedic site, we predicted that users would overlook the existing intra-
article navigation menu, thinking it is the global navigation menu. As a result,
we hypothesized that users would read some or all of the article linearly by clicking
on "Next Page" and "Previous Page" or by clicking down the left-hand navigation
menu links, but without understanding the article's overall structure. They would
be more likely to miss important information and perhaps abort reading before
reaching the end of an article, a browsing behavior that would negatively affect
their comprehension.

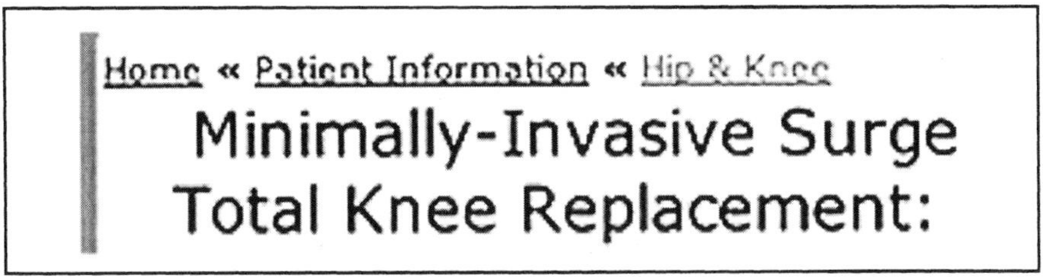

Home « Patient Information « Hip & Knee
Minimally-Invasive Surge
Total Knee Replacement:

Figure 2. Breadcrumbs provide the only form of global
navigation within an article.
Reproduced with the permission of the Department of Orthopaedic Surgery
and Sports Medicine, University of Washington.

METHODS

To test our hypotheses, we remotely administered an Internet-based study investigating the effect of four intra-article navigation conditions.

Participants

A total of 224 adult participants were drawn from naturally occurring readers of orthopedic information. A banner was placed on the UW Orthopaedics Web site to direct users to the study. Flyers advertising the study were sent to orthopedic medical offices throughout Washington State, and electronic announcements were made in online forums about arthritis.

Materials

The study Web site consisted of an article drawn from the UW Orthopaedic Web site that contained eight pages discussing a new type of total knee replacement surgery. To adapt the site for use in this study, we removed the Web site search tool and links to other parts of the site. This article's eight long pages comprised more than 8,500 words and numerous illustrations of the surgical procedure. This article was chosen for this study because it is one of the highest rated of the 80 articles on the Web site concerning medical conditions and surgical procedures.

Using PHP scripts, four versions of the site were generated such that each version incorporated a different visual representation of the intra-article navigation bar. The study used four conditions: (a) the existing intra-article navigation bar on the left; (b) an intra-article navigation bar on the left that was visually similar to the existing bar but labeled at the top with "Article Table of Contents"; (c) an intra-article navigation bar on the left that was visually distinct from the original global navigation and labeled at the top "Article Table of Contents"; and (d) an intra-article navigation bar labeled "Article Table of Contents" placed to the right of the content area, with the existing global navigation bar placed to the left of the main content area. Figures 3a–3d display these four conditions.

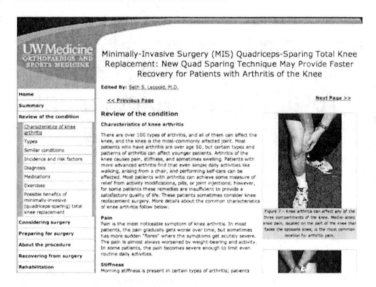

Figure 3a. The existing intra-article navigation menu is placed to the left of the main content area. This is in the same location and has the same style as the global navigation menu shown in Figure 1, left.
Reproduced with the permission of the Department of Orthopaedic Surgery and Sports Medicine, University of Washington.

Figure 3b. A slightly revised intra-article navigation menu labeled "Article Table of Contents," but otherwise visually similar to the preexisting intra-article navigation scheme.
Reproduced with the permission of the Department of Orthopaedic Surgery and Sports Medicine, University of Washington.

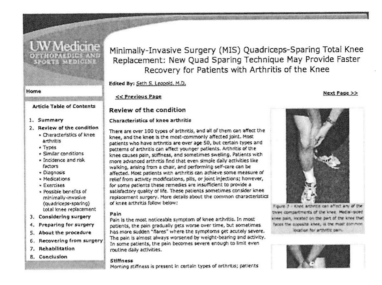

Figure 3c. A substantially revised intra-article navigation menu clearly labeled "Article Table of Contents" numbers the eight pages in the article and clearly marks the major headings for the page being viewed. This menu is visually distinct from the site's global navigation menu.
Reproduced with the permission of the Department of Orthopaedic Surgery and Sports Medicine, University of Washington.

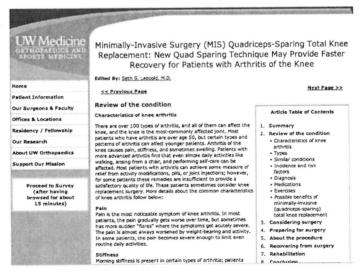

Figure 3d. The global navigation menu appears on the left and the substantially revised intra-article navigation menu (same as Figure 3c) is placed on the right, inside the article content pane.
Reproduced with the permission of the Department of Orthopaedic Surgery and Sports Medicine, University of Washington.

The study Web site was prefaced with introductory pages providing background information about the study, an informed consent statement, a demographics questionnaire, and study instructions that told participants they would be asked to answer some questions about the site when they were finished browsing and that they would not be able to return to the Web site once they entered the questionnaire. When participants were finished browsing, they answered an online questionnaire that assessed their perceptions and comprehension of the Web site.

Our toolkit for conducting Web-based experiments also recorded information about participants' clicking behaviors. The article pages were instrumented with PHP scripts so that participants' navigational behavior, such as which links they clicked, could be accurately recorded. As the participants browsed the article pages, the specific links clicked were logged, time-stamped, and associated with each participant's session. To make sure that all interactions with the site were recorded by the Web-server, each page was marked with a browser request to turn off page caching. This forced all page requests to go to the server and allowed us to identify when the browser's back button rather than a hyperlink was used to reach a page. The research team could thus determine the specific links used to navigate between pages, the approximate time spent on each page, and the order in which users visited pages.

Procedure

When visitors opened the initial page of the experimental Web site, they were randomly assigned to one of the four conditions. Each visitor read the introductory material, and if they chose to participate, they browsed the test site for about 10 to 15 minutes and then clicked the "Proceed to Survey" button.

After users clicked the "Proceed to Survey" button or any other link that would take them outside of the eight-page article, the participants were given the option to return to the article, go to the survey, or leave the study completely. The survey asked questions about their perceptions of the Web site's extent, usability, and knowledge gained. Next, the participants answered a set of factual and inferential multiple-choice comprehension questions about the article's contents. Factual questions could be answered on the basis of facts presented in the article. Inferential questions required participants to draw an inference from at least two separate pieces of information presented in the article. All questions were assessed for passage dependency, and the whole study was pilot tested. Survey results were logged with a participant ID so that they could be matched up with the participant's browsing behavior during analysis. Our toolkit included a set of data postprocessing scripts that parse our custom Web logs and disqualify participants who violate study procedure (Barrick et al., 2004).

RESULTS AND DISCUSSION

Given the random assignment of participants to conditions as they came to the study sites, each of the four conditions contained around 50 participants.

Participants, two-thirds of whom were female, were frequent users of the Web to find information but less frequent users to find medical information: about two-thirds reported using the Web daily for general information seeking while only about one-third reported using it daily or a few times a week to seek medical information.

We have analyzed a portion of the data with SPSS 11.5 at this time, and the results are very telling in terms of the experimental conditions and our hypotheses. As anticipated, a table of contents that was visually distinct from the design of the global navigation menu best facilitated comprehension. The average comprehension score for participants was highest in the third condition (visually distinct "Table of Contents" intra-article navigation on the left, see Figure 3c), whereas comprehension was lowest for participants who saw the original navigation design (existing intra-article navigation on the left that was identical in its visual appearance to the global navigation menu, see Figure 3a). The original navigation menu design suggested that the individual article pages were in fact unique lower-level pages within a tree-like structural Web site hierarchy, whereas the third condition, while containing identical text for each menu item, used a distinct visual layout more in keeping with a table of contents, and it was clearly labeled as one. Surprisingly, participants reported the least amount of perceived gain in knowledge about knee surgery when exposed to the third condition and the greatest gain when exposed to the second condition, which modified the original navigation design by adding only "Article Table of Contents" above the intra-article navigation menu links (see Figure 3b).

CONCLUSIONS
AND FUTURE RESEARCH

The findings in this study further our understanding of how users navigate through lengthy, multipage Web site articles. These findings also further the development of empirically based guidelines for the design of navigational affordances. Web designers should visually differentiate intra-article navigation from a site's overall navigation scheme. Additionally, the findings suggest that comprehension and perceptions of use do not always match: perceptual responses about Web experience or perceived performance may not correctly indicate actual performance on an important metric, such as site content comprehension. Web designers will need to decide, given the goals they have for a given site, whether they want to design for comprehension or perceptions. This study is part of an ongoing series of large-scale, rigorous empirical studies that investigate Web users' behavior, comprehension, and perceptions.

More research is needed to provide empirical evidence for Web design guidelines, especially large-scale, naturalistic Internet-based studies. In addition, more investigation is needed concerning methodological issues for conducting Internet-based studies of Web design as well as the requirements of software tools that support such experimentation.

REFERENCES

Barrick, J., Maust, B., Spyridakis, J. H., Eliot, M., Wei, C., Evans, M., & Mobrand, K. (2004). A tool for supporting Web-based empirical research: Providing a basis for Web design guidelines. In *Proceedings of the IEEE International Professional Communication Conference* (pp. 189-194). Piscataway, NJ: IEEE.

Bernard, M. (2001). Developing schemas for the location of common Web objects. *Usability News.* http://psychology.wichita.edu/surl/usabilitynews/3W/web_object.htm

Bernard, M. (2002). Examining user expectations for the location of common e-commerce web objects. *Usability News.* http://psychology.wichita.edu/surl/usabilitynews/41/web_object-ecom.htm

Bieber, M. (1997). Enhancing information comprehension through hypertext. In C. Nicholas & J. Mayfields (Eds.), *Intelligent hypertext: Advanced techniques for the World Wide Web* (pp. 1-11). Berlin: Springer-Verlag.

Croft, D. R., & Peterson, M. W. (2002). An evaluation of the quality and contents of asthma education on the World Wide Web. *Chest, 121*(4), 1301-1307.

Dieberger, A. (1997). Supporting social navigation on the World-Wide Web. *International Journal of Human-Computer Studies, 46,* 805-825.

Elkin, P. L., Sorensen, B., De Palo, D., Poland, G., Bailkey, K. R, Wood, D. L., & LaRusso, N. F. (2002). Optimization of a research Web environment for academic internal medicine faculty. *Journal of the American Medical Informatics Association, 9*(5), 472-480.

Eysenbach, G., & Köhler, C. (2002). How do consumers search for and appraise health information on the World Wide Web? Qualitative study using focus groups, usability tests, and in-depth interviews. *BMJ.* http://bmj.bmjjournals.com/misc/terms.shtml

Farkas, D., & Farkas, J. (2000). Guidelines for designing Web navigation. *Technical Communication, 47*(3), 341-358.

Fetters, M. D., Ivankova, N. V., Ruffin, M. T., Creswell, J. W., & Power, D. (2004). Developing a Web site in primary care. *Family Medicine, 36*(9), 651-659.

Freeman, K. S., & Spyridakis, J. H. (2004). An examination of factors that affect the credibility of health information on the Internet. *Technical Communication, 51*(2), 239-263.

Fuller, D. M., & Hinegardner, P. G. (2001). Ensuring quality Web site redesign: The University of Maryland's experience. *Bulletin of the Medical Library Association, 89*(4), 339-345.

Haas, S., & Grams, E. (1998). A link taxonomy for Web pages. In *Proceedings of the 61st Annual Meeting of the American Society for Information Science* (pp. 485-495). Pittsburgh, Pennsylvania.

Koyani, S., Bailey, R., & Nall, J. (2004). *Research-based Web design and usability guidelines.* Bethesda, MD: National Cancer Institute.

McCray, A. T., Dorfman, E., Ripple, A., Ide, N. C., Jha, M., Katz, D. G., Loane, R. F ., & Tse, T. (2000). Usability issues in developing a Web-based consumer health site. In *Proceedings of the AMIA Annual Symposium* (pp. 556-560). Los Angeles, California.

Mobrand, K., & Spyridakis, J. H. (2007). Explicitness of local navigational links: Comprehension, perceptions of use, and browsing behaviour. *Journal of Information Science, 33*(1), 41-61.

Pew Internet and American Life. (2006). *Seeking Health Online.* http://pewresearch.org/reports/?ReportID=65

Schultz, L., & Spyridakis, J. H. (2004). The effect of heading frequency on comprehension of online information: A study of two populations. *Technical Communication, 51*(4), 504-518.

Seidler-Patterson, K., & Patterson, M. J. (2001, July-August). Tapping into the usability dimension: Test your product before it goes on-line. *Quirk's Marketing Research Review.* http://quirkssom/articles/a2001/20010708.aspx?searchID=9652618.

Spyridakis, J. (2000). Guidelines for authoring comprehensible Web pages and evaluating their success. *Technical Communication, 47*(3), 59-382.

Spyridakis, J. H., Wei, C., Barrick, J., Cuddihy, E., & Maust, B. (2005). Internet-based research: Providing a foundation for Web design guidelines. *IEEE Transactions on Professional Communication, 48*(3), 242-260.

Wei, C. Y., Evans, M. B., Eliot, M., Barrick, J., Maust, B., & Spyridakis, J. H. (2005). Influencing Web browsing behaviour with intriguing and informative hyperlink wording. *Journal of Information Science, 31*(5), 433-445.

Yu, B.M., & Roh, S-Z. (2002). The effects of menu design on information-seeking performance and user's attitude on the World Wide Web. *Journal of the American Society for Information Science and Technology, 53*(11), 923-933.

CHAPTER 4

Manuals for the Elderly: Text Characteristics That Help or Hinder Older Users

*Floor van Horen, Carel Jansen,
Leo Noordman, and Alfons Maes*

Manuals for consumer electronics devices are often criticized for being difficult and inaccessible for many users, especially elderly people. This is an important target group, however, because within the next few decades, almost half of the population in the Western world will be older than 50. More and more elderly people will use consumer electronics devices. Lippincott (2004) argues that multidisciplinary research projects are needed in order to investigate the behavioral and cognitive differences between age groups interacting with technical communication.

In the last few years, several gerontological studies have shown that major advances have been made in adapting technology to elderly people. Hartley (1994) listed various rules of thumb for designing instructional text for elderly people. Both T. D. Freudenthal (1998) and A. Freudenthal (1999) studied elderly people's interactive behavior with complex devices in order to identify characteristics of the devices that cause problems, along with characteristics of elderly people's behavior that might explain their problems. Wright (2000) investigated the use of instructions by elderly readers.

The studies discussed in this chapter aim at contributing to the identification of characteristics of instructions that cause elderly users' problems with electronic devices. In a first phase, an exploratory study resulted in three candidate variables that may cause problems: temporal iconicity, the signaling of steps, and the absence of goal and consequence information. In a second phase, the effect of manipulating these three variables was investigated in three experiments.

TEMPORAL ICONICITY

Research on the effects of aging on the reading process has shown that stories told in a nonchronological order are harder to comprehend for older people than for younger (Smith, Rebok, Smith, Hall, & Alvin, 1983). When people operate devices, it is important that actions be performed in the correct order. Instructions should help the user to conceive the correct order of procedural steps. It seems obvious that instructions should therefore mention the actions in the order that they have to be executed.

We refer to this similarity between textual and actual procedure as "temporal iconicity." According to Enkvist (1981), "Iconicism occurs whenever the linear relations in a text stand for temporal [. . .] relations between the referents in the world described by that text" (p. 99). We expect that especially the elderly benefit from temporal iconicity in instructions.

SIGNALING STEPS

In many advisory guides for document design, the importance of segmenting and signaling procedural steps is stressed. In general text comprehension, signaling words (such as *therefore, but, because, first of all, secondly, likewise, nonetheless,* and so forth) help the reader to understand the text's structure and to build a correct and coherent mental representation (Lorch & Lorch, 1996).

Segmentation in instructions is important because it enables users to switch more easily between manual and device (Steehouder & Karreman, 2000). People read a step from the procedure, execute it on the device, and go back to the text to read the next step.

Some research has been done on older people's memory for performed tasks. Kausler and Hakami (1983) had older and younger people perform a series of tasks, after which they were given a recall task. The older participants recalled fewer tasks than the younger. Some researchers explicitly recommend giving instructions in formatted lists to facilitate this recall process (Wright, 2000). In our experiments, we expected that clear signaling of the instructions is beneficial, especially for older users.

GOAL AND CONSEQUENCE INFORMATION

Manuals can never be fully explicit. Users must always infer information from their background knowledge and from the task context. Research on the effects of aging on the process of inferential reasoning has shown that elderly people are less capable of making inferences than younger people (Cohen, 1981). If manuals only explicitly mention the action to be performed and not the context in which this action will take place, older users especially may have problems with the required inferences.

In order to decide which information is relevant, an inventory of information types in instructions is needed. Inspired by Farkas (1999), we defined four basic types of procedural information. Farkas describes the process of operating a device as bringing it from an original status into a desired or goal status. *Goal information* describes the desired status and *starting point information* describes the original status. *Action information* describes the actions that lead to the goal status. Finally, *consequence information* describes what can be observed on the device when an action is performed, in order to be able to check whether an action was performed correctly. Goal and consequence information were the objects of our investigation.

In sum, we investigated experimentally the effect of three types of variables in manuals: the iconic or noniconic order of actions, the signaling of steps, and the presence of goal and consequence information. In the experiments, people from two age groups volunteered: older participants, aged between 60 and 70 years, and younger participants, aged between 20 and 30 years. In all experiments, we balanced the number of male and female participants and the education levels between the age groups. We investigated the variables with the help of statistical tests. In this chapter, we discuss only the main effects and interactions that were found to be statistically significant.

EXPERIMENT I:
ICONICITY AND THE SIGNALING OF STEPS

The variables iconicity and the signaling of steps were investigated in an experiment with a fictitious device: a medical laser. In this experiment, 30 older and 30 younger participants were given iconic and noniconic procedures as well as instructions with different types of signaling (see Table 1 for examples of each condition). There were two text manipulations.

First of all, we constructed two iconicity conditions analogously to the materials from investigations on the processing of event order in discourse. Clark and Clark started this work in 1968, giving people complex sentences containing the connectives *before* or *after*, such as "He tooted the horn before he swiped the cabbages" and " He swiped the cabbages after he tooted the horn" (Clark & Clark, 1968). In the other text manipulation, the action steps were either not signaled, signaled visually, or signaled by verbal means (connectives).

After reading the instructions, the participants viewed a correct or incorrect simulation of the procedure on a TV screen, which they had to judge for correctness. Reading times, time that was needed to judge the simulation (reaction time), and error rates were measured. In analyses of variance for repeated measures, main effects for the factor "age group" were found. The task appeared to be harder for the older group on three dimensions. Compared with the younger, the elderly needed more time to read the procedures and to judge the simulations, and they made more incorrect judgments. The reaction times are given in Table 2. Results on the error rates and the reading times also showed main effects only for the factor "age group."

In the analyses, significant differences were found for the type of simulation. Unlike the younger group, the elderly needed more time and were less accurate in judging incorrect as compared with correct simulations. Unexpectedly, however, text differences did not affect task performance. We found no main effects and no

Table 1. Conditions in Experiment I

	Example
Iconic	Shift the power switch to <1>. Shift the limiter to <low> before you press <green> to start the treatment.
Noniconic	Shift the power switch to <1>. Press <green> to start the treatment after you have shifted the limiter to <low>.
No signals	Shift the power switch to <1>. Shift the limiter to <low>. Press <green> to start the treatment.
Visual signals	1. Shift the power switch to <1>. 2. Shift the limiter to <low>. 3. Press <green> to start the treatment.
Verbal signals	First shift the power switch to <1>. Then shift the limiter to <low>. Finally press <green> to start the treatment.

Table 2. Mean Reaction Times (in Seconds) per Simulation Type (Correct vs. Incorrect), Text Condition, and Age Group

Age group	Iconicity			Signaling of steps			
	Iconic	Noniconic	Mean	Neutral	Visual	Verbal	Mean
Correct simulations							
Old	1.821	1.629	1.669	1.750	1.786	1.860	1.751
Young	1.163	1.131	1.140	1.207	1.337	1.312	1.288
Mean	1.462	1.357		1.459	1.545	1.566	
Incorrect simulations							
Old	3.590	4.058	4.549	3.914	4.728	3.919	4.281
Young	2.663	2.787	2.744	3.143	3.056	2.469	2.885
Mean	3.018	3.274		3.382	3.573	2.918	

interactions. It is hard to interpret this outcome, especially in the case of iconicity, which turned out to be effective in research with other text genres. Perhaps the manipulations were too limited to play a noticeable role in the relatively broad judging task in this experiment.

Regarding the signaling of steps, it should be noted that switching behavior between text and device, which is necessary in natural situations where instructions first have to be read and then physically carried out, was ruled out in our experiment.

Participants were asked to judge only simulations, not to perform real actions with an actual device. This might explain why we found no effect for signaling of steps. Future experiments could be carried out to find out what happens when readers of instructions switch between text and device.

EXPERIMENT II: ICONICITY

To further explore the effects of iconicity on older and younger readers of instructions, a follow-up experiment was conducted in which participants had to execute specific tasks. A simple and straightforward task on a computer screen was created. A total of 18 younger and 15 older participants were presented with iconic and noniconic instructions (see Figure 1), and were asked to execute these instructions by pressing two keys on the keyboard. Reading times (defined as the time between the appearance of the stimulus on screen and the participant's first push on a key) were measured.

By varying the temporal connective and the position of the main and subordinate clause, we created four types of sentences, as can be seen in Table 3. For each sentence in Table 3, a second one was also used, in which the color words were switched. Each participant was exposed to 62 sentences (32 experimental sentences

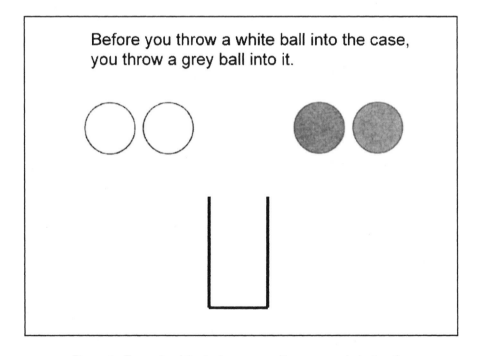

Figure 1. Example of the task screen, with an example instruction in Experiment II.

Table 3. Conditions in Experiment II. (The nature of the first clause
[main vs. subordinate clause] and the connective [before, after]
are given in the "condition" column.)

Condition	Sentence
Iconic 1 (main clause first, before)	Throw a white ball into the case, before you throw a grey ball into it
Iconic 2 (subclause first, after)	After you have thrown a white ball into the case, you throw a grey ball into it
Noniconic 1 (main clause first, after)	Throw a grey ball into the case, after you have thrown a white ball into it
Noniconic 2 (subclause first, before)	Before you throw a grey ball into the case, you throw a white ball into it

and 30 fillers with two identical color words). The results of this experiment are presented in Table 4.

We executed analyses of variance for repeated measures. As expected, the older group needed far more time than the younger. Apart from that outcome, the results were rather surprising.

We found a main effect of the factor "clause position." When the subordinate clause preceded the main clause, the reading times were shorter. In other experiments with comparable (though not instructive) stimuli, the sentences with the main clause in first position were processed and remembered better than sentences starting with the subordinate clause (Clark & Clark, 1968; Smith & McMahon, 1970). In this experiment, the subclause contains more crucial information on the task than the main clause, that is, information on the order of the two tasks. This is a likely reason for the shorter reading time of this version in this experiment.

Another surprising result was the main effect of the factor iconicity that was found: in both age groups noniconic sentences had shorter reading times than iconic sentences. This result can also be explained by the typical task situation in the experiment. The instructive sentence and the task (i.e., the balls and the case) were displayed on the same screen, so readers did not have to memorize the text or switch between reading and performing. Apparently, task execution was faster when participants could start executing the action they had read most recently.

Table 4. Overall Mean Reading Times (in Seconds) and
Means per Age Group for Each of the Two Variants of the Factors
Iconicity, Connective, and Clause Position

	Age group		
	Younger	Older	Mean
Iconicity			
Iconic	2.62	3.53	3.08
Noniconic	2.48	3.38	2.93
Connective			
Before	2.54	3.44	2.99
After	2.57	3.47	3.02
Clause position			
Main-Sub	2.68	3.68	3.18
Sub-Main	2.42	3.23	2.83

Table 5. Overall Mean Reading Times
(in Seconds) and Means per Age Group for
the Two Variants of the Factor Color Word Order

Age group	Color word order	
	White – Grey	Grey – White
Younger	2.47	2.63
Older	3.24	3.69
Mean	2.85	3.16

Another result concerned the order of the color words in the sentence. Variations in the order showed an interaction with the age group. Table 5 shows that sentences with a "white-grey" order were read faster than sentences with a "grey-white" order, especially by the older age group. An explanation can be found in the order of the balls on the screen, which was invariably white-grey, as can be seen in Figure 1.

The shorter reading times for white-grey sentences may be the result of what we may call "perceptual" iconicity, that is, the correspondence between the order of the color words in the sentence and the position of the balls on the screen. A future experiment in which the position of the colored balls is varied could shed more light on this hypothesis.

EXPERIMENT III: THE NEED FOR GOAL AND CONSEQUENCE INFORMATION

The third experiment investigated the effects of goal information and consequence information. We designed instructions in which the presence of the two information types was varied. A total of 39 younger and 35 older participants executed tasks on a central heating thermostat. They were given one of three versions of a manual.

Throughout the manual, action information was always specified. Apart from that, in one version of the manual both goal and consequence information were given. In the other two versions, one of the two information types was systematically left out. Examples of the descriptions of an action in the three versions can be seen in Table 6.

Participants worked aloud, and video recordings of their behavior were made. The elements in the manual that were read, the errors that were made, and the time that was needed to perform each action were analyzed. Performance times and the number of correct actions are given in Table 7.

In analyses of variance, main effects for each age group were found. The older group needed more time to perform actions and they made more errors than the younger group. In the performance times, we found an interaction of text version and age group. The elderly needed more time for the version without consequence information than for the other versions, whereas in the younger group no difference between the versions were found.

Apparently, the elderly benefit from information enabling them to check if an action is finished and whether it has been performed correctly. Consequence information may bring a sense of security to the interaction with a device. It is easy to imagine that this is more comfortable for elderly users, because it enables them to

Table 6. Conditions in Experiment III

Conditions	Example of an action description
+ goal information	Activate the copying function:
+ consequence information	Press the button COPY DAY once.
	The word "Copy" appears in the display. The copying function is now active.
– goal information	Press the botton COPY DAY once.
	The word "Copy" appears in the display. The copying function is now active.
– consequence information	Activate the copying function:
	Press the button COPY DAY once.

Table 7. Mean Performance Times (in Seconds) and Mean Number
of Correct Actions per Age Group in the Three Conditions
(+ goal/consequence, – consequence, – goal)

	+ goal information + consequence information	– consequence information	– goal information
Performance time			
Younger	14.58	9.55	8.88
Older	15.54	20.51	12.81
Correct actions			
Younger	26.5	26.8	26.3
Older	20.2	22.1	20.2

keep track of the procedures. Another explanation is that they may be less able than the younger participants to infer the consequence from the information in the manual, their own knowledge, and signals on the thermostat.

DISCUSSION

The goal of our research project was to identify and further investigate text characteristics that help or hinder older people's interaction with devices and manuals. The role of temporal iconicity, the signaling of steps, and the absence of goal information and consequence information was investigated. In the three experiments that we carried out, clear age effects were found. The elderly needed more time to read instructions and to execute the tasks, and with respect to performance quality, they performed worse than the younger age group. We finish this chapter with an attempt to translate the results into three cautious guidelines for manuals that meet the needs of an older audience.

Segmentation of instructions

The results of Experiment II suggest that temporal iconicity of instructions is not helpful. It appears to be more important for readers to perform an action immediately after reading about it; and in Experiment II this is only the case in the noniconic sentences. This result may be regarded as a plea for a clear segmentation of procedural steps: apparently readers want to perform the step they just read about as quickly as possible. Segmentation of instructions clarifies to the reader when to stop reading and start performing, and what text fragment to go to after performing, without erroneously repeating or skipping actions.

At first sight, this plea for segmentation may seem to contradict the results of Experiment I, which showed no effects for the signaling of steps. However, Experiment II measured text effects while people were actually performing tasks.

In Experiment I, people did not perform instructions. We think the segmenting of instructions will support readers who have to execute tasks. We expect that segmentation is especially helpful for readers who have to switch continuously between reading instructions and operating devices.

Put the Most Informative Part of the Instruction First

The reading times in Experiment II were influenced by the position of the two clauses, with an interaction with age group. We argued that this result was probably caused by the fact that the information about the order of the actions was present only in the subordinate clause. This result suggests the following principle: put the most informative part of the instruction first. The context influences which information is most informative. In Experiment II, the information that was most informative to the performance of the actions was the connective: it contained information about the order of the two actions. Document designers should adopt the perspective of the user in order to decide which information is most informative for the task at hand.

Consequence Information is Important

Experiment III yielded results that can easily be applied: it is important to describe the means to check whether an action has been performed (correctly). Apparently elderly users want to know "what will happen." Document designers should describe the results of an action and the feedback signals that can be perceived on the device.

REFERENCES

Clark, H. H., & Clark, E. V. (1968). Semantic distinctions and memory for complex sentences. *Quarterly Journal of Experimental Psychology, 20*(2), 129-138.

Cohen, G. (1981). Inferential reasoning in old age. *Cognition, 9*(1), 59-72.

Enkvist, N. E. (1981). Experiential iconicism in text strategy. *Text, 1*(1), 97-111.

Farkas, D. K. (1999). The logical and rhetorical construction of procedural discourse. *Technical Communication, 46*(1), 42-54.

Freudenthal, A. (1999). *The design of home appliances for young and old consumers.* Delft, The Netherlands: Delft University of Technology.

Freudenthal, T. D. (1998). *Learning to use interactive devices: Age differences in the reasoning process.* Eindhoven, The Netherlands: Eindhoven University of Technology.

Hartley, J. (1994). Designing instructional text for older readers: A literature review. *British Journal of Educational Technology, 25*(3), 172-188.

Kausler, D. H., & Hakami, M. K. (1983). Memory for activities: Adult age differences and intentionality. *Developmental Psychology, 19*, 889-894.

Lippincott, G. (2004). Grey matters: Where are the technical communicators in research and design for aging audiences? *IEEE Transactions on Professional Communication, 47*(3), 157-170.

Lorch, R. F., & Lorch, E. P. (1996). Effects of organizational signals on free recall of expository text. *Journal of Educational Psychology, 88,* 38-48.

Smith, H. K., & McMahon, L. E. (1970). Understanding of information in sentences: Some recent work at Bell Laboratories. In G. B. Flores d'Arcais and W. J. M. Levelt (Eds.), *Advances in psycholinguistics* (pp. 173-192). Amsterdam/Oxford: North-Holland Publishing Company.

Smith, S. W., Rebok, G. W., Smith, W. R., Hall, S. E., & Alvin, M. (1983). Adult age differences in the use of story structure in delayed free recall. *Experimental Aging Research, 9*(3), 191-195.

Steehouder, M., & Karreman, J. (2000). De verwerking van stapsgewijze instructies. *Tijdschrift voor Taalbeheersing, 22,* 218-237.

Wright, P. (2000). Supportive documentation for older people. In C. Jansen, R. Punselie, & P. Westendorp (Eds.), *Interface design and document design* (pp. 31-43). Amsterdam: Editions Rodopi BV.

PART II

Globalization:
Overcoming the Challenges of
Languages and Cultures

CHAPTER 5

Communication as a Key to Global Business

Reinhard Schäler

Communication is the tie that binds our global community. It must be conducted in such a way that its content is accessible to all and respectful of local languages and cultures. The idea of English as a *lingua franca,* as the universal medium of communication among the people of the world, is extremely appealing, but while its role is important, we believe that it is essentially a fallback, a second best. We will maintain that localization must be the key enabler for making connections in the digital world and will provide arguments based on mainstream localization practice for those wondering whether they should localize their digital content. We will argue that current mainstream efforts are not enough to deal with the exploding volume of digital content that requires localization into an ever-growing number of languages. We will put forward a case for a new approach, development localization, and introduce the Global Initiative for Local Computing (GILC).

LANGUAGE IS COMMUNICATION

The mission of the technical communicator is to help engineers make the results of their work more accessible to people, using state-of-the-art digital media. The single most important task for technical communicators today is probably to help nonnative English speakers communicate technical and scientific information effectively to other nonnative speakers using the English language as their medium of communication. In a world where people communicate using sophisticated and highly efficient global networks, which make boundaries formerly imposed by time and geography irrelevant, language as the means of communication remains as one of the last barriers on the way to global understanding.

This is so because communication is essentially about making connections between human beings using language, not between digital networks using standard protocols and fiber optic cables. To make communication possible in a multilingual, collaborative, global, and digital environment, people need to either use a common language when conveying a message (today this is mainly English), or they need to adapt the source language and culture to those of the people they want to communicate with.

The latter includes the provision of services and technologies for the management of multilinguality across the digital and global information flow. In other words, the alternative to the attempt of using a *lingua franca* for communication is the localization of its content.

WHAT'S WRONG WITH ENGLISH?

It could be argued that communication problems related to multilingualism are already solved to a large extent. English has become the language of business, science, and tourism.

Large multinational companies conduct internal communications through English. For example, Airbus, one of the world's largest aerospace manufacturers, directly employs some 52,000 people of over 80 nationalities and 20 different languages, and English is the company's working language (Airbus Today, n.d.).

In the aerospace industry, English is the language most widely used for writing technical documentation; however, it is often not the native language of the readers of such documentation (nor necessarily that of the writers). Many readers have only a limited knowledge of English. They are easily confused by complex sentence structures and by the number of meanings and synonyms that English words can have.

In the late 1970s, the European Association of Aerospace Industries (AECMA), on the request of the Association of European Airlines (AEA), assessed the readability of maintenance documentation in the civilian aircraft industry. The result of this effort was the *AECMA Simplified English Guide,* now the *Specification ASD Simplified Technical English.* The primary aim of AECMA Simplified English is to help nonnative readers of English-language documentation in the aerospace sector understand what they read. This approach has been so successful that other nonaerospace industries have adopted the principles of the AECMA Simplified English guide for their own documentation (Aerospace and Defence Industries Association of Europe, n.d.).

English is the common language of choice not just in science and technology, but also in the tourism sector. No matter whether you are in Asia, the Middle East, the Americas, or Europe, chances are that English will help you order a meal, find a hotel, or get directions (*Country Studies India,* n.d.). Every day, hundreds of political, technical, business, and academic conferences and meetings are held around the world where English native speakers, if present at all, are a minority among delegates. Yet communication is conducted through the "universal" medium of English.

Because it is widely believed—rightly or wrongly—that most of the world's population speaks English to a degree that allows them to communicate and conduct business with each other, English is still the dominant language on the Web.

English has become the medium of communication in many domains. However, there is strong evidence to suggest that this is so not by choice but out of necessity and due to the lack of an alternative.

While advances in technology, trade, and politics have made the world a smaller place, politics and business remain essentially local. People prefer to communicate and conduct business in their own language.

Willy Brandt, the former German Chancellor, once highlighted the essentially local nature of business, making a strong case for the buyer's market: "If I'm selling to you, I speak your language. If I'm buying, dann müssen Sie Deutsch sprechen [then you must speak German]." Statistics, which show that business users are three times more likely to buy when addressed in their own language, bear out this view as Luscombe (2002) shows. While people use, accept, or sometimes just tolerate English as a means of communication, they do so only as long as there is no viable alternative.

LOCALIZATION: ACCESS TO THE DIGITAL WORLD—
IN YOUR LANGUAGE

The localization industry has claimed to be fundamentally different from everything done prior to its emergence. It is the localization industry that provides the services and the technology to people who want to communicate with their friends, colleagues, customers, and clients in the digital world, not in English, but in their own language and within their own cultural reference system.

Localization is like translation—but much more. It is like global marketing—but much broader in its approach. It touches on project management, engineering, quality assurance, and human-computer interface design issues, and covers even aspects of anthropology and international law. In the context of the phenomenal growth of the World Wide Web, localizers have started to debate issues around cultural aspects of localization.

In the following sections, we will outline the emergence of the localization industry and discuss the rationale behind current, mainstream localization efforts. We will explain why people localize and introduce the three principles of localization. Following this, we will question whether current mainstream localization efforts adequately address current and future requirements for multilanguage and multicultural digital content provision.

The Emergence of an Industry

The localization industry as we know it today emerged in the mid-1980s. Ireland quickly became one of the world centers of localization because of the advantage of having English as the dominant language, a highly educated but poorly paid labor force, and exceptional government grants and tax incentives for an industry sector working under the label *international product development.*

The localization industry in Ireland was so successful in the 1990s that the country became the world's number one exporter of software, outperforming even the United States, because 7 out the world's 10 largest independent software developers had located their headquarters for Europe, the Middle East, and Africa (EMEA) in Ireland, among them Microsoft, IBM, Oracle, Novell, Symantec, Apple/Claris, and Corel. In 2003, Ireland exported €14 billion worth of software, and according to industry observers quoted by Hoffmann (2005), this figure is increasing.

An interesting but often overlooked fact is that approximately 95% of all localized products still originate in the United States, where the overwhelming majority of digital publishers now make more money from the sales of their localized products than they make from the sales of the original product. Microsoft, for example, has made more than 60% of its revenues from its international operation for years, with the revenue from localized products exceeding $5 billion. In Ireland alone and according to Balmer quoted in the *Irish Times* (2002), Microsoft carries out more than 1,000 localization projects (product/language) per year, bringing in revenues of $1.9 billion from its international sales in 2001.

The Rationale

A short survey among digital content publishers carried out by the Localisation Research Centre (LRC) seemed to indicate that the business case for localization is quite straightforward—so straightforward, in fact, that many otherwise sensible business people have not more to say than *well, it makes sense* or *everybody else is doing it.*

Even authors of business books on globalization such as DePalma (2002) present pictures of Japanese Web sites to their English-speaking readers and assert under-statedly, "If this page were all the information this company offered to world markets, it would not be the third-largest auto manufacturer in the world." Other figures often quoted in support of a localization business case are those published by GlobalReach (n.d.) in relation to the evolution of the online linguistic popula-tions and global internet statistics by language showing an enormous growth of non-English-speaking Web users.

According to IBM (n.d.), more than two-thirds of today's Internet users are outside the United States, and IDC, a global provider of market intelligence and subsidiary of IDG, the world's leading technology media, research, and events company, states that fewer than 25% of Web users in 2005 lived in the United States, with more than 70% speaking a primary language other than English.

Indeed, there seems to be plenty of examples to show that localization is the route to take if a digital publisher is planning to increase its revenue. As already mentioned, the big three (Microsoft, IBM, and Oracle) make more than 60% of their revenue from international sales. It works for them, so it must work for everybody else.

What is often forgotten, however, is that these multinational giants have almost two decades of localization experience behind them; that is, they started when the World Wide Web existed only in scientists' dreams, and PCs were just about to appear in mainstreet shops. During this time, they have not only figured out how to bring their products to international markets efficiently and effectively, they have also made crucial mistakes and learned very expensive lessons—lessons that small and medium enterprises and even midsized divisions of large multinationals could not afford to take in today's economy.

When localization started in the mid-1980s, it was a highly specialized and labor-intensive activity. Different types of professionals were involved, including software engineers, testers, translators, desktop publishing experts, and project managers. Today, the leaders in localization have adapted what we call the *localization factory*, a term first used by Jewtushenko (2002) from Oracle. Localization factories are highly automated; they rely on tools and process and file exchange standards—all covered under the broad term of "language resources." In a localization factory, labor-intensive, repetitive, costly, and tedious tasks are automated, and the involvement of large numbers of professionals becomes less important.

A typical localization factory, as described by Jewtushenko, can operate as follows:

Project constraints
- 4 million word count software strings
- 30 languages simultaneous release
- 13,000 localizable files
- Localization group in Dublin
- 5,000-person, worldwide distributed development team

Objectives
- 24/7, 100% automated process—no exceptions
- Translation in parallel with development
- Translation begins at code check-in
- Translation "on demand"—no more "big project" model

Achievements
- Current throughput: 100,000 language check-ins per month
- Two million files per month
- 98% of words are leveraged
- Average time to process a file: 45 seconds
- Fully scalable "add-a-box" model
- Simship of all 30 languages
- International version testing before U.S. release
- Reduced number of release engineers (from 20 to 2), resulting in $20 million saving per year
- Positive return on investment (ROI) within one year

The scale of the projects handled in this environment, the turnover achieved, and the level of automation go far beyond the reach of the average localization operation. Nonetheless, there is no doubt that this is the model for the localization operation of the future. The increasing demand for localized digital content in a growing number of languages, including those currently deemed to be not financially viable, cannot be serviced by traditional, mainstream operations anymore.

Just adding a line item to your budget to cover your localization costs—which many companies still calculate by multiplying the number of words in their source product with a rate-per-word and adding a percentage value for project management—no longer works and, perhaps more importantly, will no longer convince senior management to allocate the necessary budget provisions.

In addition, when making the case for localization within an organization, it is crucial to keep in mind that different groups within this organization will have different interests and reasons to localize.

The Three Principles of Localization

In our opinion, current mainstream localization efforts are driven mainly by three principles.

1. *Increase Return on Investment (ROI)*

   An already developed product is superficially adapted to the requirements of foreign markets with a minimum of additional investment and is then sold in these new markets for the same price as the original product.

   This principle implies that it does not always make sense to localize a product. If the target market will most likely not yield the returns necessary to justify the localization effort (and this has to be interpreted in the widest sense), then localization makes no sense. For example, when calculating the ROI in localization, it is not sufficient to subtract the relatively well-defined costs of localization proper from the projected return; it is also necessary to take into account other costs, such as those for market entry or product support.

2. *Use Globally Acceptable Content (LCD/I18N)*

   Developers are instructed to develop products and services using content covering the lowest common denominator (LCD): the out-of-the-box product should not offend anyone and work for all *locales* without the need for further adaptation. In other words, services and products should be *enabled* and should be subject to *internationalization* (I18N).

   Colors, symbols, sound, and signs should be recognizable and understood by as many potential users as possible, independently of their linguistic or cultural background. The less adaptation that needs to be done, the higher the potential earnings from the sales of the localized product will be. The aim is to reduce the localization effort to translation. However, while aiming for the lowest common denominator is good for short-term revenues, there is a danger that the information and entertainment value of the product or service suffers and, subsequently, leads to a decrease in its long-term market value.

3. *Reuse (Leverage) as Much as Possible*

   Translation should be automated as much as possible. Changes to the original product must be kept to an absolute minimum because each modification of the original will have to be implemented in each of the localized versions (x20, 30, or 40). Translations of previously translated, unchanged sources can automatically be inserted into the corresponding target languages of the updated version. This can be up to 80% of the total word count and offers potential savings of millions of dollars/euro.

All of the above principles focus on short-term, financial gains. Localization becomes a commodity where technologies and standards are being developed to reduce the localization effort as much as possible to an automated process, thus dramatically reducing its costs, eliminating the need for human intervention, and increasing the profits of content developers and localizers alike.

Development Localization

Although cost reductions favor localization of digital content into languages which, because of the cost implications, could previously not be considered, localizers have to broaden their horizons and look beyond short-term ROI—if not because of a sense of social responsibility, then because of the opportunities they are going to miss otherwise in the emerging markets.

The following section will introduce a number of short case studies, examples of what we call *development localization* initiatives, which go beyond short-term ROI-driven mainstream localization.

Operating Systems for the Masses

Microsoft is one of the companies that has adopted a highly innovative strategy to provide language versions of its Windows operating system for countries with an expected low ROI and for emerging markets: the *Language Interface Packs (LIPs)*.

The following is an overview of the international support currently available in Windows XP, including LIPs. There are

- 25 fully localized versions of the operating system;
- 33+ Multilingual User Interfaces (MUIs)—language-specific resource files that can be added to the English version of Windows;
- 9 Language Interface Packs (LIPs)—they create a language skin to localize the 20% of the UI that is used 80% of the time;
  - Costs less than $100,000 (not hundreds of thousands);
  - Takes 5–6 weeks (not 5–6 months);
  - Less disk space: 3.5–4 MB (not 40–80 MB).

On November 17, 2004, Microsoft published an interview with Pete Hayes, Microsoft Vice President for EMEA Public Sector, in which he stated that "technology has become an integral part of the global economy. At Microsoft we have always believed that one of the most important uses for technology is to create opportunities today and for the future. As such, we have made a broad commitment to digital inclusion and to helping individuals, communities, and nations gain the

ICT tools and skills they need to realize their full potential." As an example of this commitment, Hayes, quoted in a press release by Microsoft, highlighted programs such as Partners in Learning (PiL) and the Local Language Program (LLP) implemented by Microsoft to address these issues.

On the same day, Microsoft and the United Nations Educational, Scientific, and Cultural Organization (UNESCO) announced a cooperation agreement that would help increase access to Information and Communications Technologies (ICT) and ICT skills training in what the press release called "underserved" communities. At a formal signing ceremony in Paris, Koichïro Matsuura, UNESCO's Director General, and Bill Gates, Microsoft's Chairman and Chief Software Architect, outlined details of the agreement, which include Microsoft and UNESCO focusing on increasing the use of ICT in education and learning, community access and development, and cultural and linguistic diversity and preservation.

A Question of Rights—The European Union

The 25-member, enlarged European Union, with its 380 million citizens, has 20 official languages. (Of the 380 million EU citizens, 200 million speak only *their own* language.)

The economically highly developed European Union perceives its linguistic and cultural diversity not as a barrier but as an opportunity for development; not as a disadvantage but as a rich heritage worth preserving. It invests large amounts of resources to ensure its survival.

Europe operates the largest language service in the world, at a cost of €800 million following the expansion (compared to €500 million prior to the expansion). As the Head of the EU Directorate General Translation, Karl-Johan Loennroth, puts it: "Gone are the days when 'Copyright' was accidentally translated into French as 'the right to copy.'"

In an article on eubusiness.com (2004), he also highlights one of the essential beliefs of the Union: that being able to communicate and access information in one's own language is not a "nice-to-have" or even an option, but "a question of rights, democracy, equality, as well as being part of a peace strategy and a multi-cultural society. The possibility of limiting the number of official EU languages can be ruled out. Everyone is entitled to information in their own language."

The European Union recognizes that there are standards to meet the needs of users with respect to multilinguality covering learning objects, indexing and search, metadata, and ontologies. It believes, however, that their sheer diversity serves to act as a technical barrier—and sometimes national markets are simply too small.

So barriers not only persist, they abound. The Union therefore intervenes with programs, such as the eContent and the new eContent Plus programs, to create the conditions to overcome these barriers by focusing on methods, tools, processes, and services related to the design, development, access and distribution of high-quality digital content, while leaving the actual production of digital content to market forces and, where appropriate, other specific Community initiatives. The financial envelope for the implementation of the new eContent Plus program is proposed to be €163 million covering a period of four years (2005–2008), as reported on the Cordis Web site.

Open Source

In China, South Korea, India, Brazil, and other countries, governments are promoting the use of *open-source software (OSS)*. Adopting open-source software can reduce costs, dispel security concerns, and ensure that there is no danger of becoming too dependent on a foreign supplier. But there is another benefit: because it can be freely modified, open-source software is also easier to translate, or *localize*, for use in a particular language. Large software vendors tend to support just the most widely spoken languages. Microsoft, for example, provides its Windows 2000 operating system in 24 languages, and Windows XP in 33. The company also supports over 20 languages in the latest version of its Office software suite and is planning support for 99 languages for its Vista products.

Shikha Pillai is one of the leaders of a team in Bangalore that is translating open-source software, including OpenOffice, into 10 Indian languages. She is quoted on *The Economist*'s Web site (2003): "Localisation makes IT accessible to common people. . . . And Indian-language enabled software could revolutionize the way our communications work; even the way computers are used in India." In May 2003 Thailand's government launched a subsidised "people's PC" that runs LinuxTLE, a Thai-language version of Linux. In September of the same year, Japan said it would join a project established by China and South Korea to develop localized, open-source alternatives to Microsoft's software. Computer users around the world are discovering that open-source software speaks their language.

The open-source desktop KDE is now available in 42 languages, with an additional 46 languages in the pipeline. The open-source browser Mozilla is already available in 65 languages, with an additional 35 languages planned. The freely available OpenOffice suite has been localized into 31 locales, with another 44 coming up. Together, KDE and Gnome are available in more than twice as many languages as industry-standard desktop interfaces.

OUTLOOK

Current localization projects are, almost without exception, based on real or expected ROI, what business people call "a solid business case." The problem with this approach is that it ignores other, equally important and more long-term strategies for localization; that is, those driven by political, social, cultural, and long-term investment reasons.

The current approach contributes to the growth of the digital divide between the people and countries taking part in the digital world and those who are excluded from it. If access to the Web is a distinct advantage in business and education, then those who have no access to it (the vast majority of the world's population today) are distinctly disadvantaged. Some industry experts have even warned that languages and cultures not present in the digital world will eventually disappear, as

David Brooks observed at the First International Conference on Language Resources and Evaluation, Granada, Spain, May 28–30, 1998.

Basic barriers for the participation in the digital world remain, and basic issues are currently unresolved for developing countries in Africa and Asia. According to Unicode, the character encoding standards association, at the current rate it will take 700 years to encode the world's remaining scripts in Unicode, a standard that allows for the encoding of virtually every script. Yet the estimated cost for this effort is only in the region of $2–3 million, as Deborah Anderson (2003) observed at the Internationalization and Unicode Conference in Atlanta (September 3–5, 2003).

Chinje, Danforth, and Mori (2003) of the World Bank stated recently that Africa offers many opportunities for the development of the digital world but that innovation is needed to overcome existing barriers preventing access for African countries.

There seems to be a general agreement that current localization efforts even endanger languages and cultures; that a new approach, *development localization*, is needed to help with the removal of basic barriers that are preventing the entry of developing countries into the digital world and to break the *negative value chain* currently being applied to low ROI markets: no market—no internationalization— no localization—no digital presence—no survival of digital diversity.

In September of 2005, major organizations came together in Limerick, Ireland, to officially launch the Global Initiative for Local Computing (GILC) with the signing of the Limerick Declaration (www.gilc.info/LimerickDeclaration.pdf), which supports local computing across geographical, political, social, and economic divides. Using existing frameworks, GILC builds on the infrastructure for regional initiatives to coordinate, pool resources, raise awareness, and communicate on a global level. GILC questions commonly held beliefs about the rationale, scale, and feasibility of localization projects, and offers solutions to people who want to participate in the digital world but are not currently served by mainstream localization efforts.

As we said at the outset, language is the most important medium of communication, even in the digital world. What localization has shown us, however, is that we do not necessarily need to speak the same language to communicate effectively. To the contrary—it could well be that respect and understanding among people can be achieved only if we preserve and nurture linguistic and cultural diversity.

REFERENCES

Aerospace and Defence Industries Association of Europe. (2005). *ASD Simplified Technical English Maintenance Group (STEMG),* formerly the "AECMA Simplified English Maintenance Group (SEMG)."
http://www.asd-ste100.org
Airbus Today. (n.d.). http://www.airbus.com/en/careers/working/culture/careers_diversity.html
Anderson, D. (2003). The digital divide and the script encoding initiative. In *Proceedings of Unicode 24.* Atlanta, Georgia.

Brooks, D. (1998). Remark made in a panel session of the First International Conference on Language Resources and Evaluation, Granada, Spain, May 28-30, 1998.

Chinje, E., Danforth, V., & Mori, I. (2003). Excuse me, again: Where? In *Proceedings Localization World*. Seattle, Washington.

Cordis. European Commission. (n.d.). *The European Union eContent programme.* http://www.cordis.europe.eu/econtent

Country Studies India. (n.d.). http://www.country-studies.com/india/english.html

DePalma, D. A. (2002). *Business without borders, A strategic guide to global marketing.* New York: John Wiley & Sons.

eubusiness.com. (2004, March 31). *Lost in translation: Official EU languages rise to 20.* http://www.eubusiness.com/afp/040331144847.921jlht7

GlobalReach. (2004). *Global Internet statistics (by language).* http://www.global-reach.biz/globstats

Hoffmann, K. (2005, 26 March). How the Celtic tiger became the world's software export champ. *Der Spiegel.* http://www.spiegel.de/international/spiegel/0,1518,348682,00.html

IBM. (n.d.). *Globalizing your e-business.* http://www.ibm.com/software/globalization/story.jsp

Irish Times. (2002, 21 October). *Microsoft reports substantial growth.*

Jewtushenko, T. (2002). Use case for translating Oracle technology using Web services. In *Proceedings LRC 2002 Conference*. Limerick, Ireland.

Luscombe, H. (2002). It's not just about speaking English loudly. *Bigmouthmedia.* http://www.bigmouthmedia.com/live/articles/its_not_just_about_speaking_english_loudly.asp

Microsoft. (2004, 17 November). *Microsoft and UNESCO announce joint education and community development initiatives,* Paris, France. http://www.microsoft.com/emea/presscentre/PressRelease.aspx?file=MSUNESCO PREMEA.xml

Microsoft. (2004, 17 November). *UNESCO and Microsoft to focus on technology in joint initiative for community development, Paris, France.* http://www.microsoft.com/emea/pressCentre/UNESCO.mspx

Microsoft. (n.d.). *Windows XP professional language interface pack (LIP).* http://www.microsoft.com/globaldev/DrIntl/faqs/LIPFaq.mspx

The Economist. (2003, 4 December). Open source's local heroes—software: If the commercial sort does not speak your language, open-source software may well do so instead. http://www.economist.com/science/tq/displayStory.cfm?Story_id=2246308

CHAPTER 6

The Hidden Costs of Cross-Cultural Documentation

Marie-Louise Flacke

By the end of 2005, it is estimated that only a third of all Internet users worldwide will be English speakers (Wordbank, n.d.). For corporations trying to expand their markets, localization is essential to the success of a product in overseas markets. To reach their global customers, organizations need to localize products and documentation without putting their localization investments at stake because of cultural gaffes. Based on experience in editing localized documentation, this study shows some localization pitfalls and their indirect costs.

TRANSLATION AND LOCALIZATION

To reach global customers, organizations need to speak the consumers' language. Is translation the right step? Why localize?

Translation is converting concepts from a source language into a target language. A good translator focuses on reproducing the original text as closely as possible into another language. Translating means the translator gets into the author's shoes and provides the audience with the feeling that they are reading the original text.

However, localization goes beyond translation. It means taking into account a whole country with its culture: "Taking a product and making it linguistically and culturally appropriate to the target locale (country/region and language) where it will be used and sold" (LISA, n.d.). Indeed, "Translation alone does not make your site local" (Layden, 1997). Translation is only a part of the localization process. In fact, good translation is a key (but only one) element of localization, which is the baseline for effective localization

Localizers focus on adapting documentation to a specific culture. To customize a product for a country, professional localizers adopt the perspective of the target (local) user audience. They include the set of information associated with a place, known as "locale," into the localization project.

When going global, a corporation should go beyond translating its product information and make sure that product and documentation are properly localized.

NEEDS FOR LOCALIZATION

Because of the high revenue generated by overseas sales and because "most global end-users prefer to use a product in their own tongue rather than English, which to them is a second (or third) language" (Layden, 1997), organizations have their products and their documentation translated into several languages. Not only do users prefer a product in their own language, but they also welcome documentation that fits into their culture. "In fact, a product that is localized well will appear as though it was originally produced in that country" (Layden, 1997).

Localized products sell better, but how much does the localization cost?

TRANSLATION BUDGET

Translation costs are part of the localization budget. Various figures have circulated about high translation costs. A striking example is given by the European Union (EU), whose bill for translation will balloon by nearly 60% to over €1 billion a year to prevent the bloc from turning into a Tower of Babel after its eastward expansion. The European Commission said the annual cost of written translation was expected to grow to €807 million in the next few years, from €549 million in 2003, when Brussels' institutions already translated a staggering 1.3 million pages (Grajewski, 2005).

Because the EU aims at providing each European citizen with the most accurate information in each European language, it must render each publication understandable to each citizen. This means translating the official publications into 20 languages.

LOCALIZATION EFFORT AND COST

In the private sector, organizations invest massively in localizing products and documentation. As an example, cellular phones and the pertinent documentation are localized in 50 languages.

When going global, an organization should be aware that budgeting 50 different translations of the same source documentation is not enough. Each translation must comply with the quality standards applying to its locale.

At this stage, quality in translation and localization is of the essence. Any poorly localized product might generate considerable costs: "According to the U.S. State Department, U.S. firms alone lose $50 billion in potential sales each year because of problems with translation and localization" (Layden, 1997). Not only is extensive translation an expensive activity, but if poorly localized, a product will have a dramatically increased budget and still not reach its potential customers. Localization service providers and translation experts have searched for ways to both provide quality translation and maintain the costs within reasonable limits.

TECHNIQUES AND TOOLS

A way to reduce translation costs, as suggested by localization service providers, is using Machine Translation (MT) and Translation Memory Software (TMS). TMS helps speed up the work of translators: by comparing what needs to be translated with what has already been translated, it helps the translator to focus on the updated text and ignore the already translated and approved text. Machine translation (MT) performs an automatic pretranslation of the source text that is then reviewed and fine-tuned by a professional translator.

What impacts have these tools had on translation costs? How far can they help reduce the localization budget?

TRANSLATION COSTS

Localization costs are distributed as follows: whereas quality translation is one of the main issues in the localization process, it accounts for only 50% of the localization cost. Further, the "local approval" is between 5% and 15% of the localization cost. The remaining costs include content/file handling, project management, desktop publishing, glossary management, and translation memory management. Based on these figures, translation and local review might be 65% of the localization costs.

By streamlining the process, localization providers offering MT, TMS, and content management solutions claim a 30% cost reduction. TMS tools reduce some translation costs by identifying and reusing already translated text. Therefore, using a TMS tool to reduce translation costs is only profitable for important translation projects that are subject to updates. A one-shot translation does not benefit from a TMS tool.

Saving 30% of the costs does not apply to the whole localization cost but exclusively to the translation costs, that is, to 50% of the localization budget. At the end, the reduction shrinks to 15% of the total cost of localization. Still, considering the size of some localization projects, a 15% reduction might result in saving millions of dollars. This is a very positive step in the process: the product documentation is translated, and translation costs have been reduced.

QUALITY CHECKS

But how can we be sure the translation meets the quality level that would prevent U.S. firms from losing those $50 billion of potential sales? To reach the required level of quality, Nadine Kano (2002) stresses the essential step of checking that "translations meet the standards of native speakers with respect to grammar and accuracy of terminology." Performing a translation Quality Assurance (QA) check is a good solution. Provided a native speaker is entrusted with these proofreading tasks, the QA test might ensure a higher quality translation.

COSTS OF QA

Obviously, this quality improvement has a cost. Proofreaders are being paid on an hourly basis to review and amend the translated text. Consider, for example, that an hourly fee of €40 can tremendously increase the localization costs. Indeed, the poorer the translation quality is, the more time the proofreader needs to upgrade the translated text.

These extra review costs might neutralize the savings generated by the MT tools. The localization service provider Wordbank (2008) is well aware of this threat: "It is . . . worth noting that the application of strongly promoted translation technologies such as translation memories and machine translation can only really make a (small) contribution to reducing the costs for translation. Their use may increase the cost of the final QA."

Localization managers might be advised to first check how much translation savings that implementing an MT or a TMS tool might generate. A senior translator will certainly provide good advice.

LOCALIZATION PITFALLS

Still, localization managers have identified several other ways to reduce costs by not only considering the translation, but focusing on the local usage and, therefore, preventing costly pitfalls. Project managers who want to go global must be aware that "Now, more than ever, showing respect for your customer's culture is crucial to your product's success in the overseas marketplace" (Layden, 1997).

Translating a document or a Web site means providing a linguistically correct product. To reach the target audience in a specific country, it is essential to localize; that is, ensure the product and its documentation are culturally acceptable.

The following tips might help the project manager localize without generating unnecessary costs.

UNNECESSARY ENGINEERING COSTS

Because localization implies not only translation, but also software reengineering, it is essential to spot all potential issues very early in the process.

Performing a pilot project (PP), as defined by Microsoft localization experts Ebben and Marshall, is a good way to eliminate bugs. "A pilot project is run to find and solve localization problems before the bulk of the work starts and to streamline the localization process. When a product is localized in a few languages, running a pilot can be a time- and cost-saving exercise" (Ebben & Marshall, 1999). The PP implies first selecting one or two languages in which the product and the documentation should be localized. Step two consists of running the localization process in the selected language(s).

In fact, because running a pilot project helps the localization team "identify and resolve international issues without wasting . . . translator's time (and your money) by fixing bugs later" (Ebben & Marshall, 1999), it becomes a useful tool. The return on investment of a PP is indeed very high. Because the team does not lose time and money fixing bugs in each localized version, it maintains the costs within budget. The golden rule defined by Microsoft localization experts recommends focusing on the costs of bugs, not on the cost of a single translated word. Because

$$TotalBugs = coreBugs * Languages$$

and

$$TotalBugs = Engineering\ Hours,$$

it is essential to identify and eliminate bugs at an early stage of the first localization effort. Having several engineers fix the same bugs in 20 languages will definitely increase the manpower cost of the project.

With a machine translation tool, the team might have a chance to reduce costs by 15%. Running a PP not only saves translation costs because it translates in only one language and then fixes the bugs before launching the translation in other languages, it also saves a large number of expensive engineering hours.

UNNECESSARY TRANSLATIONS COSTS

Running the pilot project, the project manager will avoid providing the localization team with *poor quality source text.* Indeed, being faced with an ambiguous text, the translator will spend unnecessary time and energy trying to understand what the author means. Should the translator be under considerable time pressure, he or she might also misinterpret the text, resulting in an erroneous translation. Because of inaccuracy in the source text, errors might be reproduced in each language and turn into a very costly mishap.

Ebben and Marshall (1999) clearly spotted this issue: "Design flaws in the source content can cause . . . serious problems because they tend to multiply in the target (translated) content." Further, ensuring a high quality source text facilitates the use of a machine translation tool to provide a fast and accurate translation.

Country-specific terms are an example of *issues in the source text.* Selecting "Abbott and Costello" or "Helmut and Hannelore" as example names to help the end user follow a procedure might not be the best choice. How many users ever heard of Costello? Or Hannelore? How should a Maltese end user relate these names to the product documentation? How many translators have ever heard of Abbott? What should they do with this entry? Maintain this name or try to localize it? To prevent such ambiguity, product managers keen to properly localize their product documentation will check that "Text and messages are devoid of slang and specific cultural references" (Kano, 2002). This approach will definitely smooth the translation process and help provide a confusion-free translation. Further, running the pilot project, the project manager might screen the source documentation for redundant information.

A good way for professional localizers to find and erase the superfluous text is to put the end user's hat on and think locally, asking such questions as: Is this information pertinent to my target audience? Do users need these details?

Indeed, information provided to a customer should be checked for pertinence before it is translated into dozens of languages. A mobile phone company, for example, might consider eliminating the chapter describing the dual-tone multi-Frequency (DTMF) functions from its user's manual. Even though the DTMF functions are fully operational in most countries, translating this feature description in various languages means generating unnecessary translation costs. As a matter of fact, consumers use the DTMF keys of their mobile phones without knowing it. There is no point in explaining to end users what this specific function means, since they do not need this information. Only telecommunication engineers involved in mobile phone developments might be interested in details on the DTMF functions, not end users. The "DTMF ringing, sending DTMF parameters . . . etc." chapter does not need to be provided in 50 languages!

Another example of unnecessarily translated text is the *unnecessary list of technical standards* spread over several pages of end user's documentation. Translating, for example, the list of standards the product complies with, such as FCC rules, VDE, ICNIRP, GS11, ANSI, and so on, does not make much sense. The FCC rules and the ANSI standards apply in the United States only, the VDE recommendations are relevant to the German products; there is no need to have these country-specific standards translated into other languages. Localizing to EU countries requires mentioning only the European norms pertinent to the localized product, since one single norm applies to 25 countries and is marked as "EN"-standard.

LOCALIZATION PITFALLS: RELIGION

Because of the diversity of religions, it is important to check with the local vendor whether a reference to a specific religion is appropriate. For example, it does not make much sense to translate a Jewish calendar into languages spoken in countries using a different calendar. Not only would it mean unnecessary translation costs, but it might also embarrass those of a different religion.

A local vendor or a native translator would also prevent internationalization issues such as improperly localizing religious references. A worldwide software corporation had to publicly apologize for "Using chanting of the Koran as a soundtrack for a computer game which led to great offense to the Saudi Arabia government" (How 8 pixels cost Microsoft millions, 2004).

These mishaps are very costly and can ruin a project, in particular when the product is withdrawn from the target market: "The software giant managed to offend the Saudis by creating a game in which Muslim warriors turned churches into mosques. That game was withdrawn" (How 8 pixels cost Microsoft millions, 2004).

LOCALIZATION PITFALLS: CULTURE

Localization professionals should always make sure that the product is "tailored to fit the local culture" (Layden, 1997). Ignoring language and cultural usage might very easily put a product or a site at stake. On his Web site, a consultant specializing in international communication recommended to individuals interested in globalization to first collect data on the country they wanted to localize in. This is definitely an excellent recommendation. Unfortunately, the list of resources for internationalization displayed on the consultant's site contains a pitfall. Recommending to check the CIA Web site as a "fabulous resource" (Hoft, 2002, *International interest*) to get information on a specific country will certainly cause problems for some overseas citizens!

Language ignorance is also a sensitive point. Saying, for example, "German technical writers often use scholarly footnotes and references to other literature. . . . Their sentences tend to be long, full of compound words and subordinate clauses" (Hoft, 2002, *German writing*) will certainly surprise if not upset German writers. Indeed, it is a characteristic of the German language to build words by concatenating existing terms. It is, for example, grammatically correct to say "Strassenbahn-haltestelle" for "tram stop," and not "Haltestelle für die Strassenbahn." When embracing internationalization, it is wise not to measure other cultures solely with one's personal view and culture.

LOCALIZATION PITFALLS: ETHICS

Ethics is also part of each country's culture and should be addressed very carefully. References to history and weapons, for example, might be highly problematic. In Europe, anything that deals with World War II should be treated by a native localizer. A *faux pas* might cost thousands of dollars and damage the company's reputation. In one case, an Internet service provider (ISP) offered French subscribers the opportunity to trade Nazi memorabilia on the Internet. Since such trading is unlawful in most European countries, the ISP was taken to court, both in the localized country and in the United States:

> A French-based human rights group that protested the sale of Nazi memorabilia on Yahoo Auctions has filed a motion with the U.S. District Court in San Jose seeking to dismiss Yahoo's lawsuit (Barnes, 2001).

In this case, the localization costs reached an extremely high level. Apart from the translation costs of its site and the pertinent documentation, the ISP was faced with legal costs both in the United States and in Europe, not to mention loss of image. A proper localization would have prevented such a pitfall by having the legal terms of using the ISP Web site checked and adapted by a local legal counsel.

Reference to weapons is very questionable in most European countries. In one case, European papers widely spread the news about a computer manufacturer's sales policies that were displayed on the Internet. Before finalizing a personal computer (PC) acquisition, the potential customer was asked to answer questions about using weapons of mass destruction, nuclear weapons, missiles, and so on. The customers perceived these inquiries as awkward and aborted their purchase process. Since this localization bug was widely reported in the European press, the organization lost a considerable number of sales and ruined its image. In this case, localizing the legal terms—and not merely translating them—would have prevented such a business disaster.

Translating the following paragraph in 20 languages does not make sense with regard to globalization:

> Further, under U.S. law, the goods shipped pursuant to this Agreement may not be sold, leased or otherwise transferred to restricted countries or utilized by restricted end-users or an end-user engaged in activities related to weapons of mass destruction . . . (Dell Inc., 2007).

Because these rules pertain to U.S. law, they apply in the United States only. Therefore, translating these restrictions into numerous languages not only increases the translation costs, but generates a puzzled reaction from the local end user: "What should I do with such rules, since I am not based in the United States?"

LOCAL AND LEGAL?

Professional localization teams should focus on localizing the legal agreements for each country. Another example of the risks incurred by poor legal localization is the so-called €77,000 translation. An ISP was fined €77,000 for binding customers with illegal agreements. In one piece of European legislation, the ISP Terms of Use contained 22 abusive clauses and 10 illegal articles. Because the localization team merely translated the original agreements without adapting them to the local legislation, it generated a costly court decision in the target country.

Project managers involved in globalization should ensure that their localization teams do not translate legal texts, but invest in legal counsel to investigate pertinent legal issues applicable in the localized country.

LOCALIZATION PITFALLS: GEOGRAPHY

To provide a cost-effective localization, staff not only needs to be proficient in the specific language, but must also have an understanding of geography, because geography sometimes costs millions. As an example, consider this issue of coloring maps. Microsoft manager Tom Edward revealed how one of the biggest companies in the world managed to offend one of the biggest countries in the world with a software slip-up. When coloring in 800,000 pixels on a map of India, Microsoft colored eight of them a different shade of green to represent the disputed Kashmiri territory. The difference in greens meant Kashmir was shown as non-Indian and the product was promptly banned in India. Microsoft headquarters in Redmond was left to recall all 200,000 copies of the offending Windows 95 software to try and heal the diplomatic wounds. "It cost millions . . ." (How 8 pixels cost Microsoft millions, 2004).

How could a project manager prevent such a disaster? Additional training in international business and an introduction to country-specific culture would be a good start: "Staff members are now sent on geography courses to try to avoid such mishaps. Some of our employees, however bright they may be, have only a hazy idea about the rest of the world" (How 8 pixels cost Microsoft millions, 2004).

LOCALIZATION TENDENCIES

Recent tendencies in localization aim at developing a direct link between project management and an in-country individual translator for each language, thus reducing the number of agencies, subcontractors, and intermediates. The senior translator is appointed localization expert in charge of evaluating project size and issues. Depending on the project size, he or she might decide to set up a localization team made up of professional translators who are experienced native speakers. As the localization expert, the senior translator is also responsible for the localization quality.

Being in-country, the localization expert might also pay attention to ethics and make sure that "The great-nation chauvinism [is] driven away. A worldview that respects every nation, no matter small or big, weak or powerful should be advocated in localization practices" (Huatong Sun, 2002). Because of a direct connection to the project manager, the localization expert is able to quickly spot and efficiently resolve potential localization issues.

CONCLUSION

When localizing, it is essential to remember that ". . . lack of multicultural savvy attitude cost[s] . . . millions of dollars" (How 8 pixels cost Microsoft millions, 2004).

For a project manager, getting prepared for internationalization would cover these tasks:

- Learn to listen to other cultures.
- Build a team including (in-country) local experts.
- Provide the team with clear instructions: localize, don't translate verbatim!
- Provide staff with accurate information on geography, history, and ethics.
- Reduce the number of intermediates between management and in-country localization experts.

REFERENCES

Barnes C. (2001, February 8). Nazi memorabilia controversy continues. *CNET News.* http://news.com.com/Nazi+memorabilia+controversy+continues/2110-1017_3-252296.html

Dell Inc. Terms and Conditions of Sale. (2007). http://www.dell.com/content/topics/global.aspx/policy/en/policy?c=us&l=en&s=gen&~section=012

Ebben, S., & Marshall, G. (1999). *The localization process: Globalizing your code and localizing your site.* Microsoft TecNet. http://www.microsoft.com/technet/archive/ittasks/plan/sysplan/glolocal.mspx?mfr=true.

Grajewski, M. (2005). *EU faces soaring translation bill.* http://www.lisa.org

Hoft N. (2002). *German writing.* http://www.world-ready.com/stcorlando.htm

Hoft, N. (2002). *International interest.* http://www.world-ready.com/r_intl.htm

How 8 pixels cost Microsoft millions. (2004, August 29). *The Economic Times Online.* http://economictimes.indiatimes.com/articleshow/msid-823975,prtpage-1.cms

Huatong Sun. (2002). Why cultural contexts are missing: A rhetorical critique of localization practices. *Proceedings of the Annual Conference of the Society for Technical Communication.* http://www.stc.org/confproceed/2002/PDFs/STC49-00090.pdf

Kano, N. (2002). *Developing international software.* http://www.microsoft.com/globaldev/dis_v1/disv1.asp

Layden, J. (1997). http://www.halcyon.com/pub/journals/21ps03-vidmar

Localization: Essential for competing in the global marketplace. http://www.fita.org/aotm/0698.html

LISA. (n.d.). www.lisa.org

Wordbank. (2008). http://www.wordbank.com

CHAPTER 7

How to Save Time and Money by Connecting the Writing Process to the Update and Translation Process

Margaretha Eriksson

THE COST OF TRANSLATION—A BRIEF BACKGROUND

The lifecycle of a software package or product documentation follows a typical pattern: the text documents are authored and published for the first time, they are translated and published in other languages, they are then further edited or updated and published, retranslated, and so on. Every cycle introduces a cost, calculated as the number of words multiplied by the price per word multiplied by the number of languages:

Translation Cost = No. of Words * Price / Word * No. of Languages

In the following paragraphs, I describe the different components and players in this process.

DOCUMENTS AND SOFTWARE PACKAGES

A software package or the documentation of a product normally consists of program files containing text strings that make up a graphical user interface (GUI), help files, screen messages, and one or more manuals. This package is designed and written in English and then proofread before being published. Many software packages are translated into one, ten, or more language versions. Since translation charges are on a per word basis, the first step is to count the number of words to be translated. In the first version of a product, every word must be translated, since all the texts are considered new. The cost of the translation is the full translation of all words.

Later, a second version of the product is published with various updates, correc-tions, and new texts. This second version must also be translated and published as soon as possible.

By using a tool called translation memory (*Translator's Workbench Help*, 2002), the translator can recall all the phrases that were translated in the first version and reuse them in the second version. What remains are the new and modified parts, which the translator needs to translate from scratch, and which are also added to the translation memory. The cost of the second translation is obviously less than that of the original translation since only the updates and changes are translated. This saves both time and money.

Here, I argue for careful updating to avoid unnecessary translation costs further down the line. These unnecessary costs arise from grammatical "touch ups," for-matting changes, and the inconsistent use of terminology. In this chapter, I present typical cases to show how costs can be reduced by careful editing.

A translation memory is a database in which pairs of phrases are stored. For example, an English phrase (source) might be stored together with the Swedish equivalent of that phrase (target). When the English phrase first occurs in the text, it is translated into Swedish, and both the source phrase and the target phrase are stored. When a stored English phrase occurs later in the text, this phrase is immediately translated into the stored Swedish equivalent.

PEOPLE AND ORGANIZATION

Many participants are involved in the life cycle of a document, and below I define the major players, as seen from the translator's point of view.

The life cycle of a document consists of the steps create, update, and finally delete, when the document becomes obsolete (Hoft, 1995). At least five categories of specialists are involved during this life cycle—the translation customer, trans-lation vendor, author/technical writer, project manager, and translator.

The Customer and the Translation Vendor

The customer's part in the process is to deliver the texts to be translated from in-house sources or contract writers to the translation vendor. Later, the customer receives the translated texts, which are ready to be built into a localized version of the software.

The Authors/Technical Writers

The number of technical writers used, either individually or in teams, is governed by the size of the writing project. The technical writers create the content of the text documents and possibly also illustrations and layout. Some of the writers are subject matter experts (SMEs) or work in close conjunction with SMEs. The writers might have terminology experts on hand, defining project-specific terminology and glossaries. A project might also employ typographical designers or GUI designers (Esselink, 1998).

The Translators

The translators work as individual freelancers or in teams, employed on a project basis. Again, the number of translators used depends on the size of the translation project. For example, to translate a press release requires only one translator, whereas to translate and localize Microsoft Windows from English into a single language, due to its size and the time-to-market requirements, takes 50 to 100 translators. Each translator must be familiar with the terminology of the topic in the target language. Translators translate the text but leave the layout unchanged (Eriksson, 1999).

Project Managers

Project managers ensure the progress of translation projects. Files are received from the technical writers, sent for translation to individual translators, checked when they are returned in a translated state, and finally, sent to the customer for conversion into the GUI, online help, and manuals.

TOOLS

Microsoft Office and FrameMaker are the most widespread tools in the authoring community. Many corporations have chosen Microsoft Office as their generic authoring environment; others prefer to mix and match, using Frame Maker or other packages.

The choice of authoring tool is not significant from the translator's point of view. What matters most to the translator is that the source files can be handled by Trados Translator's Workbench, also known as Trados or translation memory (TM), which is a tool commonly used by translators. In its simplest form, a TM is a database in which pairs of phrases are stored, with one phrase in the source language and a corresponding phrase in the target language.

Other products providing similar functionality are DejaVu and Star Transit.

MINIMIZING COSTS WHILE MAXIMIZING QUALITY

Minimizing Translation Time

The extreme requirements of time-to-market make translation a pressured activity, placing high demands on both writers and translators. The more text material that can be reused the better.

Single-sourcing has become increasingly popular since it speeds up the process. Already created and proofed documents or parts of documents are reused, as are their translated versions. This minimizes production time.

Minimizing Costs

The cost of translation, from the translator's viewpoint, has decreased over the last 15 years. Translators are expected to work faster, using translation memories, and yet are paid less. Meanwhile, the volume of translation work is steadily growing.

From the producer's side, translation is about creating and protecting a market. Software in Swedish sells more to the general public in Sweden, than that in a foreign language, such as English. Importantly, a Swedish directive states that government agencies must purchase translated software for the usability benefits that it provides for employees.

Maximizing Quality

The quality of a translation depends on the quality of the translator and on internal quality controls implemented by the translation vendor (Samuelsson-Brown, 1998). The quality of a translation also depends on the translator's access to terminology, reference material, and previously translated versions. These needs are often ignored by project managers due to lack of time or competence, leaving the translator to rely on guesswork. Previous translations may not be available due to a change of translation vendor or personnel.

Handling Updates

Selecting the material to be updated is a delicate issue: how much text must be changed because it is incorrect; what can be presented in a more readable way by making formatting changes; and finally, what grammatical fine-tuning is needed? An observant corporation tracks updates in its internal documentation. It is then easy to send the documentation for translation and incorporate changes.

Three types of updates or changes can be made:

- Those necessary to correct errors,
- Those made for clarity or aesthetic reasons, and
- Those involving changes in formatting and template styles.

LOCALIZATION-RELATED ISSUES

Changes in Content and Formatting

A text document consists of words and formatting, which are governed by terminology, style guides, and writing guidelines. Bulleted lists and the capitalization of initial letters may improve readability and clarity but seldom change the content. The same is true for manual line breaks, which keep text together on two consecutive lines. The use of commas and periods can change the meaning of a phrase, and thus the content.

Spelling

Translators expect a document to be spell-checked and proofread before they receive it, although those expectations are not always met. Consequently, many translators routinely spell-check each document before they start to translate it.

Spelling mistakes can also arise, for example, from the differences between British English and American English. When the text is analyzed in Trados, such discrepancies show up as deviations in the source text.

Below, I illustrate several common formatting issues of which many authors may be unaware, such as the local formatting of numbers, date, and time. The choice of decimal symbol and measurement system, as well as the use of inches/feet or the metric system is also significant.

- The Calendar Type: calendar used in the country of the target language, mainly languages such as Japanese and Chinese
- Short Date/Long Date: how short and long date formats are to be localized during translation
- Time Style: how the time format is to be localized during translation
- Digit Grouping: the symbol used in the target language to group large numbers
- Decimal Symbol: the symbol used to indicate decimal values in the target language
- Measurement System: the system of measurement used in the target language

ANALYZING THE DIFFERENCES IN TRADOS

Trados Translator's Workbench incorporates a useful analysis tool that compares the source text with the phrases already stored in the translation memory. The translator uses this tool to determine the volume of the assignment, the number of repetitions, and the percentage of matches within the text files. Figure 1 shows a typical report from the tool.

When the source phrase is identical to a phrase stored in the memory, this constitutes a *100% match*. Figure 1 shows 17 segments and 17 words of this type.

When a slight deviation is found in the source phrase compared with the phrase in the memory, this is called a *fuzzy match*. Fuzzy matches are sorted in ranges: 95%–98%, 85%–94%, 75%–84%, and 50%–74%. Figure 1 shows six segments with 35 words of this type.

The result *no match* is considered to be less than 50% similar to any phrase in the memory. There are 280 segments with 3,738 words of this type. This document is considered new to a degree of 95%.

Matching Formatting Effects

Words set in *italics* or **bold** in a document should remain so in the translated document. Trados Translator's Workbench is sensitive to the formatting of words, and this is set in the Penalties function, which is used to penalize source sentences where the formatting differs from that of the matching translation memory source sentence.

Translation Memory: F:\Translation\Minne\Remote_Access.tmw
F:\Translation\Dec04\Orig\User's Guide01.doc

Analyse Total (1 file):

Match Types	Segments	Words	Percent	Placeables
XTranslated	0	0	0	0
Repetitions	43	156	4	4
100%	17	17	0	0
95%–98%	1	3	0	0
85%–94%	2	14	0	0
75%–84%	5	9	0	0
50%–74%	6	35	1	0
No Match	280	3,738	95	14
Total	354	3,972	100	18
Chars/Word	4.74			
Chars Total	18,832			

Figure 1. Example of an analyzed report log. This is a list of matches, rated by the similarity with an existing translation stored in memory.

COST-SAVING ADVICE

Below, I offer the authoring community some useful advice to help speed up the translation phase and save money.

Know the Translation Pricing Model

Keep the number of changes as low as possible in order to avoid introducing unnecessary translation costs. The translation vendor charges a fixed amount per translated word, and when the match is closer to 100%, the charge is lower. "No match" represents 100% of the fee, while "100% match" represents a small fraction of the fee.

Terminology Used During Authoring

Make sure to establish a firm terminology base in each documentation project. Make the terminology base available online to writers and proofreaders in the project. Make sure that approved terms are used consistently throughout documents.

Terminology During Translation

Make sure that approved terminology is available to translators when documents are sent for translation.

Be prepared to respond to feedback from translators, who may ask for clarification on the correct use of terms, as well as synonyms used.

Support Translators During Translation

Consider the translator to be a person who is completely new to the project's jargon and terminology. The terminology list is essential if a translator is to produce relevant and accurate translations (Eriksson, 1999).

Terminology Management During Translation

Update the terminology list with new terms when they are introduced. Use feedback received from the translators. Remember to distribute the version of the terminology to all involved parties.

Establish a terminology master and a change control board, whose responsibility is to maintain and update the terminology database.

Establish a Writing Style Guide

Be sure to establish a style guide within the organization, and make it available online for everyone in the project. Establish a style guide master and a change control board, whose responsibility is to maintain and update the style guide. These are excellent support tools for the writers.

Make sure that templates and styles are used consistently throughout documents. Translators value consistently formatted documents, as these create fewer fuzzy matches caused by formatting penalties.

Establish a Localization Style Guide

The localization style guide is as important as the writing style guide, the only difference being that it deals with the target language. This guide establishes the use of terminology, tone of voice, the use of active or passive tense, spelling rules, the use of branding, and many other language-specific details.

Establish Proofreading Guidelines

Proofreaders reduce translation costs by ensuring that there are no spelling errors and that correct terminology is used. They can also check that "fixed phrases" are used consistently throughout a document.

Writers and copyeditors should ask themselves critically if minor changes, such as the use of initial capital letters for clarity or adding a comma, are really necessary, as these small changes increase the total translation cost.

REFERENCES

Eriksson, M. (1999). Multimedia demands a new breed of translators. In J-M. Vande Valle (Ed.), *Proceedings of the XV Congress* (pp. 112-114). Mons: International Federation of Translators.

Esselink, B. (1998). *A practical guide to software localization.* Amsterdam: John Benjamins Publishing Company.

Hoft, N. L. (1995). *International technical communication.* New York: John Wiley & Sons.
Samuelsson-Brown, G. (1998). *A practical guide for translators* (3rd ed.). Clevedon: Multilingual Matters Ltd.
Translator's Workbench Help. (2002). Dublin: TRADOS Ireland Ltd.

CHAPTER 8

Technical Communication and Cross-Cultural Miscommunication: User Culture and the Outsourcing of Writing

Joseph Jeyaraj

Writing is a culturally situated activity. When writing is outsourced to other cultures, because of a lack of knowledge of the users' culture and the influence of the local culture, those doing the writing and design, despite various strategies adopted for overcoming these disadvantages, may not know how to culturally situate the writing. It is therefore important that bicultural people who know the users' culture as well as the culture of those doing the outsourced work give writing teams feedback about the users' culture.

While cultural differences depend on various categories like ethnicity, nationality, and profession, this chapter focuses on the cultural miscommunication caused by nationality, partly because in outsourcing, nationality is an important category, which causes cultural miscommunication and partly because it would take too much space to deal with the cultural differences caused by other categories. My chapter therefore examines writing situations in places like India to where writing is outsourced. I argue that although those doing the writing attempt to eliminate the effects of local influences in their writing, the problem of lack of cultural situatedness is not fully addressed.

As a solution, I suggest that bicultural people, who know both the users' culture and the culture of those doing the outsourced work, act as a resource to help those doing the outsourced writing to understand the users' culture. Finally, I give examples of culturally situated documentation and point out how such documentation greatly helps users.

OUTSOURCING WRITING
AND DESIGN

Because of recent advances in technology, it is possible to outsource various business processes. What initially began as body shopping increased in scope when North American corporations realized that instead of bringing people from other cultures to work in the United States, advances in telecommunications allowed them to take jobs overseas on an expanded scale. The success of such outsourcing also enabled corporations to realize that if people overseas can have the expertise to maintain complex North American business operations from a distance, then advanced intellectual work involving research and design could also be outsourced.

Hence, big North American corporations like Microsoft, Oracle, General Electric, and others have established cutting-edge research laboratories in places such as India. On the other hand, corporations from other parts of the world, such as Cognizant, an Indian I-solutions company based in Madras, have also started producing such products for North American markets. This trend has resulted in corporations realizing that if they can find people with good writing skills overseas, then it would be equally easy to outsource the documentation accompanying various outsourced business processes and also the documentation for various products developed overseas.

As a result, increasingly we have a form of globalization where people in one culture may not only be maintaining business processes and designing new products for those in another, but also producing the documentation for those products and processes. According to Marakand Pandit (2003), there are about 2,500 technical writers in India with scope for 10,000 more. He states that Indian technical writers produce "installation and configuration guides," "user's/administrator's guides," "context sensitive help," "application programming interface (API) documentation," and "other product support materials." Indian technical writers have also been asked to design company profiles, test applications, and review user interfaces for inconsistencies.

LOCAL INFLUENCES AND
PEDAGOGIES

As Gauri Viswanathan (1989) points out, the colonial British Indian education system focused on the study of literature, and this approach was widely adopted in most Indian universities. It is still the same today. A case in point is Madras University, located in a major site for business process outsourcing and product development. Madras University supplies thousands of graduates for the many organizations located in Madras doing work outsourced from countries such as the United States. The curriculum for the English courses mandatory for undergraduates at this university places a lot of importance on the study of various British literary works, which is complemented by the study of grammar so that students are knowledgeable about the mechanics of writing correct English.

These literary texts were written to represent, from a certain perspective, certain aspects of nineteenth- and twentieth-century British culture, and when students analyze these texts, they become deeply involved in the worlds encoded by these texts. This pedagogy, therefore, operates on the premise that by making second language and replacement mother-tongue speakers of English familiar with sophisticated English language texts, the students' English language skills are increased. This curriculum also operates on the premise that since such literary analyses develop thinking skills, doing these analyses will enable writers to think creatively in other intellectual situations, including those involving professional writing.

Of course, analyzing literary texts may improve students' English and also make them intellectually creative; however, because of advances in technology, most human beings deal with technology of some complexity in different walks of life. Technical writing has, therefore, increasingly acquired specialized forms for helping users take advantage of these complex technologies. Just reading sophisticated literary texts and writing responses to these texts will not teach students to become skilled technical writers who can communicate effectively with specific audiences. Furthermore, since outsourced product development and the technical documentation for such products is being done for users in contemporary Western cultures, studying British texts from a different era will not teach students the cultural codes of users' cultures.

As a result, the curriculum, such as the one at Madras University, seems to operate on the premise that language is a transparent medium that can communicate content seamlessly across cultures as long as one focuses on writing simple, clear, plain English. This approach does not acknowledge the manner in which culture influences language nor the fact that if one wants to write across cultures, one should be aware of such cultural influences and situate writing to account for those influences.

The lack of an appropriate curriculum for training international technical writers is further compounded by the fact that technical writers overseas, just like technical writers in North America during the early stages of the profession's development there, lack an understanding of the importance of writing. As a result, just as those without a writing background were asked to write technical documentation in North America several decades ago, today, as corporations outsource in the hope of reducing costs, they have been replicating these outdated practices by trying to recruit technical writers fairly indiscriminately. For instance, consider this job advertisement for a technical writer posted on the Society for Technical Communication (STC) India chapter's blog:

Apr 22, 2004

Job Opening at Dhyan Infotech—Chennai

Here are the details

- No. of Position: 1
- Position: Technical Writer
- Start Date: Immediate
- Work Experience: 2 to 3 yrs
- Qualification: MBA Data Analysis & possess very good communication skills.

You can get in touch with . . . (Kiruba, 2004)

This organization, in requiring a master's degree in business administration and good communication skills, evidences a lack of understanding of writing by not asking for people with good writing skills, much less knowledge of the users' culture. Hence, according to a report in the *Times of India,* people there consider "technical writing as a back-door entry to the once glamorous software industry." Others infer that technical writing is taken up by those people whose writing is not good enough to get them writing jobs and who are technically not sound enough to become programmers. "Within the software community, technical writing is relegated low down in the hierarchy, even below the quality assurance guys" (Nair, 2002). That is why I believe a roundtable discussion involving representatives from STC, the Bay Area Publication Managers' Forum, the National Writers' Union, and the director of San Jose State technical writing certificate program brought up the point that when writing is offshored, one should expect "multiple rewrites and a long learning curve even with good documentation process in place because of using writers" with, among other things, "communication/cultural differences" (Bay Area Publication Managers' Forum, 2003).

As if poor technical writing skills and lack of cultural awareness were not big enough problems, Gurudutt Kamath (2003) complains that "one of the biggest frauds being [perpetrated] in India is that it is a must for technical writers to know certain tools. If you do not know FrameMaker you are not a technical writer! If you do not know RoboHelp you don't stand a chance as a technical writer!"

LOCAL STRATEGIES AND
CULTURAL UNSITUATEDNESS

Overseas technical writers have also attempted to follow an approach based on functionality and simplicity in order to make the writing clear in the belief that avoiding complex syntax will make their writing less susceptible to errors. Hence, the observation by Kalyan Iyer (2004), an Indian technical writer, that writers should have "an obsession for writing clean, correct, and simple English." Dalvi, another technical writer, also advocates simplicity as a rhetorical strategy. She says, "Avoid long, complex sentences. Use the active voice as much as possible. It keeps the sentences short and clear" (Dalvi, 2005, p. 11).

By emphasizing simplicity, these writers, without really knowing the users' culture, try to avoid as many cultural mistakes as they can. To some extent they can be partially successful, because in writing simple English, they are able to avoid obvious mistakes that are the product of local influences. For instance, Indians tend to use more words than Americans because of cultural influences and their pedagogical tradition. An approach based on functionality and simplicity has the potential to eliminate some of these obvious local influences. However, as a strategy, it is only partially effective. Gurudutt Kamath (2002) points out that if technical writing by an Indian writer is reviewed by "a good American editor," many "errors will spew out" and the "page will be riddled with revision marks and question marks" with "some usage not understood at all." He also points out that one of the biggest problems among Indian technical communicators is their lack of under-standing of audience.

A case in point is the use of colors, which can have culture-specific meanings and associations that could affect a document's usability. A color used in one context in one culture may have certain meanings that, if used in a different context, may have inappropriate connotations. Sun (2002) points out that red as a color means danger in American culture. However, as a color it is also an "eye catcher." So how can one use red appropriately in documentation for North Americans without first knowing North American culture?

However much one may instruct writers to use simple language in writing instruc-tions, those instructions cannot be culturally situated unless writers have an in-depth understanding of the users' culture.

If bicultural people work with writers, they can give feedback that can increase cultural situatedness. Knowledge of the culture doing the outsourced work would be an added bonus, because it would enable the bicultural person to understand cultural differences and therefore offer explanations to the writers as to why these differences exist. Having such explanations would in turn enable writers to apply these concepts intelligently whenever necessary instead of needing the bicultural person to tell them what to do.

Among those who could serve as bicultural resources would be employees who have held graduate teaching or research assistantships in the target culture. These experiences have the potential of allowing foreign students to learn salient aspects of the host country's culture, especially if they have been asked to teach. Many of these international students eventually graduate and take jobs in various North American organizations, thus further developing their understanding of North American culture.

Although it is impossible to become as culturally literate as the natives, many of these former students will acquire different levels of fluency in the host culture that will enable them to function successfully in North American culture. I would argue that such bicultural people, if they also have good writing skills, know enough about the users' culture to serve as resource people and reviewers for international writers producing outsourced technical documentation for North American users. In fact, there is a mounting body of evidence that indicates that one important reason why it is easier to outsource to India as opposed to other destinations is the availability of such bicultural people.

Alternatively, it would also be helpful to have as resource people those native to the target culture who have had experiences in the culture where the outsourcing is taking place. If those native to the users' culture spend a lot of time in the culture where the outsourcing is happening, then just like the bicultural students from the cultures doing the outsourced work, they too will learn about the culture where the outsourced work is being done. Even if they have worked with groups of people from different parts of the world, they will have learned about the obvious cultural differences that exist between those cultures and the users' culture. Hence, bicultural people will have internalized the cultural templates and categories for identifying such differences even when they are asked to work in additional new cultures.

If bicultural people act as resources for overseas technical writers, they can help these writers in situations involving cross-cultural miscommunication. For instance, the use of the term *post* can create cross-cultural miscommunication. For Indians, this word can mean a pole stuck in the ground, while for Americans, it can refer to a job, something that neither an international spell checker or grammar checker can catch. A bicultural person who knows English usage in both south Asian and American cultures will have the skills to clear any confusion that can result from the different meanings this term possesses in different cultures. Or as Kuusto (2001), quoting Kenneth Keniston, points out, if bicultural resource people were to work for technical writers producing documentation for products used in Argentina, they would know that because of the communal nature of this country's culture, people from Argentina are comfortable doing group work. Hence, if they were to help create the documentation for a culturally unsituated software program that emphasized individual and not group behavior, it would be easy for such bicultural people to understand the difficulties users from this communal culture would have with such a program. They could, therefore, help the technical writers produce documentation that would improve the program's usability by offering explanations for overcoming such a lack of cultural situatedness in design.

There is a belief in international technical communication that if one strives for simplicity then that will erase local cultural features that could confuse users. Simplicity may, as I have already pointed out, enable writers to weed out obvious local cultural features. Simplicity, as a strategy, can help the writer avoid sins of commission, but it cannot proactively improve usability, because it cannot deal with the sins of cultural omission. Such problems involve aspects of communication that would be more difficult to quantify in the form of a tip or some other clearly defined piece of information. For instance, writers from countries belonging to the British Commonwealth write a version of British English. Since the British tend to be more formal in their speech, that feature spills over into their writing as well. On the other hand, Americans prefer direct communication, something that can be perceived as rude by those used to British English and culture.

As I mentioned earlier, red as a color can mean danger in American culture. However, as a color it is also an eye catcher. While creating graphics, if one follows the rule of simplicity and uses just black and white and avoids using colors, one can lose the chance of improving usability by using colors proactively. Because of its eye catching qualities for American audiences, depending on the context, it may be possible to use red proactively in order to improve an interface's usability.

CULTURALLY SITUATED TEXTS: A TEXT FOR DUMMIES

The popular American "For Dummies" series of instruction manuals is a case in point. This series takes full advantage of various cultural features familiar to U.S. audiences and produces narratives that, in proactively attempting to culturally situate documentation, help audiences deal with different applications and topics. Because of its proactive approach, this instructional material not only avoids sins of commission but also sins of cultural omission. This series has become so popular that one can find a "For Dummies" book on almost any topic, and they are even used at universities as course textbooks.

Here is a short passage from the book *Word 2000 for Dummies* (2000) involving a situation in which those using the software application Word 2000 cannot undo an action they have completed. This passage partially illustrates how this book proactively situates itself culturally:

> *Can't Undo*? Here's why . . .
>
> Sometimes it eats you alive that Word can't undo an action. On the menu bar you even see the message "Can't Undo." What gives?
>
> Essentially, whatever action you just did, Word can't undo it. This result can be true for a number of reasons: There is nothing to undo; not enough memory is available to undo, Word can't undo because what you did was too complex; Word just forgot; Word hates you; and so on.
>
> I know it is frustrating, but everyone has to live with it (Gookin, 1999, p. 58).

There are many rhetorical features in this short passage that are very appealing to American users. By positioning itself as a book for dummies and seeming to make fun of users, the text is actually saying with humor that it is going to work hard to be nice to readers. Within the passage itself, there is a high level of informality that I believe most international. And the phraseology, based on colloquial American English, is punctuated with humor. Most international technical communicators would say that the humorous fictitious reasons the narrative offers for why Word cannot undo the action are just redundant and should not be included. But the text, in allowing such redundancies for the sake of humor, communicates to the reader that it understands the users' frustration when poor product design prevents them from undoing something. Thus, it also exhibits another American cultural trait: it is okay to be vulnerable and acknowledge design problems in the product if there are any. By doing so, the instructions are not only understandable and enjoyable to American users, but also trustworthy.

Such cultural situatedness defines all aspects of this book's content. For example, among the categories for organizing content, it has a subcategory titled "technical stuff," which contains nonessential information. The visual icon indicating this category even has a box with a cartoon figure of a "nerd," a uniquely American stereotype of those considered bookish and brainy. By doing so, the narrative tells users that if they do not care about the features dealt with in this subcategory, that it is no slur on their character, because only boring, bookish people who are not very practical in the first place would find those aspects of the application useful. I believe that if bicultural communicators work with international technical writing teams, they can begin improving usability not only by avoiding obvious sins of cultural commission but also proactively avoiding sins of cultural omission.

Cultural situatedness is necessary if technical documentation is to score high on usability. Because bicultural people understand the users' culture and the culture doing the outsourcing, they have the potential to serve as reviewers and resource people for those writing the outsourced documentation. If bicultural people are able to give useful cross-cultural inputs, they can not only enable international technical communicators to avoid committing cultural *faux pas,* but can also teach them to proactively incorporate aspects of the users' culture to better facilitate communication. Doing so will greatly enhance the documentation's usability.

REFERENCES

Bay Area Publication Managers' Forum. (2003, July 24). Offshoring of technical writing: Roundtable meeting abridged notes.
http://www.bapmf.net/2003/TWritingOffSHNoteK1.pdf

Dalvi, M. (2005, September-October). Writing for the global market: Understand preferences. *INDUS: Newsletter from the India Chapter of the STC, (7)*5, 10-11.
http://www.stc-india.org/indus/092005/articlemeghashri.htm

Gookin, D. (1999). *Word 2000 for Windows for dummies.* Chicago, IL: IDG Books.

Iyer, K. (2004, March). Hiring the right writer. *INDUS: Newsletter from the India Chapter of the STC.* Retrieved October 13, 2006, from
http://www.stc-India.org/indus/032004/bestpractices.htm

Kamath, G. (2002, August 12). To err in English. *Indian Express.*
http://www.expressitpeople.com/20020812/careers1.shtml

Kamath, G. (2003, June 23). Writing right: I can learn. *Indian Express.*
http://www.expressitpeople.com/20030623/careers1.shtml

Kiruba, _. (2004, April 22). *Technical writing blog.*
http://techwriting.blogdrive.com/archive/cm-10_cy-2006_m-10_d-11_y-2006_o-10.html

Kuusto, M. H. (2001). English in technical communication—Global language, global culture? In *Proceedings of the 48th Society for Technical Communication Annual Conference* (pp. 141-146). Arlington, VA: Society for Technical Communication. http://www.stc.org/confproceed/2001/PDFs/STC58-000141.PDF

Nair, S. (2002, March 16). The write stuff. *The Times of India.* http://timesofindia.indiatimes.com//articleshow/msid-3900424,prtpage-1.cms?

Pandit, M. (2003, March). Technical writing in 1993 and 2003. *INDUS: Newsletter from the India Chapter of the STC, (5)2.* http://www.stc-india.org/indus/032003/mpandit.htm

Sun, H. (2002). Why cultural contexts are missing: A rhetorical critique of localization practices. In *Proceedings of the 49th Society for Technical Communication Annual Conference* (pp. 164-168). http://www.stc.org/confproceed/2002/PDFs/STC49-00090.PDF

Viswantathan, G. (1989). *Masks of conquest: Literary study and British rule in India.* New York: Columbia University Press.

CHAPTER 9

Presenting in English to International Audiences: A Critical Survey of Published Advice and Actual Practice

Thomas Orr, Renu Gupta, Atsuko Yamazaki,
and Laurence Anthony

The ability to deliver effective presentations in English to international audiences is an essential requirement today for professionals in a variety of fields, but especially for those in science, engineering, and business. Conferences and conventions have become increasingly international, as have meetings, projects, and clientele; and a high degree of competence in English presentation is now mandatory in many workplaces.

Effective presentation is not easy, however. Greater linguistic diversity at international events frequently means that speakers as well as listeners may be required to communicate in English, although they have limited abilities in the language. This complicates matters for speakers who learn English as a foreign language and need to convey complex ideas with limited vocabularies and hard-to-understand pronunciations. It also complicates matters for fluent English speakers, who must adjust their presentations to audiences with varying levels of English proficiency. Additional complications arise from poor presentation skills—irrespective of language skills—as well as confusion over how to apply conflicting advice that is frequently found in the self-help presentation guides readily available in bookstores. Finally, one additional factor that makes presenting well so difficult is that few professionals have been trained in presentation skills, especially with regard to the linguistic and cultural parameters involved in presenting in international contexts.

This chapter presents some initial findings from a project designed to investigate these issues by four academics who work regularly with international colleagues, students, and clients in science, engineering, and business in order to help them learn how to present in English to audiences with limited English skills, while struggling with limitations of their own in English.

PROJECT OVERVIEW

The research reported here is based on five investigative activities: (a) a brief critical survey of 12 self-help books published in English on making presentations for professional audiences; (b) an investigative survey of journal articles and abstracts in English from online databases and professional publications that address some aspect of professional presentations; (c) a brief critical survey of six books and four journal articles published in Japanese that offer advice to nonnative English speakers about presenting in English; (d) a small pilot investigation of actual presentations delivered to an international audience by three academics for whom English is a foreign language; and e) a comparison of the data generated from these four activities to identify useful information for speakers who know limited English, and to establish research objectives for further, more rigorous research.

SURVEY OF ENGLISH BOOKS

The 12 self-help books surveyed in this study (see Appendix A) were selected because they could be found on the shelves of major international bookstores or easily obtained via the Internet. Concern was not whether they were representative of all existing books on oral presentation, but rather whether they were highly visible in major bookstores or on the pages of major online book distributors, such as Amazon or Barnes & Noble. Advice gathered from these books was organized under the four categories that seemed most productive for studying the central aspects of an oral presentation; namely *content*, *language*, *visuals*, and *speaker presence*.

Content

Presentation content is clearly the central element of any lecture, for it comprises the message that speakers wish to get across to their audiences as well as the information required to communicate this message. Content selection and development is a topic, however, that is difficult to teach, as it involves social and psychological issues that extend beyond a book author's area of expertise. Few of the books surveyed gave much attention to the issue of presentation content, except for superficial treatment, assuming perhaps that speakers already know what they want to talk about. The gist of the recommendations, however, stated that oral presentations should contain the following core elements: a position on a topic, a proposal for action, and a list of benefits if the position is accepted and the actions are followed; or instruction, details, and applications. Options for structuring and packaging content linguistically and graphically included statements of fact, formulas and equations, numerical data, anecdotes, examples, illustrations, quotations, rhetorical questions, shocking or surprising information, humorous stories or remarks, images and graphics, organizational aids, and memory support. The books recommended first analyzing audience needs, attitudes, knowledge areas, environment, and demographics, and then generating suitable content through various brainstorming techniques. Disappointingly, these were not explained in depth.

Language

Language is the central medium for a lecture or speech, for it is the primary encoder and carrier of a speaker's message. Some of the language may be spoken, and some of it may be posted on slides or handouts, but the language (i.e., the vocabulary and syntax) a speaker chooses alters a presentation greatly. All of the 12 books surveyed offered advice on language, but the depth of recommendations varied, and most books failed to provide much justification for the advice except that it would hold audience attention, signpost the flow of a talk, or make presentations more interesting and understandable. When compiled into one list, advice on language choice consisted of the following main points.

- Use language that is colorful, concrete, concise, and precise.
- Use active voice.
- Use questions to stimulate curiosity, shocking statements to attract attention, and humorous language to heighten enjoyment.
- Use modifiers to soften or strengthen points.
- Use introductory clauses to signal transitions and time connectors to specify time.
- Use language that draws attention to visuals when speaking about something on a visual aid.
- Use forms of address appropriate for the occasion and the audience.

The books devoted attention to what speakers should say (or display), but they failed to provide much discussion of language at depths that would provide satisfactory rationale to readers with a limited knowledge of English. In addition, only one of the books provided specific examples of words and phrases that could be used to obtain specific effects.

Visuals

By visuals, we not only mean the pictures, charts, graphs and formulas that support a lecture but also fonts and formats, along with any other image or artifact that is used to support a speaker's message. The books we surveyed provided much advice on visuals, particularly in light of the current popularity of Microsoft PowerPoint. The most common advice among the texts can be briefly summarized as follows:

- Use slides sparingly.
- Prefer pictures to words.
- Keep slides horizontal.
- Present one key point per slide.

- Use no more than five bullets per slide.
- Use no more than five words per bullet.
- Make content big enough to see.
- Use color carefully.
- Use no more than four colors per slide.
- Don't use red for text.
- Use builds and animation sparingly.
- Average two minutes per slide.

Some books also mentioned when not to use slides (e.g., when you want the audience to look at your face), and two books even recommended not using slides at all if they can be avoided. Similar to the advice on presentation content and language, however, most of the books based advice on the expertise, experience, and authority of the author rather than on research by scholars in visual communication and related fields of scholarship.

Speaker Presence

By speaker presence, we mean the physical presence of speakers before an audience, with particular attention to their dress, body movements, attitudes, and articulation. All 12 books provided advice on different aspects of speaker presence that can be summarized as follows:

Advice on Clothing

Speakers should select attire that is professional and appropriate for the occasion and does not distract the audience from the presentation. Women should select clothes that fit well, but not too tightly; avoid wearing too much makeup; and avoid wearing jewelry that sparkles. Men should wear dark, well-tailored suits; avoid brightly colored shirts; and wear cotton T-shirts under white dress shirts to avoid showing signs of perspiration.

Advice on Other Issues

Speakers should speak loudly and clearly; not speak too fast; avoid filling pauses between utterances with meaningless sounds such as *hmmm, aaah, errr*; maintain eye contact with the audience; and continue to smile unless the message requires a different facial expression. Speakers should not use gestures unless they support the language or direct attention to a visual; and they should speak from one location, unless there is good reason for moving about.

Advice on speaker presence seemed useful with regard to the underlying principle of dressing and acting appropriately, but specific descriptions of what was appropriate as far as dress seemed narrowly limited to, say, business meetings on Wall Street rather than other international environments with different climatic and cultural circumstances.

SURVEY OF ENGLISH RESEARCH ARTICLES

In the second phase of this project, articles and abstracts from several online databases and professional publications were studied for the purpose of identifying research on topics related to oral presentations that were not covered in popular self-help guides. The intent was not to compile exhaustive survey data but rather to identify issues beyond those covered in self-help books. Five such topics were found in the research literature: perceptions of fonts (Mackiewicz & Moeller, 2004), speaking rates for nonnative listeners (Derwing & Munro, 2001), audience interaction in academic monologues (Thompson, 1997), information structure manipulation (Rowley-Jolivet & Carter-Thomas, 2005), and metaphor in cross-cultural contexts (Littlemore, 2001). Although there was research on other aspects of presentations, the topics listed here show that there is useful research that has not yet received much attention in self-help books on oral dissemination.

SURVEY OF JAPANESE BOOKS AND ARTICLES

The third research activity was to survey a small sample of self-help books and journal articles on oral presentations, published in Japanese, that are well known among Japanese engineering professionals (see Appendix B). The recommendations found in these texts were organized under the same four headings used for our survey of the English books.

Content

Surprisingly, very little advice on content selection and development appeared in the books and articles published in Japanese. For second language speakers of English, it seemed that language issues were more pressing and received greater attention. The advice on content was (a) make sure you have a main point; (b) do not present more than three points of contention; and (c) lectures on research should include background information on the project, details about the research method, and a presentation of the results, followed by some discussion and a conclusion. There was almost no information on how to select or develop this material, nor much discussion of what content and focus would be appropriate for particular speaking situations.

Language

The English language was the central concern in the books and articles published in Japanese. In fact, roughly 50% to 80% of the instruction prescribed English vocabulary, useful phrases, grammar, and organization patterns (as well as advice on pronunciation, which we will deal with later under Speaker Presence). Language advice included long lists of English phrases (i.e., 100 to 640 items) and their Japanese translations (e.g., *Ladies and gentlemen*; *If you are really dying to know*; and *I'm not qualified to answer that question.*), advice on vocabulary usage (e.g., Do not say *get a result* but rather *obtain a result.*) as well as advice for distinguishing fact from assumption and for organizing material logically.

Visuals

Visuals are very important for Japanese presenters because they can communicate a lot of information that does not need to be stated in English. This makes presentations easier to prepare and easier to deliver. Compared with the recommendations for English language usage, however, there was less advice on visuals than expected: (a) present one message per slide; (b) provide one slide to support each minute or two of speaking; (c) do not put too many words, numbers, or symbols on a page; (d) do not put more than eight lines of information on a slide; (e) top each slide with a title or the main topic; (f) present simpler versions of figures and tables than those appropriate for research papers; and (g) use graphs instead of tables.

Speaker Presence

Since speaker presence includes vocal articulation, considerable attention was devoted to this topic, although most of it involved pronunciation. This primarily consisted of how to pronounce words, phrases, and technical language such as numbers, symbols, and mathematical formulas. Advice related to other aspects of physical presence consisted of the following: (a) do not speak more than 100 words per minute; (b) speak slower than you normally would in Japanese; (c) don't read your presentation; (d) make eye contact with the audience; (e) be confident; and (f) smile, but don't use a smile as an evasive maneuver in difficult situations such as Q&A. No advice was provided, however, on clothing, and very little advice addressed gesture, movement, and other aspects of body language.

ACTUAL PRESENTATIONS

In the fourth phase of this project, presentations in English by three academics in computer science were studied to identify potentially effective practices that were missing or briefly mentioned in the English and Japanese self-help literature on oral presentations. All three speakers had learned English as a foreign language; one speaker was a Japanese male, who had been working for several years in the United States, and the other two speakers were from Russia. In both cases, the audience, which consisted of Japanese university students and international faculty, had vastly differing levels of proficiency in English. Although space does not permit complete descriptions of all that was observed, several aspects of the presentations that we noticed have not received much attention in the popular or scholarly literature that we surveyed. These practices included (a) skillful presentation of relevant background information to set the talk in context; (b) drawing on overhead transparencies to expand or highlight information (instead of using PowerPoint); (c) skipping slides when the speaker sensed that the information was too detailed, unnecessary, or not interesting for the audience; (d) using informative hand gestures to emphasize points or highlight the slope on a graph; (e) expressing small numbers with a show of fingers to parallel the presentation of information on slides that were too small to be read or pronounced too poorly to be understood; (f) effective use of color so that similar items appeared in the same color; and (g) adjusting (successfully and not) to sudden and unexpected restrictions on presentation time.

SUMMARY OF FUNDAMENTAL PRINCIPLES

Although there were both similarities and differences among the sources surveyed in this research, several fundamental principles surfaced (explicitly or implicitly) that should be at the core of all educational products and training on oral presentation skills.

- Know and understand the needs, expectations, abilities, and interests of your audience.
- Select, display, and deliver the content in ways that are appropriate for audience needs, expectations, abilities, interests, and experiences.
- Compensate for weaknesses in one mode of delivery (e.g., English grammar or pronunciation) with stronger support in other modes of delivery (e.g., visuals, body language).
- Remain flexible and continually adjust every aspect of the content, language, visuals, and speaker presence to constraints and forces that arise in the speaking situation.
- Ground your communication and physical presence in attitudes and motivations that harmonize with the message and its intended purpose.

ISSUES OF CONCERN

Based upon a critical review of published advice and actual practices, issues of concern can be summarized as follows: (a) inconsistency in the instructions across texts and sometimes within texts; (b) lack of scholarly grounding for the instruction; (c) lack of instruction for foreign language speakers in material published in English; (d) lack of depth and accuracy in the instruction for foreign language speakers in material published in Japanese (and perhaps in other languages too); (e) too little attention devoted to tailoring content and delivery for diverse audiences of different ages, language backgrounds and abilities, socioeconomic and cultural situations, and levels of expertise; (f) potentially useful information for presenters scattered across the research literature in different fields; (g) the difficulty of effectively combining a wide range of useful material into one book; (h) the lack of presentation skill training in universities and graduate schools; and (i) the variety of techniques and styles that presenters employ in real practice not mentioned in the popular self-help literature on presentations.

FUTURE RESEARCH

In order to address the issues of concern mentioned above, the following activities would be appropriate for future research: (a) a more extensive survey of the self-help and research literature on oral presentations, as well as materials published in other languages on making presentations in English; (b) more exhaustive studies of actual presentations in English by both fluent English speakers and those with limited English proficiency, in different contexts, including case studies of specific presenters; (c) studies of audience response and interaction; (d) studies of appropriate means for evaluating oral presentations; (e) studies of effective means for improving skills in oral presentation; (f) studies contrasting single presentations with serial presentations, such as seminars and lectures; (g) studies of how various technologies affect presentations; and (h) surveys of existing university and corporate training programs, as well as online training resources.

CONCLUSION

In spite of the rapid development of computers and the Internet, which has greatly advanced the production and dissemination of written communication, oral presentation continues to be an important medium for face-to-face communication in classrooms and meeting rooms, conventional halls and conference centers, as well as in corporate and government offices. With the increasing linguistic and cultural diversity of twenty-first-century audiences and speakers, skillful speaking and presentation skills are becoming increasingly necessary for professionals in nearly all fields. This chapter briefly describes one small step toward increasing our understanding of oral presentations in order to serve modern training needs in light of new constraints that complicate twenty-first-century presentations in international contexts. See Appendix A and B for other books and articles of interest.

APPENDIX A
English Self-Help Books Surveyed

Alley, M. (2003). *The craft of scientific presentations: Critical steps to succeed and critical errors to avoid.* Blacksburg, VA: Springer-Verlag.

Bienvenu, S. (2000). *The presentation skills workshop: Helping people create and deliver great presentations—A trainer's guide.* New York: American Management Association.

DiResta, D. (1998). *Knockout presentations: How to deliver your message with power, punch, and pizzazz.* Worcester, MA: Chandler House Press.

Gurak, L. J. (2000). *Oral presentations for technical communication.* Needham Heights, MA: Allyn & Bacon.

Hager P., & Scheiber, H. J. (1997). *Designing and delivering scientific, technical and managerial presentations.* New York: Wiley.

Kushner, M. (2004). *Presentations for dummies.* Hoboken, NJ: Wiley Publishing.

Mandel, S. (2000). *Effective presentation skills: A practical guide for better speaking.* Menlo Park, CA: Crisp Learning.

Powell, M. (2002). *Presenting in English.* Boston, MA: Heinle.

Reimond, P., & Reimond, C. (2003). *The short road to great presentations.* Hoboken, NJ: IEEE.

Reinhart, S. M. (2002). *Giving academic presentations.* Ann Arbor, MI: U of Michigan Press.

Urech, E. (2004). *Speaking globally: Effective presentations across international and cultural boundaries.* Rollinsford, NH: Book Network International.

Wiessman, J. (2003). *Presenting to win: The art of telling your story.* London: Financial Times Prentice Hall.

APPENDIX B
Books and Articles Published in Japanese

Hirooka, Y. (2003). 理科系のための実践英語プレゼンテーション
[Practical English presentation for science fields]. Tokyo: Asakura.

Iguchi, M. (1995). 英語で科学を語る- 国際会議における口頭発表
[Talking about science in English—Oral presentation at an international conference].
Tokyo: Maruzen.

Nagata, Y. (1988). 英語口頭発表の心得   [Tips for English oral presentation]. *Journal of the Institute of Electronics, Information and Communication Engineers, 71*(8), 779-782.

Nakayama, S. (1989). 科学者のための英語口頭発表のしかた [How to make an English oral presentation—For scientists]. Tokyo: Asakura.

Naminosuke, K. (1999). 研究者のための国際学会プレゼンテーション   [International Presentations for Scientists]. Tokyo: Kyouritsu.

Ono, Y. (2004). English for engineers and scientist: Technical writing and oral presentation in English—How to prepare presentation in English and recipe for slides and transparencies. *Journal of the Japan Society of Mechanical Engineers, 107*(1030), 64-66.

Ono, Y. (2004). English for engineers and scientist: Technical writing and oral presentation in English—How to speak understandable English: Easily understandable English expressions, to read or not to read the manuscript and tips for writing manuscripts and memos. *Journal of the Japan Society of Mechanical Engineers, 107*(1031), 53-56.

Ono, Y. (2004). English for engineers and scientist: Technical writing and oral presentation in English—Set phrases for oral presentation in English and how to address at Q&A sessions. *Journal of the Japan Society of Mechanical Engineers, 107*(1032), 33-36.

Shimura, F. (2002).理科系のための英語プレゼンテーションの技術[English presentation skills for science]. Tokyo: The Japan Times.

Toyama, M., & Toyama, K. (1999). 理工系英語論文と口頭発表の実際   [English papers and oral presentation in practice for engineering and science]. Tokyo: Corona.

REFERENCES

Derwing, T., & Munro, M. (2001). What speaking rates do nonnative listeners prefer? *Applied Linguistics, 22*(3), 324-337.

Littlemore, J. (2001). The use of metaphor in university lectures and the problems that it causes for overseas students. *Teaching in Higher Education 6*(3), 333-349.

Mackiewicz, J., & Moeller, R. (2004). Why people perceive typefaces to have different personalities. In *Proceedings of the 2004 International Professional Communication Conference* (pp. 304-313). Minneapolis, MN.

Rowley-Jolivet, E., & Carter-Thomas, S. (2005). Genre awareness and rhetorical appropriacy: Manipulation of information structure by NS and NNS scientists in the international conference setting. *English for Specific Purposes, 24*(1), 41-64.

Thompson, S. E. (1997). *Presenting research: A study of interaction in academic monologue.* Unpublished doctoral dissertation, University of Liverpool.

PART III

Health and Safety: Informing Society of Risks and Dangers

CHAPTER 10

Public Professional Communication in the Antiterror Age: A Discourse Analysis

Catherine F. Smith

OVERVIEW

In an undeclared war on terror, the United States federal government routinely assesses the risk of attack on the nation. Wide-ranging risk assessments are instrumental to broad rewriting of national law and large-scale reorganization of the federal government for homeland security. One risk identified in a cumulative assessment by the National Intelligence Council is psychological and emotional attack, or creating a psychology of fear (National Intelligence Council, 2005).

The creation of a psychology of fear is the topic here. My focus is on government's creation of fear in public deliberation. Here I am less concerned with what attackers might do and more concerned with what U.S. federal lawmakers say in order to create fear in everyday American life. I proceed from a skeptical view of public policy that relies on fear to motivate agreement on governmental priorities. Here, I consider linguistic and paralinguistic evidence that the 108th Congress used fear generation to create perceived need for new antiterror legislation. In the information exchanges of a Senate committee hearing discussed here, my analysis shows the manifestation of a perspective that finds potential terror wherever it looks. I argue that this perspective—call it the terror perspective—functions to establish the relevance of information for antiterror public policymaking. Terror is abstract. Its practical meanings are found by application. Here, I discuss applications by a Congressional committee chair and expert witnesses to interpret everyday operations of industry, business, and consumption as vulnerable to attack. The analysis presented here is generally relevant to professional and technical communication. It shows a normal condition of governance, policymakers calling on specialized expertise to help define problems and to inform the choice of policy solutions. It is particularly relevant in post 9/11 U.S. Congressional deliberations. During the conduct of a war on terror, specialists inside and outside the legislature are called on to relate their expertise to antiterror policymaking. To meet difficult communication challenges, specialists need, generally, to recognize the influence of perspective on the creation, reception, and use of information.

THEORETICAL APPROACH:
PERSPECTIVE IN PUBLIC POLICY DISCOURSE

In the visual arts from which the concept derives, perspective pulls together a viewpoint, features of objects, and horizon to effect "a form of representation by which the parts of an object or the elements of a complex state of affairs and their interrelations are construed and presented as if seen from a given point of view" (Graumann, 2002, p. 26). More generally for human knowledge construction, perspective relates features of objects to background expectations. When the perspective itself remains implicit and unrepresented, objects nonetheless come to us "perspectivized," or presented according to a set of expectations.

In communication, perspective is discourse-based or, more fundamentally, action-based. It is manifested in utterance but also in extralinguistic phenomena such as institutional culture and contextual activity. Within a communicative event, perspective is evident "in the interplay between cues in the object and schema-providing cultures supplied and made relevant in the contexts of the communicative event" (Linnell, 2002, p. 43).

In public policymaking, perspective equates to a viewpoint that selects objects and highlights features of the objects according to expectations. Perspective functions to problematize, or to define something as problematic according to a viewpoint. The public policy process begins with a perceived problem (Coplin & O'Leary, 1998, pp. 3, 7). Somebody, an individual or a collective, perceives a wrong, thus initiating a governmental process of defining that wrong as a problem that public policy (usually government action) might solve. Even when it remains implicit or transparent, perspective or viewpoint is substantive; it is part of the problem as perceived and defined. It is therefore salient for analysis to examine how an existing condition becomes defined as a policy problem.

EMPIRICAL EVIDENCE

The communication event considered here is a Congressional committee open hearing. Legislative hearings are relatively informal discussions in public view by elected officeholders and representatives of interested people to consider matters pertinent to policymaking. Unlike a trial or deposition in judicial proceedings, and unlike floor debate in the Congress prior to a vote, a committee hearing is conversational, albeit ritualized. Statements and subsequent interaction do not follow prescribed rules for allowable questioning, types of disclosure, admissibility of sources, or determination of relevance. Except in hearings to investigate wrong-doing or to confirm nominations for administrative appointments where witnesses might testify under oath, there are no general guidelines and few constraints on the introduction and use of information. Legislative committees and subcommittees generally set their own procedures for conducting deliberation. The committee chair, who is always a member of the political party holding a majority in the parent governing body, sets them.

Paralinguistic influences on deliberation in a hearing are institutional setting, political context, and communication situation. Institutional setting includes the legislative branch of government, the assembly (House of Representatives or Senate), the jurisdiction of the committee holding the hearing, specific legislation in process, and the hearing's purpose for that process. Political context is primarily the expectations of the majority party as implemented by the committee chair and majority staff; another political context is the constituency interests of committee members. Those influences, along with the written and spoken statements that shape face-to-face interaction, create the affordances for discourse developments in the hearing as a type of communication situation (Smith, 1994).

A hearing held in 2003 by the U.S. Senate Committee on Government Affairs (later renamed the Committee on Homeland Security and Government Affairs) is selected for analysis here. The institutional setting and larger political context include single-party (Republican) majority control of the Senate, the House of Representatives, and the presidency. The immediate context is the legislative agenda of the committee's chair, Senator Susan M. Collins, a Republican from Maine. Her agenda, as indicated by her sponsorship of legislation, includes addressing risk of biological warfare as a likely method of terrorist attack. She called this hearing to address the potential for biological attack on the American food supply. Her stated purpose was to examine everyday operations of business and industry in food growing, production, distribution, and consumption in order to identify potential for disaster.

ANALYSIS

Communication in this hearing shows discursive development of the terror perspective. The perspective is manifested through rhetorical uses of language influenced by institutional role performance.

Opening Statement by Senator Collins

In opening the hearing, Senator Collins defines the problem she calls agro-terrorism by means of two linguistic devices: assembled meaning and recontextualization.

Assembled meaning is meaning-by-aggregation, or a communicated association of items. This meaning relies on many-to-one reduction, which sweeps unlike items under one heading. The relevance of their association is not inherent; rather, it is provided. Collins deliberately constructs three assemblies: a sector of the American economy, a paper trail, and a set of administrative agencies with shared responsibility.

First, she aggregates farming, food processing, food service, consumption, food-related sciences, and transportation into a single economic sector:

> Nothing is more at the heart and core of our economy than our agriculture and food industry. It is a $1 trillion economic sector that creates one-sixth of our gross national product. One in eight Americans works in this sector. It . . . encompasses a half-billion acres of croplands, thousands of feedlots, countless processing plants, warehouses, research facilities, and factories for ingredients, ready-to-eat foods, and packaging, as well as the distribution network that brings food from around the Nation and around the world into the neighborhood markets and restaurants via virtually every mode of transportation (*Agro terrorism: The threat to America's breadbasket*, 2004, p. 1).

Second, she compiles a paper trail of disparate publications to imply a commonality:

> Hundreds of pages of U.S. agricultural documents recovered from the al Qaeda caves in Afghanistan early last year are a strong indication that terrorists recognize that our agriculture and food industry provides tempting targets. According to a new RAND Corporation report, . . . the industry's size, scope, and productivity, combined with our lack of preparedness, offer a great many points of attack. . . . A CIA report . . . confirmed that the September 11 hijackers expressed interest in crop dusting aircraft. . . . This horrific page is from *The Poisoner's Handbook*, an underground pamphlet published here in the United States that provides detailed instructions on how to make powerful plant, animal, and human poisons from easily obtained ingredients and how to disseminate them. It was found in Afghanistan. . . . Last spring, a Saudi cleric who supports al Qaeda . . . issued a fatwa, a religious ruling, that justified the use of chemical and biological weapons, including weapons that destroy tillage and stock (*Agro terrorism*, 2004, p. 1).

Third, she refers broadly to administrative overlap to imply ineffectiveness: "Should there be an attack, more than 30 agencies may be involved [as shown by] the 30 agencies that would be involved in . . . an outbreak of foot and mouth disease" (*Agro terrorism*, 2004, p. 1).

The other rhetorical device used by Senator Collins, recontextualization, places an old topic in a new context. Citing instances of the 1997 outbreak of swine foot and mouth disease in Taiwan, the 2001 outbreak of cattle foot and mouth disease in Great Britain, and the 2002 outbreak of poultry exotic Newcastle disease in California, she claims

> to call these three cases naturally occurring ignores an important point. Each was caused by human error, by carelessness, by a lapse in security. In Taiwan, it was one infected pig imported from Hong Kong. In Britain, it was one batch of infected feed at one farm. In California, it was one infected rooster smuggled across the border from Mexico. The ease with which terrorists could replicate these events is alarming (*Agro terrorism*, 2004, p. 1).

This recontextualization by one-to-many expansion transforms single conditions into potential weapons of mass destruction.

In summary, Senator Collins selects objects for consideration, leading me to ask "why those objects?" My analysis suggests that expectation of terrorist attack directs her selection and highlighting of features to cue the objects' relevance for policy she intends to propose. As a scene is rendered according to a perspective in visual art, the American food supply is here portrayed as fearful according to a viewpoint. Collins's opening statement rhetorically accomplishes the construction of a schema for interpreting information that she and others expect to bring out in the hearing. The language reflects her power in Congressional culture as committee chair with authority to call hearings, set their topics, and invite subject experts to testify. Consequently, following her opening statement, several panels of witnesses testify. Two expert testimonies are discussed in selective detail next.

Testimony by Thomas McGinn

The first witness is a veterinarian and expert in animal disease, as well as administrator for agriculture in state government. His state, North Carolina, has an interest in defining agroterrorism as a problem. The state economy would lose by attack on agriculture and gain from federal funding allocated to prevent it or prepare for it. Therefore, he represents a constituency. However, that is probably not the reason he has been invited to testify. Rather, as the chairman says in introducing his testimony, he is there as a specialist in animal medicine who is active in state-level disease control. He is also experienced in preparing technical data used in governmental risk assessments. The rhetorical choices shown in his testimony suggest that he has been invited by the hearing's organizers to testify because he is a credible authority on agriculture, and he is sympathetic to the agenda of improving homeland security.

Witness McGinn amplifies the hearing's topics by addition and by multiplication. First he adds characteristics and details to the chair's examples. He characterizes agriculture as "perfect" for use as a weapon or target. To Senator Collins' cast of characters, terrorists and U.S. government administrators, he adds first responders to disasters as well as citizen victims of disaster. He adds a list of needs for funding appropriations to pay for state-level antiterror research, laboratories, and response mechanisms. More persuasive than addition, however, is McGinn's multiplication. Visual rhetoric in animated PowerPoint slides accompanied by his "what-if" narration projects compelling scenarios of the impacts of animal disease used as weapon. "My next slide will be a simulation that demonstrates the intentional introduction of foot and mouth disease into multiple locations in our country. . . . Over 700,000 people would be needed [to respond to the disaster]. . . . Our Nation is not prepared to be able to respond with that kind of response . . ." (*Agro terrorism*, 2004, p. 9).

> Imagine the fear that would result from [the intentional introduction of pathogens into food processing]. . . . We have become a Nation concerned about receiving anthrax in our mailboxes. Imagine what it would be like to be a Nation

concerned about opening our refrigerators and anthrax being in our refrigerators as well . . ." (*Agro terrorism*, 2004, p. 9).

McGinn is employing a favored methodology of threat assessment: the construction of scenarios based on varied kinds of modeling. A National Intelligence Council summary assessment explains why the method is favored:

> While straight-line projections are useful in establishing a baseline and positing a mainline scenario, they typically present a one-dimensional view of how the future might unfold and tend to focus attention exclusively on the "prediction." Scenarios offer a more dynamic view of possible futures and focus attention on the underlying interactions that may have particular policy significance. . . . Scenarios help decision makers to break through conventional thinking and basic assumptions so that a broader range of possibilities can be considered— including new risks and opportunities (National Intelligence Council, 2005, p. 21).

McGinn's visual rhetoric brings interactivity into the hearing. While the circumstances of committee hearings do not permit observers to interact with testimony materials, this witness's animated graphics encourage imagination to engage the possibilities he narrates. Like scenario construction, interactivity is a favored method of engaging varied participation in threat assessment. The National Intelligence Council provided for broad domestic and international participation in its cumulative assessment by means of "an interactive, password-protected Web site to serve as a repository for discussion papers and workshop summaries. The site also provided a link to massive quantities of basic data for reference and analysis. It contained interactive tools to keep our foreign and domestic experts engaged and created 'hands-on' computer simulations that allowed novice and expert alike to develop their own scenarios" (National Intelligence Council, 2005, p. 23).

In summary, witness McGinn uses visual and spoken storytelling to engage the C-SPAN viewing audience for this televised hearing and to persuade committee members in the hearing room. The rhetorical achievement is to popularize the chair's concerns. Like the chorus in early Greek tragic drama, his testimony appeals to, and speaks for, public interests in the action.

> The protection of our food supply, therefore, is central to our culture and central to our government's stability. As consumers, we are looking for government agencies to speak with one voice. We are looking for them to actually give us the roles and responsibilities . . . of the private sector, and then of the citizens themselves. We were looking for funding on the state level to actually do the sorts of things that can't be done on the national level . . ." (*Agro terrorism*, 2004, p. 9).

Testimony by Peter Chalk

Peter Chalk is a risk analyst for the research organization RAND Corporation and author of its report on biological warfare and agriculture cited by the committee chair in her opening statement. He testifies following McGinn in the hearing. Chalk counters the discourse developed between the chair's opening statement and the first witness's testimony. Initially, he makes measured acknowledgment of the validity of Collins's and McGinn's claims. While acknowledging agriculture's vulnerability, he qualifies the risk. "Now, although vulnerability does not translate to risk, and there are few reported actual incidents of terrorists employing biological agents against agriculture, a realistic potential for such a contingency certainly exists" (*Agro terrorism*, 2004, p. 14). He goes on to apply probabilistic reasoning to constrain inferences. "The problem is that you can't extrapolate [a disease outbreak in poultry] to the general agricultural industry because the referent . . . experience is not there" (*Agro terrorism*, 2004, p. 22).

Chalk then draws attention to the constructed nature of scenarios and disputes their value as a method of risk assessment. "The one thing I would like to stress is that . . . we are always dealing in scenarios when it comes to agro terrorism; I have only come up with two documented cases of the . . . use of biological weapons deliberately as a political strategy against livestock" (*Agro terrorism*, 2004, p. 31).

Chalk goes on to rank the risk comparatively. "Despite the ease by which agricultural terrorism can be carried out and the potential ramifications. . . . I don't think that it is likely to constitute a primary form of terrorist aggression. . . . However, I think [such attacks] could certainly emerge as a favored secondary form of aggression . . ." (*Agro terrorism*, 2004, p. 17).

Without referring directly to the RAND report that he authored, Chalk effectively disassociates that report from the paper trail in which Senator Collins had earlier placed it. In doing so, he exercises control over use of his knowledge.

In summary, the rhetorical achievement of Chalk's testimony can be described as double voicing, or polyphony (Gunther, 2002). He asserts while, simultaneously, he evaluates other assertions. He deliberates the abstract possibility of terror while countering claims about its scope of actual applicability. Thus, he disrupts the perspective that Collins and McGinn have co-constructed in the hearing. The disruptions draw attention to that perspective, making it evident and showing its limits. With the loss of transparency, abstract terror is exposed as a way of seeing that is also a way of not seeing.

CONCLUSION: PREPARING PROFESSIONALS

Antidote to uncritical acceptance of a prevailing perspective is a need found in many workplaces (Linnell, 2002). In settings of public policy work, perspective explicitly or implicitly comes with the territory, and a prevailing perspective likely comes with each political context. Critical discourse analysis can provide the antidote of "recognition work" for professionals who communicate in public policy settings (Gee, 1999, p. 20). Skills of recognition and response are especially important for professionals who want to communicate skepticism or disagreement in those settings.

Teachers and trainers might offer preprofessional students and professionals in continuing education the tools of recognition. For example, we might provide opportunity to read transcripts or view broadcasts of governmental public hearings. To prompt analysis of the communication choices shown there, we can apply visual techniques. Students and trainees might map or use spreadsheets to graph the information exchanges between office holders and invited witnesses. These techniques help to identify present viewpoints on the data and to speculate on the absence of other viewpoints. Or participants might practice conceptual framing skills by defining a problem differently according to different viewpoints. Or they might perform theme analysis by tracing original information through its recontextualizations in a single hearing.

We can borrow recognition techniques from political satire to prompt recognition of hyperbole, or deliberate overstatement. For example, if I were to show a videotape of the agroterrorism hearing in an academic class or professional training seminar, I might use as a pedagogical tool the satiric technique of reducing experience to a formula. I might ask participants to index the hyperbole in that hearing using this mock formula:

Sector defined by hypothetical terrorist attack = risk

Risk multiplied by inferential assessment = fear

Fear divided by probability = hyperbole

In doing that exercise, I would not intend to suggest that public policy communication is fundamentally hyperbolic. Cynical mistrust of government and contempt for politics are not the objectives. Rather, I would intend to show rhetoric's presence in public deliberations and to illustrate rhetorical choices made by deliberators to communicate risk under conditions of ethical and political uncertainty (Sauer, 2003, p. 19).

REFERENCES

Agro terrorism: The threat to America's breadbasket. (2004.) Washington: U.S. Government Printing Office.
http://frwebgate.access.gpo.gov/cgi-bin/getdoc.cgi?dbname=108_senate_hearings&docid=f:91045.wais

Coplin, W. D., & O'Leary, M. K. (1998). *Public policy skills* (3rd ed.). Washington: Policy Studies Associates.

Gee, J. P. (1999). *An introduction to discourse analysis: Theory and method.* London and New York: Routledge.

Graumann, C. F. (2002). Explicit and implicit perspectivity. In C. F. Graumann & W. Kallmeyer (Eds.), *Perspective and perspectivity in discourse* (pp. 25-39). Amsterdam and Philadelphia: John Benjamins Publishing Company.

Gunther, S. (2002). Perspectivity in reported dialogues. The contextualization of evaluative stances in reconstructing speech. In C. F. Graumann & W. Kallmeyer (Eds.), *Perspective and perspectivity in discourse* (pp. 347-374). Amsterdam and Philadelphia: John Benjamins Publishing Company

Linnell, P. (2002). Perspectives, implicitness and recontextualization. In C. F. Graumann & W. Kallmeyer (Eds.), *Perspective and perspectivity in discourse* (pp. 41-57). Amsterdam and Philadelphia: John Benjamins Publishing Company.

National Intelligence Council. (2005). *Mapping the global future: National Intelligence Council's 2020 report.* Washington: U.S. Government Printing Office. http://www.dni.gov/nic/NIC_home.html

Sauer, B. (2003). *The rhetoric of risk: Technical communication in hazardous environments.* Mahwah, NJ: Lawrence Erlbaum Associates.

Smith, C. F. (1994). "Is it worth fixing this plane?" The rhetorical life of information in a Congressional oversight hearing on the B-1 bomber. In B. Sims (Ed.), *Studies in technical communication: Selected papers from the 1993 CCCC and NCTE meetings* (pp. 111-146). Denton, TX: University of North Texas.

CHAPTER 11

Challenges to Effective Information and Communication Systems in Humanitarian Relief Organizations

Christina Maiers, Margaret Reynolds, and Mark Haselkorn

There are substantial and diverse challenges to the development and use of an information and communication system (ICS) in support of effective delivery of humanitarian relief during complex emergencies. These challenges generally go far beyond technology considerations and often relate to core organizational issues of mission, culture, environment, and communication.

Not only must ICS support basic transportation and logistics issues, but it also must support organizational communication that is greatly complicated by a diverse landscape of players. These players include the United Nations, donor governments, multi- and bilateral agencies, governments of countries affected by the crisis, nongovernmental organizations (NGOs), philanthropic foundations, corporations, the giving public, and those who have suffered during the crisis.

A clear and comprehensive communication system is critical to managing relationships among players in the relief landscape. Such a system consists of far more than information and communication technology (ICT)—even more problematic are human, political, and organizational aspects of an effective ICS. For this discussion, then, ICS means not only IT but also people, practices, policies, and organizational environments.

In order to reduce human suffering in the face of natural disasters and man-made emergencies, organizations need established communication channels, infrastructures, strategies, agreements, education, and training in place to adequately respond. The technology component is usually the easiest part. As Harley Benz of the USGS

National Earthquake Information Service put it in the case of a Southeast Asia Tsunami warning system:

> Putting in the sensors is the easy part. The difficult part here would be coordination between emergency-response agencies in the region. Then, you have to deal with education, preparedness and training issues (Haselkorn, 2005).

It is too late to begin establishing the necessary ICS infrastructure, including agreements, policies, and practices, after an emergency has occurred. Even when a relief organization is not in emergency response mode, establishing an effective ICS infrastructure is not easy. The communication challenges facing organizations involved in international humanitarian relief, particularly NGOs, are unusual in their complexity and criticality.

For NGOs, complex communication challenges occur not only within their own organizations, but also among the political, military, and numerous other non-governmental organizations that operate alongside them—particularly when these diverse nonprofit and governmental organizations strive to enhance relief effectiveness by increasing cooperation. Challenges arise in all aspects of evolving relief efforts, including preparedness and early warning, rescue, relief, and recovery. These efforts are themselves composed of complex, interconnected operations such as logistics, supply chain management, human resources, informal and formal agreements, evaluation and assessment, lessons learned, and institutional learning. Perhaps most importantly, communication challenges exist between relief actors and the general public whom they are committed to serve.

This chapter explores communication issues and associated challenges revealed during international humanitarian relief efforts and identifies potential areas of interest for further exploration. We focus on issues and challenges that exist within NGOs (intraorganizational) and among NGOs, as well as between NGOs and the other types of organizations involved in humanitarian relief, including the people being served (interorganizational).

METHODOLOGY AND ORGANIZATION

This chapter draws from two types of research conducted in 2004 (prior to the southeast Asia earthquake and tsunamis): a headquarters-level assessment of upper-level management perspectives on organizational communication issues and strategies; and a field-level assessment conducted in Africa, intended to identify key communication challenges facing NGOs today. For the headquarters assessment, information was gathered through an open-ended survey administered face-to-face or over the phone to IT managers, directors, and operations managers of prominent Northern hemisphere humanitarian relief NGOs. For the field-level assessment, field researchers traveled to Kenya and Ethiopia to gather information through in-depth exploratory interviews with and participatory observation of key NGO personnel. These field studies were conducted in cooperation with the Fritz Institute; John Snow, Inc.; USAID; and World Vision International.

The following discussion divides NGO communication issues and associated challenges into two categories: intraorganizational communication and interorganizational communication. It is important to note that while this division makes discussion easier, in practice these categories are highly interdependent.

INTRAORGANIZATIONAL COMMUNICATION

The state of the internal information and communication systems within an NGO is an integral component of how successfully the organization may be able to respond to complex humanitarian emergencies. An internal ICS is not only connected to the technological capacity of an NGO, but also to its mission, culture, structure, people, policies, and administrative strategies. Although this is true for all organizations, NGOs and other relief organizations face particularly complex issues and challenges to the establishment and management of an effective ICS. Here follows a brief analysis of the internal issues and challenges most common to the relief sector.

Complications from a Decentralized Organizational Structure

NGOs operating in the developing world typically have a decentralized organizational structure in which field offices exhibit a high level of autonomy with minimal oversight by headquarters (HQ). The main advantage of this type of structure is that NGO field offices can develop a firm understanding of the local situation, needs, languages, politics, and cultural nuances of the country where the disaster has occurred. This in-depth understanding of the locality helps an NGO respond more rapidly and appropriately, and is a critical success factor in disaster response.

While there are critical benefits of a decentralized structure, it also considerably complicates the implementation and management of an organizationwide ICS infrastructure. In our NGO interviews, the tensions between an organization's decentralized organizational structure and the demands of establishing a cross-organizational ICS infrastructure were strongly present. As one IT director described his job, "I am responsible for persuading the field that IT is important in completing their work and the overall mission of the organization. They do not see the direct benefit." Below are some reasons for this disconnect:

- The field is not interested in gathering information; they regard it as a nuisance and are busy operating (NGO administrator).
- There is a general disconnect between systems mandated at HQ and availability or usability in the field. This situation has evolved because it is easy to mandate down to the field, and it is sometimes hard for HQ to understand how things work in the field (NGO field manager).

In some cases, the goals of the field and of HQ can conflict. For example, field workers operating in resource-poor environments may choose unique local systems to spur economic growth in the local economy, while HQ is attempting to promote cost-effective operations by implementing compatible systems across the organization. When field offices can operate at their own discretion, choosing to use separate software systems or not to use them at all, an organization's ability to communicate clearly across international offices and headquarters can become extremely complicated.

Despite the need for a central ICS organizational strategy, mandating such a strategy from HQ (top-down) is typically not effective or feasible. Many HQ offices function as nonoperational, fundraising components of the organization, with little or no oversight, making it difficult to field test and implement new communication strategies. In addition, mandating policy from an HQ level is not compatible with the consensus-building leadership style of NGOs (and nonprofits in general). Even though NGO field offices often consider recommendations on all levels by HQ, they are rarely required to implement them.

Need for User-Centered Design Strategies

Our headquarters-level NGO research found that one key to effective ICS implementation and use is to ensure that systems meet the unique communication and environmental needs of the local office.

> HQ implemented Web-based timesheets. They think it is great, but it is not practical in the field because of connectivity and time pressures (NGO field worker).

In the NGO world, the local communication needs and contexts in the African offices are likely to be very different than needs in the Latin American offices. In these varying environments, user-centered design becomes an even more critical but extremely challenging activity. The major challenge is to develop systems and strategies that can address diverse needs, users, and conditions without becoming chaotic (i.e., developing systems that are *flexible*, but not *ad hoc*).

During research interviews, interviewees in the field characterized many HQ-driven ICS projects as developed and managed without adequate consultation with local staff.

> The Commodity Tracking System program may assist with HQ needs, but there is not as much benefit on the field level (NGO field manager).

Initiatives to enhance activities like supply chain management (SCM), which have strong information and communication components, were viewed quite differently from the HQ and field perspectives.

> It would be very useful to have the program people see what SCM entails and have them learn more about the logistics process on the ground (NGO field office).

One area of needed improvement is getting [local] SCM staff to better understand the financial structures and the budget process. We have had a lot of budgeting problems, because there is a lack of understanding of the financial process (NGO HQ).

The results of ICS projects in which field workers were not "co-owners" of the effort and differing valid perspectives were not aligned caused friction between local staff and HQ, and in some cases even reinforced asymmetrical power relations between developing-world and HQ-level staff teams. A number of potentially valuable ICS software (FACTS and Humanitarian Logistics Software) were abandoned or had limited impact in the relief and development sector in part because local needs were inadequately represented or appropriate buy-in from local offices was not obtained during the design and development phases.

Despite many negative incidents, we observed a positive example in Africa of how recognizing local communication needs can improve the success of NGO ICS projects. An organization decided to implement a commodity tracking system that allows an NGO, both field office and HQ, to track their goods along the supply chain. Because they had inadequate resources to develop their own software, the HQ began looking at already developed software packages while incorporating their field staff in the decision-making process every step of the way. By bringing local staff to the United States and hiring software consultants to assist with appropriateness and usability issues, the HQ and local office together were able to conduct a program that addressed the needs of both the local office and HQ.

Weak Information Management

An NGO's ability to store and manage information and knowledge is a critical component of organizational capacity, disaster response, postdisaster assessment, and institutionalization of lessons learned. Knowledge management tools and strategies are just being recognized in the sector as potentially valuable ways to improve and refine performance for future disasters. In the past, humanitarian relief organizations have focused on response activities, but now there is increased interest in learning activities as well. If NGOs are to move from a focus on doing well in the current emergency to doing a better job the next time, they will need to develop and apply ICS to the capture and application of past experiences.

Despite the growing recognition of the importance of information and knowledge management, this activity is generally handled poorly across the humanitarian relief sector, and to a great extent, the sector reinvents itself with each new catastrophe. While it is important to understand the extreme difficulties of operating in highly chaotic, resource- and information-poor environments, operating within chaos is not the only factor that works against effective information management in NGOs. Other major constraining factors include insufficient time, energy, and financial resources; workforce turnover and lack of professional standing; multiple organizational perspectives on the appropriateness and role of information infrastructures;

focus on technology rather than on organizational culture; and differences in the value and implementation of ongoing assessment and improvement strategies.

Need for Cross-Organizational Program Development

Cross-organizational sharing or communication among multiple departments within an NGO, is a vital component of program planning and organizational success. When planning project proposals for disaster mitigation or response, each department (finance, programs, development, etc.) must work collaboratively to form financially viable, organizationally feasible, and well-planned programs.

Despite this challenge, proposals are often written without adequate consultation of support departments, such as ICT and logistics, and create huge long-term management problems. Inaccurate project budgets and unrealistic expectations of price and services from support departments are a few examples of problems associated with a lack of cross-organizational communication.

For the sector to more effectively respond to humanitarian crises, it is critical that NGOs recognize the value-added by the use of a coordinated approach and implement information and communication policies that support increased coordination.

Lack of Funding for ICT Strategic Planning and Implementation

Humanitarian relief organizations generally view an ICS as overhead rather than as a fundamental activity. To make matters worse, relief donors generally view overhead costs as detrimental to a proposed project, so they are kept to a minimum. In addition, since most funding is project-based, there are few if any program resources that can be used to address longer-term, organizationwide infrastructure needs.

In addition, donor governments, foundations, corporations, and the giving public focus relief donations on immediate solutions for immediate situations, targeting funds toward water and sanitation, medicine, food, and shelter in direct response to visible human suffering.

> Field training, supervision, lack of institutional memory . . . donors do not fund to help with these things (NGO administrator).

Where donor funding goes beyond basic needs, it is generally allocated toward tangible infrastructure projects, such as the restoration and building of schools and hospitals, without complementary financing for the long-term administrative and strategic support of these facilities. Although donations for basic needs and traditional infrastructure are critical, resources for strategic ICS solutions and management are just as critical.

> A child is far more compelling than a satellite phone, but a well-placed satellite phone can help reduce the suffering of many children (Haselkorn, 2005).

For these reasons, finding adequate funding for a cross-organizational ICS is a common problem in NGOs. The restricted and short-term nature of donor funding makes it very difficult for organizations to invest more strategically in long-term planning and discourages organizations from adequately investing in strategic ICS infrastructure. Unfortunately, an inadequately planned and implemented ICS negatively impacts critical activities like contingency planning and preparedness. This effect forces organizations into a reactionary mode in which information and communication needs cannot be adequately addressed "on the fly."

Barriers to Cross-Organizational Information Sharing

Many of the issues discussed thus far make it difficult for NGOs to effectively share information across the organization. Decentralized structures and field offices located in geographically dispersed areas of the world complicate NGO efforts to aggregate common experiences and disseminate lessons learned. Many NGOs have begun building internal libraries, attempting to create information repositories that can be accessed from field offices and other locations. Unfortunately, these efforts are not generally integrated within an organizationwide, developed strategy for how information and communication will be used.

Most IT directors we spoke with believe that creative use of ICS can help meet the challenge of communicating with dispersed field offices. Some focus on a centralized information library; others believe that the most effective way to encourage organizational information sharing is to build better and more effective search engines. Most acknowledge the importance of a common ICS strategic plan.

> A common information strategy and reliable and accurate information systems can help field directors have more confidence in the information, which will encourage them to access it when they are faced with an unfamiliar situation or emergency (NGO IT director).

One of the most important reasons for developing a common information strategy is to allow diverse experiences from all over the world to fuel the institutional knowledge of an organization. In the NGO world this is extremely complicated, because a typical organization is developing one strategy for 80 to 90 unique field offices, each with its own unique organizational processes and communication systems, in addition to differing cultures, languages, and experiences. Every NGO surveyed in our research was struggling with the enormous challenge of developing standard systems in an extremely diverse environment.

Another challenge related to the establishment of cross-organizational information systems is the widespread concern both at HQ and in the field that IT is a distraction rather than an essential support of organizational objectives.

> IT is not a high priority for senior management (NGO IT director).

> Senior administrators are beginning to see IT as essential to the program, but it is still somewhere in the middle (NGO IT manager).

While appeals to increased efficiency and accountability may be persuasive at HQ, they are less likely to affect field workers.

> Our primary objective is to serve people in need. First we concentrate on getting the goods there and saving lives and then our secondary consideration is the bottom line/costs (NGO field worker).

Based on our interviews, we concluded that ICS is not universally perceived as important to the basic functions of NGOs. ICS advocates in NGOs face a considerable challenge to demonstrate to both HQ and field personnel how a developed ICS infrastructure and strategy would serve the organization's central mission.

Short-Term Focus Complicates Long-Term ICT Infrastructure Issues

Thorough planning of clear communication strategies and systems *prior to* a disaster is perhaps the most essential step toward attaining effective communication systems within NGOs. But although ongoing strategic planning is essential, internal issues and challenges confronting NGOs make this an extremely difficult thing to do.

The challenge of giving equal weight to long-term planning as well as short-term relief is a major issue within the humanitarian relief sector on many different levels. It can be seen in the short-term immediate funding tendencies of donors and in the tendency of NGO field workers to focus on short-term information needs while being resistant to the "disruptive" longer-term informational needs for assessment and capture of lessons learned.

Lack of Trained Personnel

Long-term versus short-term planning issues are further complicated by the often temporary nature of NGO workers. NGO field workers experience up to 80% annual turnover. This fact makes it more difficult for these workers to invest time and energy into longer-term strategic initiatives.

Not surprisingly, our research found that human capacity can be much more critical to a long-term effective communication system than technological capacity. As an administrator from a large international NGO told us:

> The biggest challenge for me is the lack of trained personnel and human resource [personnel]. . . . We need people who are competent and ready when a disaster strikes.

The numerous and varied challenges to establishing an effective ICS within an NGO become even more challenging when we consider the essential communication and collaboration that needs to occur across the entire humanitarian relief sector.

INTERORGANIZATIONAL COMMUNICATION

Within the last decade organizations have increasingly realized the value of having a coordinated response to humanitarian emergencies. In 1991 the United Nations formed the Office for Coordination of Humanitarian Affairs (OCHA). The objective for creating OCHA was to provide coordination among the various UN bodies responding to humanitarian emergencies.

> Humanitarian coordination is based on the belief that a coherent approach to emergency response will maximize its benefits and minimize its potential pitfalls—in short, that the whole will be greater that the sum of its parts (UN Office for the Coordination of Humanitarian Affairs, n.d.).

The UN has recognized the need to promote collaboration among international NGOs as well. The UN OCHA now acts as the central coordinating body for NGOs on the ground, working to more effectively deliver aid to those most in need. However, NGOs usually are mobilized and on the ground long before the UN has arrived.

Despite the increasing recognition of the need for more effective coordination among the UN, NGOs, and the military (either acting as peacekeepers or delivering aid), a number of barriers have prevented the establishment of a clear and effective interagency information and communication strategy.

Need to Increase Coordination and Interoperability While Maintaining Organizational Autonomy

The actors who respond to humanitarian emergencies are diverse, with different constituents, missions, and objectives. While they all share the objective of alleviating human suffering, commonalities typically end there. Given the challenges inherent in devising a coordinated strategy among extremely diverse players, organizations have begun to focus on interoperability as a key to creating environments that support cooperation.

NGOs have deep organizational roots and cultures, and they are strongly committed to their various, often unique missions. For this reason, the maintenance of organizational autonomy is often cited as a barrier to increased coordination and interoperability. For example, field workers in Africa told us that a shared warehouse might well increase their efficiency, but they could not participate if it meant sacrificing the ability to respond independently.

Given NGOs' strong desire for autonomy, interoperability is best viewed not as sharing common systems, but as "creating conditions that enable separate organizations to share information toward a common end" (Solomon & Brown, 2004). This definition of interoperability does not require NGOs to relinquish organizational sovereignty but rather focuses on the underlying conditions that make information sharing beneficial to all parties.

Need for Increased Security and Coordination with the Military

In addition to increased cooperation among NGOs and the UN, the necessity of a cooperative relationship between the military and NGOs is also becoming more accepted. Within the last five years, NGOs have been operating in increasingly insecure environments. The number of humanitarian aid workers attacked, kidnapped, and murdered has risen considerably, leading many organizations to put security much higher on their list of priority issues, and even leading some to scale down relief efforts in certain areas. It has become critical that NGOs be able to accomplish their mission while providing for the safety and security of their personnel.

If NGOs are to secure the safety of their workers while continuing to serve people living in high-risk areas, they must coordinate with military organizations. There are, however, obvious challenges to this communication and coordination need.

The military operates in one of two ways in an emergency situation. They may either serve in a peacekeeping function where there are warring parties or ethnic strife, as in Afghanistan and Kosovo, or they may directly administer aid, as in the Asian tsunami relief. Each of these operations requires interaction with other actors, but the military is used to operating independently and is not likely to share secure information. In this environment, cooperation among military and nonmilitary entities is a challenge.

NGOs are also put in a difficult situation when seeking better coordination with the military. On the one hand, an NGO's mission depends in part on remaining politically unbiased; an NGO aligning itself with the military could jeopardize its mission. On the other hand, not seeking military information and coordination can put its employees and volunteers at a considerable security risk. How can NGOs maintain an image of impartiality even as they increase efforts to promote communication and information sharing with the military?

Need to Integrate Incomplete Information Among Various Organizations

At the onset of an emergency, information such as assessments, statistics, and census reports is needed immediately and must be as accurate as possible to gauge the necessary level of response. Despite this need, the typical reality in disaster response is that existing information is either outdated, hard to find, scattered among different sources, or unreliable for political or other reasons. The difficulties in sending assessment teams to a site without accurate information are extreme, often resulting in wasted time and resources.

The negative effects of unreliable data were demonstrated in the NGO response to the Darfur conflict. Soon after the conflict started, NGOs needed to get estimates on the number of people in the geographically dispersed and hard-to-reach areas of Darfur to plan for the response. Roads, airfields, and other transportation networks were either nonexistent or in very poor condition within the region, preventing NGOs from engaging in much field-level preassessment work. NGOs were often forced to rely upon outdated census information from the government. In one case, an NGO initiated a full-scale response for one area of Darfur, only to discover that the 25,000 people thought to be living in the area were no longer there. Significant time, money, and resources were wasted. This example illustrates the drastic repercussions of not having timely and accurate information to help plan a response.

This event also points toward areas of possible information cooperation among NGOs. For example, a geographic information system (GIS) can be quite powerful in tracking the migration and movement of large populations. A shared humanitarian GIS data center might well have prevented some of the waste of time and resources in Darfur or could be used in warning systems and postdisaster recovery. A recent collaboration among Mercy Corps, the Pacific Data Center, and the University of Washington is exploring this possibility (Paulson, 2005).

The development of a coordinated system for relief assessment and information sharing has been generally seen as the province of the UN. OCHA and the UN Joint Logistics Centre both function as information clearinghouses to relief actors and provide operational coordination as well. While each of these agencies has struggled with providing much needed coordination, their unique role within emergencies is critical.

Overcoming Reluctance of Organizations to Share Information

Although NGOs are nonprofit entities, they have been increasingly forced to compete for limited available resources and "market share," leading to a type of "corporatization" of NGOs. Although NGOs voice the desire and willingness to cooperate, the pressure of competition is enormous, presenting challenges to joint communication and information sharing. There is a general reluctance of organizations to share information, especially information that is considered proprietary or significantly valuable to organizations typically competing for funding from the same sources.

For both NGOs and funders, feelings about competition versus cooperation remain mixed. An advantage of NGO competition is that those organizations who do not provide adequate services or maintain the values of accountability and transparency will not receive valuable contracts. On the other hand, competition creates secrecy and an atmosphere of seeking competitive advantage rather than serving the people. The contradictory nature of this challenge makes it one of the most important to be addressed by the NGO community.

Challenges of Working in Underdeveloped, Disaster-Affected Environments

Although poor physical infrastructure is inherent within the nature of disaster response work and is largely expected, the degree to which poor physical or communication infrastructure impedes operations is substantial. The challenge of physically reaching victims often determines the immediate effectiveness of an NGO. Physical infrastructure, such as railroads, roads, and bridges destroyed by war, earthquakes, or tsunamis often makes the work of reaching victims nearly impossible. In addition, the sheer remoteness of a location or operating in a country with little existing infrastructure also impedes an organization's ability to reach recipients. For example, roads of sand in Sudan have created major obstacles for NGOs trying to transport large loads of supplementary foods to needy villages. In addition, many poorly built roads in Ethiopia totally prevent access to relief supplies by many villages during the three-month rainy season. These two examples are not exceptional but extremely common infrastructure problems NGOs must face.

An effective information and communication infrastructure among NGOs can offer possibilities for alleviating the constraints imposed by underdeveloped or destroyed physical infrastructure. If NGOs can communicate about what roads have been wiped out and what roads are functioning, they may be able to reach victims faster. If an isolated worker at an emergency site can speak easily to field headquarters or other organizations involved in relief, that communication can make a major difference in the response. Although poor physical conditions cannot be changed immediately during an emergency, a well-planned, strategically implemented communication infrastructure can contribute to a more successful response to disasters and emergencies.

CONCLUSION

NGOs can improve their effectiveness and efficiency by focusing not only on direct relief and development, but also on strategic infrastructure and management. A well-planned ICS infrastructure can enhance overall organizational capacity, especially in areas such as coordination, strategic planning, preparedness, accountability, lessons learned, education, and research.

There are, however, numerous complex issues and challenges to the effective use of an ICS by humanitarian relief organizations. It is possible for the humanitarian relief industry to learn much in this area from the private sector, but solutions cannot be taken off the shelf and be expected to be completely applicable. Rather it is critical that NGOs adapt these solutions to their own particular conditions and needs.

The humanitarian relief sector is, unfortunately, a "growth industry," attracting tens of billions of dollars each year.

> We need to change the way we support this critical and courageous industry. We need to empower its organizations and people, invest in their education, conduct research that provides them with better tools and techniques, and support the development of human and technology infrastructure that will enable workers to not only conduct their complex work this time, but do it better the next (Haselkorn, 2005).

Helping NGOs overcome the many challenges to effective use of an ICS is a critical component of this vital support.

REFERENCES

Haselkorn, M. (2005, January 14). Improving humanitarian relief for the next big disaster. *The Seattle Times.*
http://seattletimes.nwsource.com/html/opinion/2002150504_haselkorn14.html

Paulson, T. (2005, March 24). Data crunchers to help rebuild Sri Lanka: GIS experts help map out tsunami recovery. *Seattle Post-Intelligencer.*
http://seattlepi.nwsource.com/local/217339_satmap24.html

Solomon, R., & Brown, S. (2004, January 13). *Creating a common communications culture: Interoperability in crisis management.*
http://www.usip.org/virtualdiplomacy/publications/reports/17.html

UN Office for the Coordination of Humanitarian Affairs. (n.d.). *Coordination of humanitarian response.*
http://ochaonline.un.org/webpage.asp?Nav=_coordination_en&Site=_coordination

CHAPTER 12

Using Role Sets to Engage and Persuade Visitors to Web Sites That Promote Safe Sex

Michaël F. Steehouder

Informing people about HIV/AIDS and persuading them toward safe sexual behavior is one of the most important weapons in the struggle against AIDS. Numerous campaigns have been started in past years, some of them worldwide, some on a national level. One of the obstacles for effective communication about HIV/AIDS and safe sexual behavior is shame. Since discussing sexual behavior is taboo in most cultures, young people rarely have access to clear and accurate information on sexual matters, leading them to indulge in risky sexual behaviors. How to communicate about such a taboo is clearly an important issue in HIV/AIDS prevention.

The purpose of this chapter is to provide a theoretical framework for communicating safe sexual behavior, based upon the notions of *face* and *politeness* as analyzed by Brown and Levinson (1987), and the concept of *altercasting*, as discussed by Pratkanis (2000). Although most of my argument is applicable to paper materials (such as brochures) as well, the emphasis will be on the use of role sets in Web sites. This chapter can be considered as an elaboration of the role-playing framework set by Coney and Steehouder (2000).

FACE THREATENING ACTS (FTAs) IN TALKING ABOUT SAFE SEX

Every member of a society wants to be respected, or, as Brown and Levinson (1987) formulate it, everyone claims for a "public self-image." This notion of face includes two aspects: the freedom to act as one chooses, unimpeded by others

133

(*negative face*) and the desire to be positively appreciated by others (*positive face*). Since we all want to "keep our face," we normally try to respect each other's face by allowing each other freedom in acting and restraining from disapproving judgments about each other's personality or behavior.

However, in most forms of communication, it is almost impossible to maintain each other's face to the full extent. As soon as we try to persuade others to a certain behavior (e.g., by giving advice or by warning about hazardous behaviors), we threaten their negative face by putting pressure on their actions. And whenever we express our point of view on a certain matter, there is the risk of implying disapproval of other persons' opinions and thus harming their positive face.

Brown and Levinson (1987, pp. 65-68) list a large number of categories of so-called *face threatening acts* (FTAs), both negative and positive. Among these, three are particularly relevant when we try to persuade people to engage in safe sexual behavior.

- *Advice, suggestions, warnings, and guidelines.* As soon as we recommend or promote forms of sexual behavior (such as the famous *ABC:* abstinence, being faithful, condom use), we attempt to curtail someone's freedom.
- *Disapproval, criticism, or disagreement* with the recipient's opinions or behavior. When promoting "good" behavior, we imply (or even state explicitly) that our audience is at least inclined to "bad" behavior, and thus we imply a disapproval of the other.
- *Mentioning taboos.* A taboo is (by definition) something we don't talk about, or discuss only in guarded terms. If we talk freely about sexuality, we neglect the fact that such talk might be a taboo for the addressee, and we suggest that we do not respect his/her values.

Brown and Levinson argue that communicators have to balance the pros and cons of three intentions: to communicate the message clearly and unambiguously, to be efficient, and to maintain the face of the recipient. As a result of the balancing, we can opt for several different strategies.

- *Going baldly on record:* Committing the FTA directly, clearly, and unambiguously. If we choose this option, the message is communicated efficiently, but there is a considerable risk of harming the recipient's face.
- *Going off record:* The FTA is not communicated directly but *suggested* by the content of the message. Going off record is a strategy that maintains the recipient's face, but it makes the message less clear with the risk of the intention not coming across.

Between these two strategies lies the possibility to *add redressive actions.* This means that we commit the FTA in such a way that the recipients understand that it is not our intention to harm their face. When adding redressive action, the message can be well communicated, and the risk of harming the recipient's face is lowered, but the communication might be less efficient than when we go baldly on record, since we use extra content. There are two types of redressive action:

- *Positive politeness* means that we show appreciation for the recipients by recognizing their desires and values or by emphasizing our good relationship with them.
- *Negative politeness* means that we ensure that we respect the recipient's freedom of choice and that we want to interfere only minimally.

Of course, there is also the option of not committing the FTA after all. In that case, there will be no hard feelings for the recipient's face, but we can also be sure that the message is not communicated.

It is not simple to predict which of the strategies is the best in a given situation. Brown and Levinson (1987) argue that a number of criteria must be taken into consideration.

- *The payoffs of each strategy.* By going *baldly on record*, we can, for instance, be credited for honesty and for the fact that we trust the addressee. But by going *off record* we can be credited for being tactful and for giving the other the opportunity to act spontaneously. By adding redressive actions, we can maintain or even strengthen the good relationship with the recipient.
- *The social relationship.* If the social distance between the communicating parties is larger, the risk of harming the face is also larger, and there will be a stronger tendency toward indirectness or redressive action. Also the power distance is important: those who are high in power are more readily allowed to perform strong FTAs than those who are less in power.
- *The ranking of a particular FTA in a specific culture.* For instance, asking someone to lend us money is much more tolerated in some cultures than in others. And so is refusing such a request.

Although Brown and Levinson's theory is not unquestioned (e.g., Glick, 1996), it is still the leading framework for studies on indirect speech and politeness, with application in such divergent fields as business communication (Campbell, 2006; Pilegaard, 1997) and technical communication (Riley, 2003).

FTAs CAUSE REACTANCE

Brown and Levinson's analysis is based on the claim that every competent language user will try to save the other's face, which is considered as a universal basic need. However, from another perspective it can be argued that it makes sense to save the other's face as a strategy to avoid *reactance* to our persuasive messages. Reactance refers to defiance and resentment toward a form of persuasion that appears to threaten an individual's behavioral freedom (Brehm, 1966). When individuals perceive that their behavioral freedom is threatened, they will change their attitude to the opposite of what is advocated in the persuasion ("boomerang effect") in an attempt to reclaim the threatened freedom. The typical example is the message "do not press the red button," which evokes the uncontrollable desire to press the red button. Whitehead and Russell (2004) conclude from their literature review that reactance occurs in particular as a response to health educators who take a dominant and authoritarian role.

Both the politeness strategy and the reactance theory suggest that face-threatening persuasive messages should be presented indirectly or with redressive action. This approach seems to be the best way to maintain the other's face, as well as to avoid reactance. However, such messages may also offer an escape for their receivers. After all, indirect messages can easily be neglected. The recipients may argue that the message is a "general" message that does not directly apply to their actual behaviors.

The dilemma can be illustrated by comparing the following examples from the FACT Web site hosted by the University of Stellenbosch, South Africa (formerly located at www.admin.sun.ac.za/aids; the texts were downloaded in the spring of 2006 but were removed from that site later). The first is a fragment that describes the so-called ABC measures against HIV infection (abstinence, being faithful, condom use). Instead of baldly recommending these behaviors to the addressee, the writers use an "off record" strategy by just mentioning them. As a result, the passage *suggests* behavioral advice, but leaves it to the reader to take that suggestion. The passage can also be interpreted as "just information."

> Not having (abstaining from) sexual intercourse is the most effective way to avoid STDs, including HIV. For those who choose to be sexually active, the following HIV prevention activities are highly effective:
> • Having intercourse with only one uninfected partner
> • Using latex condoms every time you have sex

As an alternative, advice can be formulated much more directly "on record," as in the following passage from the same Web site:

> You need to use a new condom every time you have sexual intercourse. Never use the same condom twice. Put the condom on after the penis is erect and before any contact is made between the penis and any part of the partner's body. If you go from anal intercourse to vaginal intercourse, you should consider changing the condom.

The FTAs in this passage are much more direct: the pronoun *you* and the imperatives refer directly to the reader and his sexual behaviors, and taboos (like anal intercourse) are mentioned without restraint. The reader cannot neglect the persuasive intention. But now there is the risk of the message being offensive and therefore evoking reactance against the advice.

CREATING ROLE SETS FOR ALTERCASTING
TO PREVENT REACTANCE

A possible solution to the dilemma may lie in the use of *author and reader personas,* which allow us to be more direct without causing a face threat and thus reactance. Brown and Levinson (1987) argue that the force of FTAs is influenced by (among other things) the social relationship between the communicating parties. Some FTAs can be committed without really causing "social damage" if the relationship is appropriate. For instance, a manager can give orders to employees, an officer can command the crew, and parents can "push" their children without really affecting the face of the other party. Intimate friends or peers can speak freely about very personal things that may be taboo for others. Whether a particular FTA is acceptable or offensive (or in-between) depends on the roles of the speaker and the listener in a particular situation.

In many forms of mass communication, participants (readers and writers) do not know each other personally, nor do they have a particular relationship. This holds for the majority of the messages used in Web communication about HIV/AIDS: the Web sites are hosted by anonymous organizations that have no personal or social relationship with their visitors. In such cases, roles and role sets are not *given,* but they can be *created* in messages, as relationships between fictitious personas.

Scholars in rhetoric have long been aware of the potential of role playing to understand the nature of any communication, to better predict its success, and to understand where it has gone wrong (Coney & Steehouder, 2000). They argue that communicators take on a role that serves a particular function in the communication and that serves the purposes of each participant. Creating role sets to persuade people is comparable to the persuasion strategy of *altercasting* (Pratkanis, 2000). Altercasting means that we "force" an audience to accept a particular role that makes them behave in the way we want them to behave. Pratkanis distinguishes two basic forms of altercasting:

- In *manded altercasting,* we explicitly "tell" people who they are (or are supposed to be) by making them aware of a role that they already have, or by attributing a role that. For example, if we say to someone, "You are a responsible person," the addressee will start to feel him- or herself as such, irrespective of whether he or she really is.
- *Tact altercasting* means that we put ourselves as senders in a role that "evokes" a natural counterrole for the other. For example, if we present ourselves as health care adviser, the other will unconsciously take the role of someone who needs health care advice.

Both forms of altercasting are considered very powerful persuasive tactics because social roles are very important motives for human behavior.

The theoretic framework can now be summarized as follows: Messages that promote safe sex will inevitably include face-threatening elements such as advice, warnings, criticism, and taboos. Because social norms force us to spare others' face, and because face threats can result in reactance, it seems sensible to present our messages indirectly (off record) or to add politeness elements. However, by doing so, we allow the reader to take the message less seriously, as it is less intrusive than a bald on-record message would be. An escape for this dilemma might be to create personas and role sets that allow us to talk straightforward and to give direct, even pressuring advice.

ROLE SETS IN WEB SITES PROMOTING
SAFE SEX

This section presents an analysis of some examples of role sets found in Web sites that promote safe sex, HIV testing, or other HIV/AIDS-related behaviors. The analysis is not based on a systematic, quantitative form of content analysis. The purpose is just to identify some typical role sets and to develop hypotheses about their potential effectiveness.

Expert-Ignorant (E-I)

An expert is an individual with specialized knowledge. Experts manifest themselves in texts by providing information without reference to sources for argumentation. The expert provides knowledge and explains. If the author persona of a Web page behaves as an expert, he or she creates a role set that puts the addressee in the role of an ignorant individual. The E-I role set is particularly manifested when information is presented in a schoolbook-like manner. A typical example is the following (from the FACT Web site):

> **What Happens when HIV Enters The Body?**
> When HIV enters the body, it attaches itself to the wall of the white CD4 blood cell (also called the helper T cell). This cell, or lymphocyte, belongs to a class of lymphocytes called T cells. T cells form a critical part of the body's immune system as they organize the overall immune response to a variety of infectious diseases.

This fragment shows several characteristics of an "expert style" of arguing:

- The heading has the form of a factual question.
- There is a strong focus on terminology (synonyms and explanations).
- The text does not explicitly refer to the persona of the expert or of the ignorant addressee.
- The information is presented in a general, abstract manner (it does not, for instance, mention "your" body but "the" body).

Since the E-I role set requires a very neutral, impersonal tone, FTAs will usually be performed off record. The on-record mode would be inappropriate because keeping face is very important in distant relationships. Adding positive or negative politeness does not fit into this role set either, as the expert is not supposed to have any "feelings" about the ignorant.

Consultant-advice seeker (C-A)

This role set resembles the Expert-Ignorant role set, in that a consultant is somebody who also has more knowledge than an advice seeker. The distinction between the role sets is, however, that in the C-A role set the topic of discussion is framed as an individual problem of the advice seeker, related to behavior or feelings. An example of a passage in which the C-A role set is created is the following (from FACT Web site again).

I Tested Positive, Now What?

A positive test result means that you have HIV antibodies, and are infected with HIV. You will get your test result from a trained counselor or healthcare professional who should tell you what to expect, and should let you know where to get health services and emotional support. Testing positive does not mean that you have AIDS. Many people who test positive stay healthy for several years, even if they do not start taking medication right away. If you test negative and you have not been exposed to HIV for at least three months, you are not infected with HIV. Continue to protect yourself from HIV infection.

How is the C-A role set created in this particular passage? First, the question-answer combination suggests that the reader (or reader persona) takes the initiative of asking for advice and in doing so he or she defines the role set. Secondly, the question frames the topic as a personal problem of the advice seeker, reinforced by the direct way he or she is addressed. The use of *you* is probably the most obvious characteristic of the C-A role set.

Of course, the *you* in this fragment is not really the reader or visitor to the Web site, but an anonymous, maybe fictitious, person who put the question. The role set will work only if the reader identifies him- or herself with the questioner. For this complicated framework of rhetorical role playing, see Coney and Steehouder (2000).

The C-A role set also seems very useful for preview passages wherein the visitor can choose a topic by clicking; for example, the following from *Khomanani*, hosted by the South African Government (www.aidsinfo.co.za):

HIV and AIDS can be prevented. Here's an important area for you to learn about sex education, the use of condoms, and how to negotiate safer sex with your partner.

Such previews suggest that the role set will be continued in the pages that appear after clicking. However, this assumption is only partially true. After this preview, passages appear, such as the following, where distant and closer language alternate.

Anyone who is in a sexual relationship should know about HIV and AIDS because HIV can be passed from one person to another during sex. Most people who are infected with HIV do not know they are infected, and you cannot tell if a person is infected just by looking at them. It is important to talk to your sexual partner about the risk of infection with HIV. There are a number of ways to have safer sex including using condoms, or having sex where no penetration or contact with body fluids occurs. Some couples in serious relationships choose to have an HIV test. This helps them make choices about their sexual practices and their future. Couples who are planning to have a baby should know that the baby can also be infected with the virus during pregnancy, birth, or through breast feeding. Only some babies born to infected mothers become infected with HIV.

This fragment shows all the characteristics of the E-I role set. However, the page continues with a fragment that seems to assume the C-A role set again. This shifting of role sets seems perfectly natural without suggesting that the text is written by an unskillful writer:

If you are in a sexual relationship:
- talk to your partner about HIV and AIDS
- practice safer sex by using condoms
- find out other ways to have safer sex
- know the facts about HIV and AIDS .
- consider having an HIV test

You and your partner have the right to say no to sex, and to practice safer sex. Respect your partner, and work together to prevent HIV and AIDS.

The C-A role set seems appropriate for persuasive messages because it allows for a much more straightforward use of FTAs than the E-I role set for various reasons. Straight advice is perfectly acceptable within this role set. Moreover, the advice seeker is supposed to take the initiative for discussing the topic and, by doing so, he or she permits the other to give straight behavioral advice. And finally, the C-A relationship is more personal than the E-I, which opens the possibility of positive politeness ("I respect you"). Within the C-A role set, it is even possible to use imperatives without offending the negative face of the addressee ("Continue to protect yourself from HIV infection").

Instructor-Follower (I-F)

In some passages, the C-A role set becomes an I-F role set: the advisor provides procedural instructions, as in the following example (from the FACT Web site).

How can I get these medicines?
- Go to a doctor as soon as you can and ask about anti-retroviral medicines that could reduce the risk of getting HIV. . . . You should ask the doctor to give you an HIV test.
- . . . While you are waiting for the results of the HIV test, the doctor may give you the medicine so that you can start taking it immediately. . . . Ask the doctor about things you can do to look after yourself when you have HIV.

- If you only get a starter pack, go back to the doctor to get the results of your HIV test. . . .

The I-F role set allows for an even more straightforward presentations of FTAs since the instructor has a greater authority than an advisor.

Peers

Occasionally, the suggestion of intimacy between the expert and the unknown is created, such as in the following passage from Lovelife, South Africa's national HIV prevention program for youth (www.lovelife.org.za). The passage appeared in 2005 on the "Ask Gerald" section, where questions from teenagers were answered by a persona called Gerald:

> Question:
> Hi G, I'm Kitty (14) and have been very naughty; I think it's peer pressure. This boy asked me to walk him to a garage after school and we ended up in the toilet having sex without a condom. I don't want to get pregnant. Help me!

> Gerald replies:
> Yo Kitty Kat! Yeah, I can understand the panic! I am too nice to tell you that "spyt kom altyd agterna" (being sorry afterwards)! If you had unprotected sex you can still get the morning-after pill from any pharmacist or clinic, so that a pregnancy can still be avoided within 72 hours after the act. I hope for your sake that you are not pregnant or got a nasty sexually transmitted infection or HIV. You should have an HIV test within the next six weeks to be sure you didn't get HIV—and again after three months. Go to your local clinic and talk to a nurse, a doctor, or a counselor about your risk of infection and options if you're pregnant. You know enough to know having casual sex—and without a condom—was a big mistake. Good luck, Kitty!

The "chatty" tone of the Ask Gerald section creates an intimate atmosphere, where both parties are more or less peers—albeit Gerald is the more knowledgeable of the two.

A noticeable characteristic of this role set is that the concern for face might be less careful than in other role sets. It allows strong positive politeness ("I can understand you") as well as strong positive FTAs ("was a big mistake") without offending the relationship. Moreover, within a relationship of peers, the taboo of talking about sexuality is probably weaker than in other relationships.

THE EFFECTIVENESS OF CREATING APPROPRIATE ROLES

In the previous section, I illustrated possible advantages of creating adequate role sets in Web sites promoting safe sex. Those particular roles sets are not by definition better than others. The appropriateness of role sets depends on many factors, a number of which were already mentioned and illustrated in Coney and Steehouder (2000):

- The author role has to be credible and inviting. The reader of the text (or visitor to the Web site) has to "believe" in the role that the author persona takes, whether it is expert, advisor, instructor, or peer. Although one may speculate about factors that make personas credible and trustworthy (such as consistency and attractiveness), there is little research that enables us to predict the effectiveness of particular roles.
- The reader role, on the other hand, has to be attractive enough for the audience of the Web site. How attractive is it for the target group of safe-sex-promoting Web sites to "play" the role of an unknown, a consultant, a follower of instructions, or a peer of the author?

An interesting and challenging question is how a credible presence of particular role sets can be created. In my analysis of some Web pages, I have suggested some features that create, for instance, an expert-ignorant role set (factual information, attention for terminology) or an advisor-consultant role set (framing the topic as a personal problem, using personal pronouns). But these features are far from complete, and a careful analysis of many more examples is needed to get a deeper insight. And, finally, it is important to realize that credibility and persuasiveness of role sets are a particularly culture-dependent matter. It is very likely that some role sets are more or less successful in one culture than in another. And it is important not only to take into account differences between national cultures, but also differences between generations, sexes, and cultural groups within nations.

The theoretical framework needs experimental testing. Some studies indicate that the use of role sets indeed influences the face threat perceived by readers, and subsequently the persuasiveness of the message. Steehouder, Ten Broeke, and Boer (forthcoming) used messages about obesity to investigate the effect of various role sets on the perceived face threat and the persuasiveness of messages. Their results showed (among other things) that *criticism* leads to a higher perceived face threat if given by a child to an adult, than if given by a doctor to a patient, while it was lowest if given by a peer to a peer. Moreover, the study showed that the persuasiveness of messages is negatively correlated with the perceived face threat: the more readers feel their face threatened by the message, the less they are convinced by it. In summary, this study seems to support the theoretical framework presented here.

Although further research is needed to verify whether such effects can also be found with other topics and other role sets, the theoretical framework might already serve as a source of inspiration and critical thinking about the way we promote topics like safe sexual behavior. Most of the current research literature about persuasive texts is oriented toward content (e.g., fear appeals) or presentation (e.g., visuals). It seems important to also consider the rhetorical and social perspective, in particular the personas that create the communicative context of a message.

REFERENCES

Brehm, J. W. (1966). *A theory of psychological reactance*. New York: Academic Press.

Brown, P., & Levinson, S. C. (1987). *Politeness: Some universals in language usage.* Cambridge, MA: Cambridge University Press.

Campbell, K. S. (2006). *Thinking and interacting like a leader: The TILL System for effective interpersonal communication.* Chicago: Parlay Press.

Coney, M., & Steehouder, M. (2000). Role playing on the Web. Guidelines for designing and evaluating personas online. *Technical Communication, 47*(3), 327-340.

Glick, D. J. (1996). A reappraisal of Brown and Levinson's politeness: Some universals of language use, eighteen years later. *Semiotica, 109*(1-2), 141-172.

Pilegaard, M. (1997). Politeness in written business discourse: A textlinguistic perspective on requests. *Journal of Pragmatics, 28*(2), 223-244.

Pratkanis, A. R. (2000). Altercasting as an influence tactic. In D. J. Terry & M. A. Hagg (Eds.), *Attitudes, behaviour and social context: The role of norms and group membership* (pp. 201-226). Mahwah, NJ: Lawrence Erlbaum Associates.

Riley, K. (2003). *About face: Comparing positive politeness in dummies and conventional software documentation.* Paper presented at the IPCC 2003: The shape of knowledge, Orlando, Florida.

Ten Broeke, A., Steehouder, M., & Boer, H. (Submitted for publication). *The effect of role sets and indirectness on the perceived face threat and perceived persuasiveness of anti-obesity messages.*

Whitehead, D., & Russell, G. (2004). How effective are health education programmes— Resistance, reactance, rationality and risk? Recommendations for effective practice. *International Journal of Nursing Studies, 41*(2), 163-172.

CHAPTER 13

Physicians and Patients: How Professionals Build Relationships Through Rapport Management

Kim Sydow Campbell

We now have clear evidence that communication between physicians and patients is central to medical care in that it is ubiquitous (Ong, de Haes, Hoos, & Lammes, 1995) and associated with crucial outcomes. More specifically, for example, Epstein, Campbell, Cohen-Cole, McWhinney, and Smilkstein (1993) estimate that the average primary care physician performs around two million medical interviews over a 40-year career. Further, physician-patient communication quality has been linked to patient adherence/compliance (Squier, 1990), satisfaction (Roter, Hall, & Katz, 1987), and malpractice claims (Levinson, Roter, Mullooly, Dull, & Frankel, 1997).

Although researchers agree in general about the importance of both instrumental and affective behavior for effective doctor-patient communication, their relative importance is somewhat controversial. In this chapter, I explore how recent research in leadership communication might provide a normative theoretical foundation for understanding how physicians can develop better relationships with patients during medical interviews. First, I focus on a competing values framework in order to categorize physician communication goals during interactions with patients. Second, I propose a theoretically founded explanation for the effects of verbal communication on rapport. Third, I define three communication strategies and explain how these are used to manage rapport effects successfully during interaction.

THE COMPETING VALUES FRAMEWORK

While working to understand what makes an organization effective, Quinn and Rohrbaugh (1983) developed a cognitive map of management, which was extended to describe managerial communication (Quinn, Hildebrandt, Rogers, & Thompson, 1991) (see Figure 1).

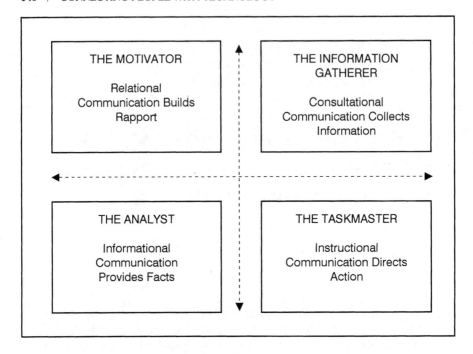

Figure 1. Competing values model of management communication
(adapted from Quinn et al., 1991).

Two axes create four quadrants of values in this model. Each quadrant reflects a different value orientation on the part of a leader toward interaction with a subordinate (Hart & Quinn, 1993):

- Informational interaction establishes clear understanding with the subordinate. The role of the manager is that of an analyst.
- Instructional interaction directs actions of the subordinate. The role of the manager is that of taskmaster.
- Consultation stimulates subordinate contributions. The role of the manager is that of information gatherer.
- Relational interaction establishes credibility, generates trust, and builds rapport with the subordinate. The role of the manager is that of motivator.

Directly opposing quadrants suggest competing values or goals. Thus, interactions in which the leader directs the subordinate's behavior (see the lower right-hand quadrant) conflict with his or her goal to build rapport (see the upper left-hand quadrant).

Leaders show strong preferences for communication styles and roles typified by a single value quadrant. However, the message of this model is that effective interaction requires attention to all four value quadrants. Thus, the traditional "command-and-control" manager stuck in the bottom quadrants is not ideal; rather, the most effective leaders are those whose interactions with subordinates include not only informing and directing, but also consulting and relating. In other words, effective leaders fulfill all four roles: analysts, taskmasters, information gatherers, and motivators.

There are similarities between leaders and physicians because of their status as "professionals" who interact with individuals in nonequal positions of power in situations that require close cooperation and deal with emotionally charged issues (Ong et al., 1995, p. 903). This certainly describes the relationship between leaders and subordinates as well or, for that matter, between all professionals and their clients/customers. Thus, the competing values framework might be useful for describing physician communication behavior (and roles) with patients. The lower quadrants of Figure 1 represent instrumental behaviors, while the upper quadrants represent affective behaviors. As with business leaders, the most effective physicians will interact with patients in ways that reflect all four quadrants. In the following section, we turn our attention specifically to rapport or relationship building (upper left-hand quadrant of Figure 1) and verbal physician behavior.

RAPPORT AND VERBAL COMMUNICATION

Rapport is a concept used to describe relationship quality and has two facets: enjoyable interactions and personal connection (Gremler & Gwinner, 2000). Rapport management refers to the use of language to manage social relations. Building from Goffman (1967) as well as Brown and Levinson (1987), Spencer-Oatey (2000) established a sociolinguistic theory of rapport management composed of two forms of face wants (quality face and social identity face) and two forms of sociality rights (autonomy and association). Let's consider the brief examples in Table 1 to illustrate how these concepts apply to a physician's verbal communication with a patient. (The examples are numbered for easier reference.)

Examples 1A–1B and 2A–2B involve a medical encounter in which a female family physician is informing the mother of a male infant patient that putting the baby on his stomach to sleep increases the risk of Sudden Infant Death Syndrome (SIDS). Examples 3A–3B and 4A–4B involve a medical interview in which a female family physician is directing her adult male patient to take his hypertension medication every day.

Example 1A is likely to threaten the baby's mother's quality face wants (her desire to be seen as a competent individual), whereas example 1B (i.e., *Although most mothers used to . . .*) explicitly tends to her quality face wants while still providing the same information. In example 2A, making a negative comment about the mother's mother is likely to threaten her social identity face wants (her desire to have her family group respected), whereas example 2B (i.e., *It used to be common*) explicitly tends to the mother's social identity face while disagreeing.

Example 3A might threaten the male patient's autonomy rights (his freedom to act as he wishes), whereas example 3B (i.e., *I know you don't always feel like you need . . .*) tends to his right for autonomy by acknowledging the imposition while the

Table 1. Rapport Effects of Physician Contributions

Example Number	Rapport effects on patient face wants and sociality rights	Physician contribution
[A1]	Threatening **Quality Face** Wants[a] → Lower Relationship Quality	*When you put your baby on his stomach to sleep, you increase the risk of SIDS.*
[1B]	Tending **Quality Face** Wants → Maintained or Higher Relationship Quality	*Although most mothers used to place babies on their stomach to sleep, we know now that it increases the risk of SIDS.*
[2A]	Threatening **Social Identity Face** Wants → Lower Relationship Quality	*Your mother's advice to put your baby on his stomach to sleep increases the risk of SIDS.*
[2B]	Tending **Social Identity Face** Wants → Maintained or Higher Relationship Quality	*It was common for mothers to place babies on their stomach to sleep when you were a baby, but we know now that it increases the risk of SIDS.*
[3A]	Threatening **Autonomy** Rights[b] → Lower Relationship Quality	*You must take your medication every morning.*
[3B]	Tending **Autonomy** Rights → Maintained or Higher Relationship Quality	*I know you don't always feel like you need it, but you must take your medication every morning.*
[4A]	Threatening **Association** Rights → Lower Relationship Quality	*You must take your medication every morning* [walks toward door].
[4B]	Tending **Association** Rights → Maintained or Higher Relationship Quality	*Why do you need to take your medication every morning* [listens before walking toward door]?

[a]"Quality face" is basically the same as POSITIVE FACE (Brown & Levinson, 1987).
[b]"Autonomy rights" represent an expanded view of NEGATIVE FACE (Brown & Levinson, 1987) based on later sociolinguistic research.

physician explains why the imposition is justified. Finally, when the physician removes herself from the interaction in example 4A, she clearly threatens the patient's right to association with her (as well as his quality face), whereas she tends to his association rights (i.e., *Why do you need to take your medication . . .*) listening to his response before ending the medical encounter in example 4B.

Roter and her colleagues (Hall, Roter & Katz, 1988; Roter & Hall, 1992; Roter et al., 1987) found that the mean frequency of overtly "positive talk" (i.e., agreeing, showing empathy, reassuring, laughing) ranged between 1% and 31% of the interview. Such physician contributions explicitly tend to a patient's face wants and sociality rights. In contrast, they found that the mean frequency of overtly "negative talk" (i.e., disagreeing, confronting, showing antagonism) ranged between 0.5% and 2.5% of the interview. As those researchers write,

It is probably a good guess that while negative talk is not often made explicit by physicians, the intent is still expressed and negative emotional messages are conveyed. . . . Our research implies that physicians find other ways to express displeasure. Reprimands may be expressed as forceful counseling or imperatives on the need to follow recommendations better (Roter & Hall, 1992, p. 84).

Thus, despite the fact that physicians rarely engage in explicit threats to patient face wants and sociality rights, such threats are communicated.

In sum, a physician's contributions during a medical encounter with a patient have an effect on rapport by influencing a patient's perception of enjoyment and personal connection during interaction with the physician. More specifically, negative rapport effects are the result of threats to the patient's face wants and sociality rights; such threats lower the quality of the relationship between physician and patient. In contrast, positive rapport effects are the result of tending to a patient's wants and rights, which maintains or enhances the quality of the relationship. At this point, it will be helpful to document more clearly those rapport effects that are intrinsic to the four categories of physician goals identified in Figure 1.

The physician's primary goal in examples 1A–1B and 2A–2B in Table 1 is to inform the mother of the infant patient that her current behavior puts her baby at risk (lower left quadrant of Figure 1). It is very common for the physician to focus on informational goals during a medical encounter. In their meta-analysis of research on medical interviews, Roter and Hall (1992) report the mean frequency of a physician's information-giving behavior during an office visit is 25% to 35%, although the range reported was from 4% to 60%. Information giving would include both of the bottom quadrants in Figure 1. Such informational goals are threatening to a patient's face wants since medical encounters often involve the following, all identified by Brown and Levinson (1987) as intrinsically face-threatening: mention of taboo topics, bad news about the patient, and emotionally charged topics (pp. 66-67). In addition, directive goals (like "doctors orders" in examples 3A–3B and 4A–4B in Table 1) are clearly threatening to a patient's autonomy.

Although we provided no specific examples in Table 1, consultational goals are also common for the physician during a medical encounter. Roter and Hall (1992) found the mean frequency of "information seeking" behavior on the part of physicians (upper right quadrant of Figure 1) to be around 20% of the medical interview with a range of 6% to 40%. Those researchers also found the mean frequency of "partnership building" behavior (upper right quadrant of Figure 1) to be around 10% of the interview, ranging from 3% to 25%. Consultational goals of the physician often threaten a patient's face wants and autonomy since the physician must sometimes push the patient to discuss taboo and emotionally charged topics (Brown & Levinson, 1987, pp. 66-67). On the other hand, consultational goals intrinsically tend to a patient's association rights, thus constituting affective behavior (upper half of Figure 1) on the part of the physician.

Relational communication goals are the least common during a medical encounter. Roter and Hall (1992) found the mean frequency of "social conversation" behavior on the part of physicians (upper left quadrant of Figure 1) to be around 6%

of the medical interview with a range of 5% to 10%. Obviously, a physician's relational goals tend to the quality face wants and association rights of a patient. In the following section, we'll turn our attention to the communication strategies that fulfill relational goals.

COMMUNICATION STRATEGIES AND RAPPORT MANAGEMENT

Within sociolinguistics, the verbal means for managing rapport are called "politeness" strategies. In the remainder of this section, I define three such communication strategies and clarify their effective and ineffective use for managing rapport by providing examples from medical interviews.

The Off Record strategy is the most indirect or ambiguous means of communicating a goal. For example, consider this explanation given by a cardiologist to a patient.

> 1. *OK, Mr. Marsden, what we have here is a lesion in the left anterior descending artery, looks like about a 90% occlusion, and then there's a 100% occlusion of the first perforator* (Coulehan & Block, 2001, p. 257).

The underlying goal of the physician appears to be informing the patient of test results. The use of the Off Record strategy makes the physician's message unclear. In this case, the Off Record strategy is implemented through the use of medical terminology. Jargon is one linguistic means for understating (saying less than is expected). Other linguistic tactics for implementing the Off Record strategy include using irony or metaphor (Campbell, White, & Johnson, 2003, p. 180).

As should be clear from the example above, the Off Record strategy is rarely the most effective choice in a medical interview. However, the following interaction shows how the Off Record strategy can be used effectively.

> 2. Doc: *Good morning, Mr. Lee. How are you feeling today?*
>
> Patient: *Better than I did a week ago.*
>
> Doc: *I'm glad of that. We have some very serious matters to discuss regarding your health. Do you feel ready for this discussion?*
>
> Patient: *Well, I want to know.*
>
> Doc: *It's hard to ever be ready for bad news. This is not easy. I need to let you know that we got the results of your test back. . . . As we had feared, the lump is a malignant tumor, cancer* (Coulehan & Block, 2001, p. 227).

Note that several of the physician's contributions should be considered Off Record: *How are you feeling? We have some very serious matters to discuss. Do you feel ready for this discussion? It's hard to ever be ready. This is not easy.* These contributions do not clearly inform the patient of the diagnosis of a malignant tumor. Rather the physician overstates and hints at the information up to this point.

However, the physician then changes to a more direct, less ambiguous strategy: *the lump is a malignant tumor, cancer.* Because of the probable negative emotional response of the patient to the physician's message, the physician has a patient-centered reason to begin the interaction in example 2 with the Off Record strategy.

We'll return to the specifics of this example in the following section. For now, it's important to note that the Off Record strategy is not likely to be effective as a single or primary communication strategy in medical interviews because vagueness or ambiguity in achieving a goal is rarely appropriate within a professional-client relationship. The only exception appears to be the use of Off Record tactics to prepare a patient for bad news.

In contrast to the Off Record strategy, the On Record Plainly strategy is the most clear or unambiguous means of communicating a goal. As one example, reconsider the dialogue in example 2. Although the physician uses the Off Record strategy as a preface to bad news, the bad news itself (*the lump is a malignant tumor, cancer*) is stated On Record Plainly. Linguistic tactics for implementing the On Record Plainly strategy include explicitly stating the goal, using canonical syntactic form (e.g., an imperative form for directives), and using metaphorical urgency (e.g., *Look . . .*) (Campbell et al., 2003, p. 179).

Now let's consider the interaction below initiated by a physician via telephone.

3. Doc: *The bad news is that you have a brain tumor. The good news is that we think it's a meningioma, which means it'll be easy for us to get to.*

   Patient: [long pause] *What, what are you saying? I don't know what you mean?*

   Doc: *I mean it's a probably a benign tumor on the outside of your brain, so we can remove it by surgery.*

   Patient: *Uh, I don't know what to say. . . . Can I come in and talk with you about this?*

   Doc: *Okay, yes, we can do that. Call Judy. Let's make an appointment for next Tuesday.* (Lind, Good, Seidel, Csordas, & Good, 1989, p. 584).

In this interaction, the physician states first and clearly that the patient has a brain tumor. The physician's use of the On Record Plainly strategy is ineffective because of a total lack of tending face wants and sociality rights. The physician completely ignores the patient's association rights by informing the patient via telephone rather than in a face-to-face meeting.

The On Record Plainly strategy is the most effective choice in a medical interview in two situations: when there is no threat to face wants or sociality rights, or when urgency is more desirable than politeness (e.g., in an emergency room situation). Neither of these situations appears to describe the context of example 3.

Let's consider another example involving an interaction in which a physician uses the On Record Plainly strategy to clarify the plan of action for a patient suffering from back pain.

4. *There's your prescriptions, here's the Percocet, only take that as needed for extra pain. The Motrin I want you to take one, four times per day: breakfast, lunch, dinner, and bedtime, and you should take that continuously. . . . And remember, take it with meals or with something in your stomach because it can irritate your stomach* (Coulehan & Block, 2001, p. 111).

In example 4, the physician uses the imperative syntactic form for most directives (*only take that as needed* or *remember, take it with meals*). The use of the On Record Plainly strategy seems effective in this situation since there appears to be relatively little threat to face wants and only a moderate threat to the patient's autonomy rights. (Clearly, the patient has invited the physician to give instructions on how to deal with the patient's back pain.)

The On Record Politely strategies are less clear than the On Record Plainly strategy but more clear than the Off Record strategy. There are two subcategories: those based on tending to face wants and those based on tending to sociality rights. For instance, in example 4, the physician tends to the patient's face wants by adding an explanation focused on the benefit to the patient of following the instructions for taking Motrin with food: *because it can irritate your stomach* (Coulehan & Block, 2001, p. 111).

Linguistic tactics for implementing the Tending Face Wants strategy include showing interest in the patient or his or her social role, using in-group markers, and seeking agreement (Campbell et al., 2003, p. 182). Linguistic tactics for implementing the Tending Sociality Rights strategy include listening, being intimate, questioning or hedging, being pessimistic, impersonalizing, minimizing imposition, giving deference, apologizing, and incurring a future debt (Campbell et al., 2003, pp. 184-185). Consider the following example in which a physician responds to a patient who insists on the need for a diagnostic test.

5. *I can see that this seems to be really important to you to have an MRI. I want to reassure you that if one is indicated, I will order it. But it would really help me to understand what you think it would show us right now* (AMA, 2000, p. 80).

In this situation, the physician tends to the patient's association rights by carefully acknowledging that he or she listened to the patient (*I can see that this seems to be really important to you*) and then by asking the patient to tell him or her more (*it would really help me to understand*).

Let's consider one final example involving a situation in which a physician tends to the patient's autonomy rights.

6. *What I think we should do, I want to check your x-rays that you had. I want to review those. I think you should get off of your feet at least for a day or two. Is that, are you able to do that* (Coulehan & Block, 2001, p. 110]?

In example 6, the physician communicates his or her recommendation for treatment using the On Record Politely strategy and tends to the patient's right to determine his/her own treatment (e.g., *What I think we should do . . .* ; *I think you should*; and *are you able to do that*?). The On Record Politely strategies are often an effective choice in medical interviews because they offer physicians the opportunity to communicate goals clearly but also to tend to their relationships with patients at the same time.

The discussion of politeness strategies in this section shows that they fall along a continuum of clarity: they range from the most ambiguous (Off Record) to the most clear and direct (On Record Plainly), with the On Record Politely strategies occupying the area in between. In actual practice, we've seen that the strategies are often combined in a single medical interview. Nevertheless, it is fairly simple to identify the individual strategies within such dialogues.

CONCLUSION

Relationship building is a crucial skill for professionals, because their success depends upon the trust and loyalty of their clients. For physicians, it has become commonplace to recognize the importance of both instrumental and affective behavior in interactions with patients during medical interviews (Balint, 1957; Bird & Cohen-Cole, 1990; Keller & Carroll, 1994; Levenstein, McCraken, & McWhinney, 1986). In this chapter, I have extended the Rapport Management Model, developed to explain how verbal communication is used by leaders (Campbell et al., 2003) and other professionals (Campbell & Davis, 2006), to physicians. A normative theory, the Rapport Management Model incorporates communication strategies for providing biopsychosocial or "complete" care (Engel, 1977). More specifically, the model shows how physicians can simultaneously achieve conflicting goals (e.g., directing a patient's behavior while also building a relationship).

Perhaps most importantly, the Rapport Management Model shows how physicians can communicate effectively even when their primary goal is intrinsically threatening to the relationship by tending to patient's face wants or sociality rights with the On Record Politely strategies. The Off Record strategy is rarely appropriate within professional settings, but can be used as preparation for bad news that is communicated using one of the On Record strategies or with patients from higher power distance or higher context cultures. The On Record Plainly strategy appears to be effective when there is no face wants or sociality rights threat in the physician's message or when the situation is urgent. To reiterate, professionals like physicians must be able to predict the likely rapport effects of their communication goals on their individual patients, and know linguistic tactics (e.g., hedging with *I think*) for mediating negative rapport effects in order to build and maintain relationships.

REFERENCES

AMA. (2000). *Communicating with your patients: Skills for building rapport*. Chicago, IL: American Medical Association.

Balint, M. (1957). *The doctor, his patient, and the illness*. New York: International Universities Press.

Bird, J., & Cohen-Cole, S. A. (1990). The three function model of the medical interview: An educational device. In M. S. Hale (Ed.), *Methods in teaching consultation-liaison psychiatry* (pp. 65-88). Basel: Karger.

Brown, P., & Levinson, S. A. (1987). *Politeness: Some universals in language usage.* (Studies in interactional sociolinguistics, Vol. 4.) Cambridge, MA: Cambridge University Press.

Campbell, K. S., & Davis, L. (2006). The sociolinguistic basis of rapport management when overcoming buying objections. *Journal of Business Communication, 43,* 43-66.

Campbell, K. S., White, C. D., & Johnson, D. E. (2003). Leader-member relations as a function of rapport management. *Journal of Business Communication, 40,* 170-194.

Coulehan, J. L., & Block, M. R. (2001). *The medical interview: Mastering skills for clinical practice* (4th ed.). Philadelphia, PA: F. A. Davis.

Engel, G. L. (1977). The need for a new medical model: A challenge for biomedicine. *Science, 196,* 29-36.

Epstein, R. M., Campbell, T. L., Cohen-Cole, S. A., McWhinney, I. R., & Smilkstein, G. (1993). Perspectives on patient-doctor communication. *Journal of Family Practice, 37,* 377-388.

Goffman, E. (1967). *Interaction ritual: Essays on face-to-face behavior.* Garden City, NY: Random House.

Gremler, D. D., & Gwinner, K. P. (2000). Customer-employee rapport in service relationships. *Journal of Services Research, 3,* 82-104.

Hall, J. A., Roter, D. L., & Katz, N. R. (1988). Patient-physician communication: A descriptive summary of the literature. *Patient Education and Counseling, 12,* 99-119.

Hart, S. L., & Quinn, R. E. (1993). Roles executives play: CEOs, behavioral complexity, and firm performance. *Human Relations, 46,* 543-574.

Keller, V. F., & Carroll, J. G. (1994). A new model for physician-patient communication. *Patient Education and Counseling, 23,* 131-140.

Levenstein, J. H., McCraken, E. C., & McWhinney, I. R. (1986). The patient-centered clinical method: A model for the doctor-patient interaction in family medicine. *Family Practice, 3,* 24-30.

Levinson, W., Roter, D. L., Mullooly, J. P., Dull, V. T., & Frankel, R. M. (1997). Physician-patient communication: The relationship with malpractice claims among primary care physicians and surgeons. *Journal of the American Medical Association, 277,* 553-559.

Lind, S. E., Good, M., Seidel, S., Csordas, T., & Good, B. J. (1989). Telling the diagnosis of cancer. *Journal of Clinical Oncology, 7,* 583-589.

Ong, L. M. L., de Haes, J. C. J. M., Hoos, A. M., & Lammes, F. B. (1995). Doctor-patient communication: A review of the literature. *Social Science and Medicine, 40,* 903-918.

Quinn, R. E., & Rohrbaugh, J. (1983). A spatial model of effectiveness criteria: Towards a competing values approach to organizational analysis. *Management Science, 29,* 363-377.

Quinn, R. E., Hildebrandt, H. W., Rogers, P. S., & Thompson, M. P. (1991). A competing values framework for analyzing presentational communication in management contexts. *Journal of Business Communication, 28,* 213-232.

Roter, D. L., & Hall, J. A. (1992). *Doctors talking with patients: Improving communication in medical visits.* Westport, CT: Auburn House.

Roter, D. L., Hall, J. A., & Katz, N. R. (1987). Relations between physicians' behaviors and analogue patients' satisfaction, recall, and impressions. *Medical Care, 25,* 437-450.

Spencer-Oatey, H. (2000). Rapport management: A framework for analysis. In H. Spencer-Oatey (Ed.) *Culturally speaking: Managing rapport through talk across cultures* (pp. 11-46). London: Continuum.

Squier, R. W. (1990). A model empathic understanding and adherence to treatment regimens in practitioner-patient relationship. *Social Science and Medicine, 30,* 325-339.

PART IV

Biotechnology:
Reporting Its Potential and
Its Problems

CHAPTER 14

Connecting Popular Culture and Science: The Case of Biotechnology

Susan Allender-Hagedorn and
Cheryl W. Ruggiero

Much is written on how modern science and technology influence popular culture, but the reciprocal process, how popular culture influences science and technology, is largely ignored or even vehemently denied. Science is, according to science writer Julie McClafferty (2005), "the act of taking something we don't understand, breaking it down into little pieces until we figure it out, and putting it back together again, ideally in a way that benefits society." In this definition, the benefits flow in one direction, from science to the world around it, and our everyday experience confirms this perception.

We are bombarded with science talk. Medicine, communications, and biotechnological plant and animal breeding practices are but a few examples that deeply impact everyday life. Students have trouble imagining a world without instant messaging, labeling of genetically engineered foods is hotly debated internationally, SETI enlists private computers to analyze data, and "E.T. phone home" is a tag line understood across many cultures. We are overwhelmed by the influence of science on our lives, even while we are somewhat—perhaps profoundly—ignorant of how that science is conducted and how it will or should be applied.

However, the world of science is often equally ignorant about how the rest of the world, including popular culture, deeply influences its work. (Witness the reoccurring "Science Wars" controversy.) In this chapter, using biotechnology (specifically advertisements aimed at biotechnologists) as an example, we hope to show how research into professional communication can become the catalyst to open up a new nonpolarizing and interdisciplinary dialogue about this two-way interaction.

157

As teachers of professional communication, we stress two concepts new writers and editors must research diligently: audience and purpose. Our proposed dialogue about how science researchers are connected to their own popular culture can improve our students' effectiveness by deepening their understanding of the public audience they must one day address. We hope to open a door to a line of research that can allow the previously polarized camps to find nonantagonistic grounds for agreement. We want to spark truly interdisciplinary research, bringing together groups that operate in the same arena where we are sending our professional communication students. We hope to deepen our students' analytical skills, and we also hope that they will *not* discover that their workplace is a battleground. We agree with Stephen Jay Gould (2004) that the central claim of each side is correct: "Science is, and must be, culturally embedded; what else could the product of human passion be? . . . Culture is not the enemy of objectivity but a matrix that can either aid or retard advancing knowledge."

THE SEPARATION BETWEEN SCIENCE AND CULTURE

Few would argue that science has a profound and pervasive influence on everyone alive today. However, there seems to be an accepted division between those who conduct science and everyone else. Participants in science and technology have their own reasons for believing and fostering the idealization of scientific isolation. First, this mythic separation partially reflects researchers' actual experiences with the dangers of interaction with the public, both historically and currently. Scientists might want to avoid confrontations with the segment of the public that reacts with fear or anger to new discoveries they do not comprehend. Conversely, many in the public want to keep the conduct of science on a pedestal. The public is concerned with the products of science, not the exacting details of a scientist's day-to-day schedule. Personally, we would rather believe that the scientist who discovered our blood pressure medicine was noble and high-minded, working every minute of every day for the good of all—not preoccupied with wondering what his or her spouse was doing or who was going to pay for lunch!

For a scientist, separation can also save time and involvement. During every annual meeting of the American Society for Microbiology, for example, news reports tout potential benefits of research that are soon to be a reality. Although frequently these reports misrepresent the way science proceeds, afterwards, many researchers are besieged with pleas for instant cures, leading to inevitable disappointments when they explain that benefits can be a year—or even a decade—in the future. Keeping science above the everyday fray lessens demands on a scientist's time and emotions. Further, many of today's researchers find themselves isolated by the social and economic structures surrounding their work. A granting sponsor is often the filter between the public and the scientist.

Another reason that scientists themselves may value the separation is that loss of such isolation could equal loss of objectivity. It is vital to science that its participants deal in observable, verifiable fact, that they are swayed as little as possible by what moves the mob, whether opinion, religion, image, icon—or myth. Thus, many in science and technology might characterize themselves, at least in the pursuit of their work, as uninvolved with the whims, moods, passions, or other trappings of popular culture.

It appears, then, that both the public and researchers participate in creating and maintaining the popular image of the idealized, isolated scientist. Like any good myth, this image embodies truths that the creating cultures (both scientific and public) hold to be so important that they must be storied and symbolized. But also as can happen with any myth, we may let the image replace experience. We might look in a number of places for practices that show researchers to be more influenced by popular culture than the myth suggests, and one such place is biotechnology. According to sociologist Sam Paden (1997), "indeed, this new and rapidly expanding field of [bio]technology is by no means some 'politically neutral' futuristic vision (such as that presented at Disney's EPCOT Center)."

One obvious interaction area is funding. Recent headlines show that as conservative thinkers and moralists become more influential, policies based on these cultural influences can proscribe some research avenues, such as stem cell sources. We have seen recent large increases in allocations for projects related to defense and homeland security, at the expense of research in other areas. According to one summary, while other programs received minimal increases, the federal budget released in February 2004 allocated large increases to defense: "The Department of Defense would capture close to $7 billion for R&D, more than 5 percent after inflation over last year, while the Department of Homeland Security would experience the largest boost, a 14 percent increase" (Goho, 2004, p. 86). So-called orphan diseases not in the public eye are not well funded, and thus little research is done into finding a cure. Popular culture can be seen in all these cases as determining what can and cannot go on in the lab. But there are other, less obvious areas of interaction.

ADVERTISEMENTS DIRECTED TOWARD SCIENTISTS

Biotechnology research is very expensive, and competition for funding is fierce. A proposal from one lab that asks for less money to accomplish more is likely to be the one funded. If a lab cannot afford a particular expensive piece of equipment, then it cannot pursue research that requires that equipment. However, since scientific grant proposals are competitive, the competition for the grant dollars by scientific vendors is even more so. A great deal of vendors' money is spent studying demographics to support the sale of scientific equipment and supplies, leading to competitive advertising practices.

While many scientists deny that they are influenced by popular culture, effective and profitable ads aimed at them suggest otherwise. For example, the largest professional organization for biotechnologists is the American Society for Microbiology. Each year, at the society's annual meeting, over 8,000 scientists are joined by nearly 3,000 vendors. Amidst scientific presentations, news releases, and poster sessions, a marketplace is set up to connect the scientists with almost any laboratory equipment, research tool or software, certification updating class, or professional contact that their hearts could desire.

From the 2004 meeting, here is a sampling of enticing giveaways available: as well as laboratory equipment and supplies, complete lobster dinners for two flown to the winner's residence, handheld computers, umbrellas (covered in sponsors' advertising), canvas tote bags, stuffed animals, instant cameras, pure maple syrup, pens, luggage ID tags, books, magazine subscriptions, calculators, bottled water, t-shirts, and enough candy to put a conscientious "shopper" into sugar shock. These are the tangible giveaways—the intangibles include behind-the-scenes wangling for discounts, service contracts, and free add-ons to expensive equipment.

Many of these gifts are not scientific tools but perks that carry cultural allusions to television, movies, environmental causes, and humor. For example, one company has adopted as its icon the toucan—a startlingly beautiful and exotic bird. The company's name also plays off of the name of the bird. When asked why he chose that particular icon, the president of the company stated that he personally believed in recycling—and did we notice the use of recycled paper in his business cards? The bird was noticeable (and the company might be remembered that way), and the color of the bird's beak contrasted nicely with the tan color of the cards.

A company that deals with test kits to analyze fecal samples for hospitals displays a one-foot-high talking toilet as part of its exhibit. It is a no-lose situation for a merchant to gain good will if a potential customer walks away with something, no matter how small or trivial, even a laugh, free—everyone is a winner for a few minutes! This conference is just one yearly occasion of many. It's even more mind-boggling to think about how these merchants seek to influence scientists monthly, weekly, and even daily through advertisements in professional magazines.

ADVERTISEMENT ANALYSIS

As we analyze ads, it is important to remember the research that has gone into the advertisements—millions of dollars each year are spent on audience analyses to find the most effective ways to sell scientific products. Most of our examples here are drawn from the most widely circulated biotechnology industry magazine, *Genetic Engineering News* [*GEN*], "the very first trade publication in biotechnology, and the most widely read biotechnology trade publication worldwide" (Liebert, 2005). The newsletter is distributed monthly, with a circulation of several hundred thousand copies.

Many *GEN* ads are straightforward, with text describing a company or a product, or presenting actual, if rather prosaic, pictures of equipment for sale. However, many ads use both obvious and subtle cultural appeals to sell the companies' products. *GEN*'s readers are all science specialists, so obviously, the many cultural references in the ads are intended to catch the eye of the scientist, not the general public, and to entice him or her to investigate the company or product further. For example, in one ad the headline is "Speed Dating—Redefined" (Charles River Laboratories, 2004). This headline is guaranteed to catch the eye of often-single bench scientists in their 20s and 30s. The ad cleverly ties the headline to the picture where the "personal" ad in a newspaper reads "single white male Lewis rat, looking for transgenic mate." Other cultural appeals have included ads with sports images that suggest that perhaps even the lab scientist can throw off his or her geeky stereotype and become a sleek, speedy athletic star in science.

PIERCE ADVERTISEMENT

We would like to focus on one particular advertisement campaign from the Pierce Company, merchant of supplies for the biotechnology laboratory. In Figure 1, in an interesting switch, the great majority of *images* in the full-page ad do not have a cultural referent—but the text does. The company's name is at the top. The five major images are of gel plates using the Western Blot technique. The four side images present successful results (and not coincidentally, the company can provide all of the supplies necessary to achieve such a success). The middle image is blurred and foggy—a useless result. It is crossed out with a large white X, a universal symbol for "not" or "unacceptable." There is a colorful image on each side of the bottom of the ad—on the left is simply a reproduction of the cover of the company's *Western Blotting Handbook*, and on the right an industry certification award appears. Nothing discussed so far is particularly tied to any popular or public referent. However, the center text tells another story:

"Bad blot, Bad blot, whatchya' gonna do? Don't let a bad blot happen to you."

Of course, no scientist would want an unacceptable result. However, the words above are a direct reference to an extremely popular song, a television show, and spin-off movies in the United States. The song, "Bad Boys," by Inner Circle, was first recorded in 1987 and became the theme song for the long-running television show *COPS*. Compare the refrain from the song and the ad as seen in Table 1. In addition, note a subtle but major cop reference: in the upper right of the ad is a frosted donut with sprinkles, a direct reference to U.S. stereotypes of police officers and their desire for donuts! The connection between the ad and the song, the show, and the movies is further cemented by more subtle clues. As shown in Table 2, we worked with Williamson's (1978) methods for decoding advertisements.

A second 2005 spin-off ad (Brian Johnson, personal communication, October 19, 2004) from Pierce showed a young man with the familiar black digital mask applied to criminal suspects. Failure of science equipment has now taken on a human—and criminal—face; faulty equipment is added to the long list of things, from shrinking candy bars to crowded buses, that we decry with the popular idiom "It's a crime!"

CULTURE, ADVERTISING, AND SCIENCE

Our preliminary examination of ads aimed at biotechnologists provides evidence that popular culture influences science advertising. But is there any proof that culture/advertising actually affects scientific practices and practitioners? We have linked culture to science ads, but is there a corresponding link from the ads to

Figure 1. Pierce advertisement.
© 2004 by Pierce Biotechnology, used with permission.

Table 1. Words to Original Song and Pierce Advertisement

Song	Advertisement
Bad boys, Bad boys,	Bad blot, Bad blot,
Whatcha gonna do?	Whatcha gonna do?
Watcha gonna do when they come for you?	Don't let a bad blot happen to you.

the science? Early information from an ongoing research project indicates a solid affirmative in one of the simplest measures of influence: profits.

According to Pierce ad director Brian Johnson, "a major advertising campaign often costs $100–$200 thousand. For one ad campaign last year I received a fourfold return on investment in 12 months—this was an easy one to measure because the trend for the product line was stable and there was nothing else going on with the line other than the advertising I did" (personal communication, October 19, 2004).

Table 2. Advertisement Evaluation

• **Font choice**: The company's name in heavy black large type, with a gray background, at the top of the page implies strength, reliability, and stability.

• **Color choice**:
  o The (slightly changed) song lyrics for the most part are in large, rounded-off letters in a dark blue, but the refrain "whatcha' gonna do?" is in aqua, the same color used to label the "good" Western Blot results, transforming the success of the blots into an answer to the question.
  o Supporting the company's name is a "shelf" of blue which matches the background color of the "good" blots.

• **Jargon**: The street jargon used definitely takes the lyrics out of the laboratory, but the substituted word "blot" brings them back in.

Moreover, scientists themselves acknowledge the advertisements' effectiveness. According to water quality specialist Annie Hassall, scientific advertising does affect both the purchasing of scientific supplies and equipment and the resultant research using that equipment and those supplies:

> Of course the quality and quantity of advertising is important in science. More times than not, the advertisements in the various trade magazines and journals are less than appealing—a picture of the company's feature product, some contact information, and that's it. When a science company puts forth the effort to come up with an advertisement that has a sense of humor, it jumps off the page. Companies like Pierce, with their 'Bad Blot' slogan, playing off of the TV show 'COPS,' are a refreshing, and I would imagine, successful example of what science advertisements can be" (personal communication, March 11, 2005).

However, there is another affirmation of the culture-ad-science connection: the ads *are* culture. The science-culture barrier was crossed the first time a supply company placed even a colorless ad in a science magazine, the first time a vehicle for intrascience information dissemination became also a vehicle for commerce. Commerce's servant, advertising, is so much a part of contemporary culture (as it has been a part of historical culture from Roman circuses to the American snake-oil circuit) that its very appearance in a highly technical biotech journal is an ingrowth of culture in the pure realm of science.

Advertisements lie on desks and in labs, and they are thumbed by the very hands that make media, count colonies, read gel plates, and *order supplies and equipment*. The juxtaposition of ads like Pierce's between articles on drug discoveries, manufacturing processes, discoveries in cell activity, and professional job ads places popular culture smack in the middle of science. Even if the ads had no effect on how scientists purchase equipment (though Pierce's experience shows the opposite), their presence in some of the information lifelines of science would indicate that culture/commerce is inextricably tangled and linked with science/scientists.

APPLICATIONS OF RESEARCH

Writing about one of the many technological venues for professional writers, creating an intranet, Lisa Ann Jackson makes one of the strongest statements in the literature about the need for analysis of users/readers: In determining the objectives "only three things matter: audience, audience, and audience" (2004, p. 268). Jackson quotes Judith Ramey's advice, from a 1997 IEEE conference presentation: "Don't start the design of a communication from the source point of view. Instead, begin the design from the user point of view" (2004, p. 268).

Wise professional communicators/instructors have counseled writers to analyze their readers' needs in just about every writing textbook, and the advice is certainly sound. A survey and compilation of the audience analysis sections in several of today's most widely used professional writing textbooks produces the following basic rubric: (a) Who will read this document? (b) How will they use it? (c) How technically expert (or not) are the readers? (d) What do they already know about the subject? (e) What cultural differences might affect how they respond?

On the question of culture, especially for nontechnical audiences, writers are urged to consider differences. Among the many familiar examples commonly given are generalized international cultural observations about preferences for directness or indirectness, familiarity or formality. Certainly, such differences are potential stumbling blocks to communication, and writers are well-advised to consider them. However, the rubrics for audience analysis seem to maintain the mythic separation between writer and audience, scientist and public, expert writer and nonexpert reader, the isolated scientist and the ignorant/innocent townspeople. Even our brief examination of a single strand of communication (advertising) in a single arena (biotechnology) has shown that such isolation is not as complete as we might wish to believe, that scientists are full members of the very public that they must bring themselves to address.

We propose, therefore, that a potentially fruitful new line be added to such audience analysis: (f) What cultural features do the audience and writer share? Examining the differences between writer and audience is very important. However, what seems to be presently ignored is the equally important research into shared experiences. Emphasis only on differences will continue to highlight those differences and make the task of the professional communicator more difficult. Advertisements have been described as constituting "sites where an exchange of meanings can take place. The purpose of this exchange is to generate currency—the social form of value—for a commodity. Advertisers try to encode a sign by prompting an exchange of meanings. But, it is on the decoding side of this 'forced' exchange that a sign is either valorized or not. Advertising has become a form of internal cultural colonialism that mercilessly hunts out and appropriates those meaningful elements of our cultural lives that have value" (Goldman, n.d.). We want our students' writings to be read and understood—we want to bridge differences, not perpetuate the divide of C. P. Snow's *The Two Cultures* (1959). We propose research into how writer-audience cultural connections could help to bridge the mythical, and mostly damaging, artificial gap between science and the public.

CONCLUSION

Science is increasingly conducted less as an individual enterprise and more as a collective endeavor (Allender-Hagedorn, 2001). Modern science presents ups and downs for the science-oriented merchant. On one hand, as research and knowledge expand along with the proliferation of new technology to support research, markets expand. However, with the need to validate scientific results and decrease incompatibilities across countries as well as between laboratories and individual researchers, competition between those selling similar merchandise has become intense. This exhilarating but frightening arena is the very workspace where many of our graduates will find the highest-paying employment. The cultural connections in advertisements are but one window into the study of the relationship between science and the public. Knowing how and why advertisements are influential is necessary because, as Williamson writes, "they are one of the most important cultural factors moulding and reflecting our life today . . . [they form] a vast super-structure with an apparently autonomous existence and an immense influence" (Williamson, 1978).

We are not suggesting that the research presented here is the only method to consider for a complete science audience analysis, but we are suggesting it as a valid but not often considered method. A great deal of inquiry in this direction was shut down by the extremely polarizing rhetoric of the Science Wars. We feel we are simply opening a window to alternative, less antagonistic interdisciplinary research that can have broad implications in cultural and science studies as well. We feel we are drawing connections, not pointing out disparities. Closer to home, and perhaps more selfishly, we want to present our professional writing students with even deeper skills in audience analysis that can be applied when they leave academia for the wider workplace. We find our validation in the successes of our students.

REFERENCES

Allender-Hagedorn, S. A. (2001). *Arguing the genome: A topology of argumentation behind the construction of the human genome project.* Doctoral dissertation, Virginia Tech.

Charles River Laboratories. (2004, August 11). Speed dating: Redefined. *Genetic Engineering News, 24*(11), 7.

Goho, A. (2004, February 7). Money crunch: Tight budget leaves scientists disappointed. *Science News, 165*(6), 86.

Goldman, R. (n.d.). *Advertising & the production of commodity signs.* http://www.lclark.edu/~goldman/contradictions/poleconsv3.html

Gould, S. J. (2004). Shields of expectation—and actuality. *The Exchange, 11*(3), 3.

Inner Circle. (1987). Bad boys. On *One way* [CD]. Washington, DC: RAS Records.

Jackson, L. A. (2004). The rhetoric of design: Implications for corporate intranets. In J. M. Dubinsky (Ed.), *Teaching technical communication: Critical issues for the classroom* (pp. 265-276). Boston, MA: St. Martin's Press.

Liebert, M. A. (2005). From the publisher. http://www.liebertpub.com/about.aspx

McClafferty, J. (2005, January 12). *Science and the nontechnical public: Putting the pieces together.* Virginia Bioinformatics Institute Seminar, Blacksburg, Virginia.

Paden, S. (1997). *A discussion of the social effects of biotechnology.* http://www.lclark.edu/~soan221/97/SAm's.GENETIC.HMPG.html

Pierce Biotechnology. (2004). Pierce: Grasp the Proteome. *Genetic Engineering News, 24*(16): 3.

Snow, C. P. (1959). *The two cultures.* Cambridge, MA: Cambridge University Press.

Williamson, J. (1978). *Decoding advertisements: Ideology and meaning in advertising.* London: Marion Boyars.

CHAPTER 15

Biotechnology and Global Miscommunication with the Public: Rhetorical Assumptions, Stylistic Acts, Ethical Implications

Steven B. Katz

Clarity, brevity, *simplicity*. What Richard Lanham (2003) calls the C-B-S theory of style is arguably the three major principles that underlie most discussions of style in technical communication (note: I have modified Lanham's third category, "sincerity," for the purpose of this chapter). But the question is always: clarity, brevity, and simplicity—**for whom?** Clarity, brevity, and simplicity are not *a priori* or universal categories applying across the board to all audiences and situations, but emerge from and are defined by particular audiences and situations, and the goals, values, concerns, and knowledge of those audiences. The C-B-S theory does not take the existence of different audiences into account. The C-B-S theory of style is arhetorical. In fact, the C-B-S theory of style can be understood to be based on an information theory model of communication that as a mathematical ideal also underlies risk communication, used widely by industries and governments worldwide to communicate with the public—including communication about biotechnology.

   The information theory model of communication actually has a history stretching all the way from the ancient Greek philosopher Plato to Shannon and Weaver's model of information transfer that they developed at Bell Laboratory in 1948 based on the laws of thermodynamics (1964, 1949). But it has a more recent reincarnation as well—as the basis of risk communication. This model, consisting of a sender, a receiver, a channel, a message, noise, and a feedback signal, has become the standard in the fields of mass communication and communication psychology, and has been adopted widely by industry and government agencies, including, as we will see, the Canadian Biotechnology Advisory Committee (CBAC). In fact, it is deeply embedded in our scientific and technological culture.

As depicted in Figure 1, in the information theory model of communication, a sender simply encodes A, and a receiver simply decodes A.

In this model, the only problem is (or should be) white noise in the system, which is regarded as interference to be eliminated or dismissed. In controversies surrounding biotechnology, this "noise," created by protesters, environmentalists, and political action groups, is regarded by experts as irrationality that interferes with the clear message of science. The information theory model that underlies risk communication works well for electronic equipment. But we know from common experience that this model does not really represent the way humans themselves actually communicate, and leaves much to be desired as a description of or a heuristic for studying human communication. The information theory model of communication ignores the audience—the inevitable role of values, goals, concerns, and emotions in interpretation—and as I will discuss in the second part of this chapter, the role of language as the medium of expression.

Assumptions, values, and emotions are "uncontrolled variables" that a more rhetorical model of communication tries to take into account. As you can see in Figure 2, the rhetorical model of communication tries to describe the way values, goals, concerns, and emotions of audiences may affect what is regarded as the creation and interpretation of communication. It acknowledges that while the speaker may intend A, the listener may interpret A "prime," or B, or Z!

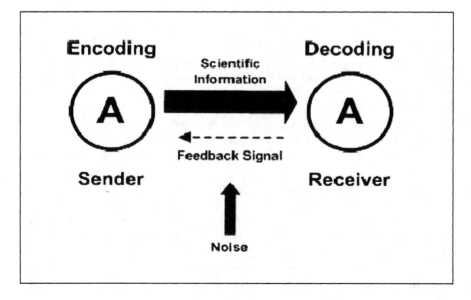

Figure 1. Information theory model of communication of scientific information.

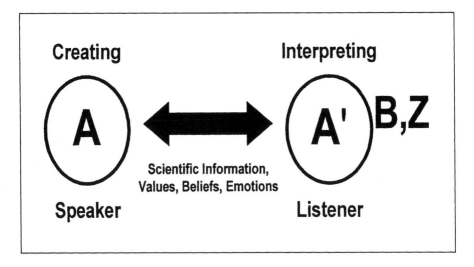

Figure 2. Rhetorical model of communication of scientific information.

The results of not acknowledging or taking the role of creativity and interpretation in human communication into account (or wishing to eliminate it) are perhaps most evident in the history of failed attempts to communicate with the public about potentially hazardous products and risk technologies. Cases abound, not only in the United States, but also Canada and Europe, of sciences and technologies that have been significantly slowed or completely halted by public opposition, biotechnology being only one of the latest examples. In previous research, Carolyn Miller and I (1996) studied the public controversy surrounding the siting of a low-level radioactive waste facility in North Carolina. We identified four major assumptions of risk communication embedded and revealed in language and action of the Low Level Radioactive Waste Authority, which had legal responsibility for siting the facility.

1. **Language is simply a conduit.** The conduit view of language entails the assumption that at its best, language is merely a *clear* channel, an invisible pipeline through which ideas are transmitted and should flow freely, unobstructed by emotions, values, and words. Philosophically it assumes that ideas can be separated from language, that language merely contains ideas, rather than also creating and constituting them. The ideal of language as a disappearing medium is rooted in the philosophy of Aristotle, who thought that facts should speak for themselves, unaided by organization, style, and delivery, but admitted that style was necessary "owing to a defect in our hearers" (1984, III. 1404a5). The notion of language as a conduit informs the empirical philosophy of John Locke (1965) and underlies the plain style movement of the 16th-century Royal Society instigated by such notables as Thomas Sprat, who held that rhetoric cheats the senses and "ought to be banished out of all civilized societies" (1667, p. 111). The conduit assumption

finds modern expression in a word that has become the buzz in the bio-technology industry: *transparency*. (I'll return to this word later.)

2. **Communication is the conveyance of information.** The conduit view of language leads to the common understanding that communication is a "conveying" of information. Communicating through the conduit is a receiving of facts. Thus, terms like *educating* and *informing*, used to describe communication campaigns for consumers/the public, are understood as a process of "information transfer." The assumption here is that listeners or readers are passive receptors; that public audiences have little to contribute to the communication or decision-making process; that if the information is clear, the message brief, the logic simple, listeners or readers should respond rationally and change their views to match the incoming transmission. Emotions and other values are noise in the system.

3. **Communication processes are controlled by authority.** In the conduit view of language, words like *inform*, *convey*, and *educate* also reflect a view of communication as a one-way process—from expert (scientist, industry rep, government official) to public. Implicit within this model of communication are philosophical assumptions about the relationship between thinking and feeling, and about what constitutes validity and knowledge. Suffice it to say that experts assume they've got it and that the public doesn't. As far as scientific knowledge goes, the experts are right; but in any situation there is more to decision making than just scientific knowledge, and these other values and concerns need to be seriously "integrated into the equation."

4. **The public is held in contempt.** Given the view that communication processes must be controlled by experts, the public's continued mistrust and questioning is regarded as "misconception," as "unreasonable fear," as "emotional hysteria." The proclivity to perceive public reaction this way increases when we apply the information theory model of communication, thereby precluding any possibility of resolving communication problems. We've seen this in the biotech industries. The public fears possible long-term and as yet unknown risks to health and the environment that no amount of scientific assurance seems able to assuage; they distrust the decision-making process that they see as much political and economic as scientific, and they question the role of industry in assessing the safety and efficacy of their own products. On the other hand, based on the information theory model of communication, hapless researchers attempt to provide the public with clear, up-to-date information and to explain the scientific logic of their reasoning; government agencies attempt to deal with the crisis in public confidence by developing expensive public information and education campaigns, and in the face of seemingly insurmountable resistance, the optimism of scientists, industry representatives, and public officials inevitably gives way to negative *emotions* of incredulity, outrage, and contempt for the public that appears to them to be unreasonable and ill-informed. This is what happened in North Carolina, and after massive expenditures of money, time, and labor, the facility was never sited.

As I wrote in a piece I presented at the American Association for the Advancement of Science and subsequently published in *AgBioForum* (2001), these four assumptions, and the predictable reactions to them, also appear to be contained and communicated in U.S. government press releases. These assumptions inherent in risk communication and the C-B-S theory of style can be seen in the language of biotechnology in Canada as well—perhaps one of the most conscientious countries when it comes to communicating biotechnology with its public. The need to address a wide range of audience concerns is acknowledged as the goal in a report entitled "Meeting the Public's Need for Information on Biotechnology," prepared for the Canadian Biotechnology Advisory Committee (CBAC): "Recognizing and addressing consumer beliefs, perceptions and concerns is an essential component of understanding consumer behaviour around consumer products. Without this understanding, an effective and integrative risk communication strategy cannot be identified and observed" (Einsiedal et al., 2000, p. 8).

This statement, and the study it introduces, is made within the framework of risk communication. Turning our attention to the language of these reports prepared for the CBAC, we see that the underlying assumptions about human communication become *stylistically* prominent in this same section "III: Consumers and Information: What the Research Tells Us": "The discussion that follows is based on an information processing model of the way people process and store information that is later used to make decisions, for example, about which foods to buy. Specifically, the model describes how message recipients deal with perceived information and the fate of that information as it is coded, transformed, associated, stored, rehearsed, recalled and potentially, forgotten" (Einsiedal et al., 2000, p. 8).

How do recipients deal with perceived information? It is "**coded**" (there's no discussion of language here), "**transformed**" (but we don't know how without looking at the total value, emotional, and mental system of the audience), "**stored**." The human capacity (and capriciousness) for creativity and interpretation is reduced to "**multiple incoming audio, visual or other sensory stimuli**" that need to "**exceed the necessary threshold to break through the sensory register of an individual**," where, in "**short-term memory** . . . all **processing** of information occurs, and **information** is **chunked**. Individuals are typically only capable of thinking about **7 units of information**." A hypothetical long term memory consists of "**nodes**" where concepts or ideas are **stored** along "**associative paths**" and retrieved "to help make a decision in a **purchase environment**" (Einsiedal et al., 2000, p. 8.)

This is what the information theory model of communication leads to: incoming messages to a passive receiver in an automated process. In the information model of communication, the receiver has no active control in the reception, storage, or retrieval of information. In the information model of communication, *the consumer has no control*—even over the process of thinking about biotechnology! That is what the style of this report assumes about and communicates to its readers, even as it talks about the need to involve the public in discussion and decision making. The necessarily reductive nature of the information theory model that attempts to understand the black box of the brain as a rational entity in a well-defined environment (as Herbert A. Simon depicts it in *The Sciences of the Artificial* [1982]) can be seen in the input-output flowcharts referenced in the appendices of the report. It is upon these reductive computer metaphors of human thinking and communication that multimillion dollar public information and education campaigns are built. The economic, political, and moral implications of this mechanistic model are enormous. In describing the way consumers think and behave and communicate in this way, the set of assumptions and the C-B-S attitude toward style are bound to lead to a failure to even understand consumers/the public, let alone communicate about biotechnology with them.

Given this information theory model of communication, it is not surprising that another, final report prepared for the CBAC, "Secondary Analysis of Public Opinion: Research Regarding Genetically Modified Food and Related Biotechnology Issues" (Environics Research Group, 2001) should make "transparency" a primary focus. Transparency in relation to the visibility of regulatory activity, the origin of the term in the biotech industry, is perfectly reasonable. But based on the C-B-S approach to style and the information-theory model that underlies risk communication, the concept of transparency also is applied to language and, indeed, the entire communication process. In this "Secondary Analysis," the concept (image) of transparency is extended through a web of hidden metaphors. Here's a paragraph from that report with the metaphors highlighted:

> The issue of **openness** and **transparency** has been discussed in various **focus** group sessions . . . conducted among the general public. Overall there is a desire on behalf of the general public for the government to be more **open** and **transparent** in its dealings in the biotechnology **arena**. For the public, a **clear sign** of this **transparency** is the **availability of information**. While most Canadians will not **seek out or read** all the **available information**, their **comfort level** increases by knowing that the **information is accessible** for those who wish to **review** it. The fact that **information is freely available** seems sufficient to convince most that there is no **hidden** agenda; **transparency** seems to **indicate** that government is properly motivated and committed to **informing** citizens (Environics Research Group, 2001, p. 11, emphasis added).

Notice the visual nature of the metaphors—including *arena*, a public spectator event. Notice how many repeated words (ploce), grammatically related words (polyptoton), and metaphors are grounded in the sense of sight (in the context of the other visual metaphors, the word *availability*, used three times in the last three sentences, means "visible"). Notice the passive construction of the sentences. Also notice the contrast between human emotions and the motives—**desire, dealing, seeking, knowing, wishing, convincing, motivating,** and **committing**—and the mechanistic processes implied here by the visual metaphors. On that one page of the report, the word *transparent* is repeated in some grammatical form eight times, giving this concept a high level of what Perelman in the *The Realm of Rhetoric* (1982) would call "presence," and the whole phrase "openness and transparency" is repeated three times.

This page of the report also contains variations in phrases where the lack of clarity is a negative, such as: "There seems to be a lack of clear information available to Canadians on features of the regulatory system," "Canadians are unclear," and "behind closed doors" (Environics Research Group, 2001, p. 11). A conservative count of nouns (in subject and object positions, exclusive of formal citations) related to the transparency/clarity equation is 33 out of 76—almost half the total number of nouns on this page, a very high percentage.

Both the reports and the CBAC itself ultimately seem to subscribe to the notion of "availability" as clarity, brevity, and simplicity, as we see in this second, final report in a discussion of labeling, which (unlike the United States) Canada instituted for its consumers on a voluntary basis on the recommendation of this report. But here too, the value of labeling is centered in the metaphorical word cluster of clarity/utility:

> Canadians want labels that are **clear, accurate**, and **simple**. . . . Part of the **clarity** and **utility** in labels might be **found** not only in the wording but in other **aspects** such as **design**. . . . In addition, label wording has an effect on the **level** of consumer understanding and there is a further **link** between this understanding and the **perceived value** of a **label message**. . . . Canadian consumers definitely know when label wording is unappealing, **unclear**, and misleading, but are not at all definite on the wording that they would **see as clear** or desirable (Environics Research Group, 2001, pp. 27-28, emphasis added).

In addition to an affective intuition noted by Cicero (1942) on the part of the public to sense what is not right in language, you'll note again the conflict embedded in the style between clarity and desire, which are presented as parallel if not synonymous.

What follows in this final report is a good discussion of what phrases consumers found distasteful. But I would hazard to say that these successful findings are not so much based on the risk model of communication used to frame and support the study as on a commonsense rhetorical understanding of the affective and intuitive responses of the public. It is a conflict of metaphors, which is a conflict of models of thinking and a conflict of goals. The result is a conflict of messages and meanings created and carried by a conflict of stylistic forms. What's particularly interesting here is not only how the "clarity" (and utility) of "label wording" translates into "understanding," which is then converted into "the perceived value of a label message," but also how the visual metaphor of "availability," like the metaphor of transparency, is about access, and hence about control of information by expert authorities. In Canada at least, there are no signs of contempt for the public on the part of government officials—not yet, anyway.

But a mechanistic model of understanding can only lead to a mechanistic model of value and emotions. "Transparency," and its legal, political, and economic implications, becomes apparent in an interim report issued by the CBAC for Canadian government ministers in 2001, "Improving the Regulation of Genetically Modified Foods and Other Novel Foods in Canada" (Biotechnology Ministerial Coordination

174 / CONNECTING PEOPLE WITH TECHNOLOGY

Committee, 2001), which also recommended voluntary labeling. Based on the belief that transparency is the correct approach to communication, a belief that is grounded in the information model of risk communication and entails the C-B-S theory of style, effectiveness, and transparency also become parallel if not synonymous recommendations to the Canadian federal government, even though there is no *clear* idea of what the transparency should reveal. I would suggest that the problem may not be an insufficient emphasis on transparency but too much emphasis on it. I would suggest that style is not separate from content, but a part of it. Biotechnology is anything but clear, especially to the public. Rather than transparency, what may be needed is opaque language that makes biotechnology "clear"—or perhaps I should say "tangible, even palpable." What the public needs is to be able to see and experience meaning in style; "clear" meaning is stylistically opaque and consistent meaning. The medium of language itself should constitute and demonstrate ideas, not contradict what is meant or said. What we need is not risk communication but rhetoric.

I am not some American cowboy-rhetorician riding up to Canada, or across the ocean, to tell anybody what to do. In fact, I think Canada has done a much better job communicating biotechnology with its public than the United States has. Crop Life Canada (formerly the Crop Protection Institute of Canada) does this exceptionally well, as you may tell from a reductive list of prominent rhetorical features found in its publication, *Crop Protection: In Context* (Crop Protection Institute of Canada, 2001):

- Full definitions based on the emotions, values, and concerns of the audience
- Comprehensive and well-developed background information
- Fully balanced treatment of benefits and risks
- Extensive discussions of regulations and safeguards
- Ample use of logically sound examples from areas of the readers' knowledge and experience
- Language addressed to the senses

Like the C-B-S concept of style, the information theory model of communication fails to take into account the creative nature of human communication, the ambiguity of languages as sets of arbitrary symbols governed by normative rules, and the affective role of style in the creation of meaning. Changing communication models probably will not resolve the problems and frustrations of communicating biotechnology with the public, but it may be a necessary first step.

REFERENCES

Aristotle. (1984). The rhetoric. Book III. In W. R. Roberts (Trans.), J. Barnes (Ed.), *The complete works of Aristotle* (pp. 2152-2269). Princeton, NJ: Princeton University Press.
Biotechnology Ministerial Coordination Committee. (2001). *Improving the regulation of genetically modified foods and other novel foods in Canada.* Interim report to the government of Canada Biotechnology Ministerial Coordination Committee. Canadian

Biotechnology Advisory Committee.
http://cbac-cccb.ca/epic/site/cbac-cccb.nsf/vwapj/BackgrounderInterimReport_english
Aug21.pdf/$FILE/BackgrounderInterimReport_englishAug21.pdf

Cicero, M. (1942). De oratore, Book III. In E. W. Sutton & H. Rackham (Trans.), *De oratore Book III, de fato, paradoxa stoicorum, partitiones oratoriae* (pp. 1-185). Cambridge, MA: Loeb-Harvard University Press.

Crop Protection Institute of Canada. (2001). *Crop protection: In context.* Niagara Falls, Ontario, Canada: Crop Protection Institute of Canada.

Einsiedal, E., Finlay, K., & Arko, J. (2000). *Meeting the public's need for information on biotechnology.* The Canadian Biotechnology Advisory Committee. http://cbac-cccb.ca/

Environics Research Group. (2001). Secondary analysis of public opinion research regarding genetically modified food and related biotechnology issues. Final report. Canadian Biotechnology Advisory Committee.
http://www.cbac.cccb.ca/epic/internet/incbaccccb.nsf/vwapj/Environics_Published_f.pdf/
$FILE/Environics_Published_f.pdf

Katz, S. (2001). Language and persuasion in biotechnology communication with the public: How to not say what you're not going to not say and not say it. *AgBioForum 4.* http://www.agbioforum.org

Katz, S., & Miller, C. (1996). The low-level radioactive waste siting controversy in North Carolina: Toward a rhetorical model of risk communication. In C. Herndl & S. Brown (Eds.), *Green culture: Environmental rhetoric in contemporary America* (pp. 111-140). Madison, WI: University of Wisconsin Press.

Lanham, R. (2003). *Analyzing prose.* New York: Continuum.

Locke J. (1965). *An essay concerning human understanding.* J. Yolton (Ed.). London: Dent.

Perelman C. (1982). *The realm of rhetoric.* W. Kluback (Trans.). South Bend, IN: University of Notre Dame Press.

Shannon, C., & Weaver, M. (1964, 1949). *The mathematical theory of communication.* Urbana, IL: University of Illinois Press.

Simon H. A. (1982). *The sciences of the artificial.* Cambridge, MA: MIT University Press.

Sprat T. (1667). *The history of the Royal-Society of London, for the improving of natural knowledge.* London: Royal Society.

CHAPTER 16

The Need for Technical Communicators as Facilitators of Negotiation in Controversial Technology Transfer Cases

Dale L. Sullivan

We take it for granted that technological innovation is a good thing, and that it will be adopted if we make it easy to understand and use. However, not all scientific and technical innovation is widely accepted as beneficial. In such cases, the task of the technical communicator needs to be more than that of an advocate for adoption who translates complex knowledge into simple language. If technical communication is going to set itself apart from public relations and marketing, its practitioners need to seek ways of becoming negotiators of technology, facilitating understanding, and creating opportunities for new interpretations and common ground to emerge.

In this chapter, I explore the need for negotiators who help set conditions for the interpretation of controversial technology. I will get at this issue by telling the story of Monsanto's attempt to release transgenic wheat in the upper midwest of the United States. It is my belief that we in technical communication should study cases of this kind to learn more about potential roles for technical communicators.

MONSANTO AND TRANSGENIC WHEAT RELEASE

There has been a long history of controversy about genetic engineering. Craig Waddell's study (1990) of the moratorium on genetic engineering research in Cambridge, MA, analyzes the arguments and emotional appeals employed by those who testified before the Cambridge Experimentation Review Board. Genetic research and engineering at that time was confined to the laboratory; in the last decade, however, genetically modified organisms have spread throughout the environment in the form of genetically modified plants. Introduced for commercial production in 1996, genetically modified corn and soybeans have enjoyed remarkable success in the United States. For instance, Kathleen Hart reported that farmers planted 1 million acres of Roundup Ready soybeans in 1996 and 12 million acres in 1997 (17% of the crop). By 2001, more than 60% of the soybean crop in the United States was Roundup Ready (Hart, 2002, p. 5). The *Fargo Forum* reported, "Gene-altered soybean varieties are expected to make up about 83 percent of Minnesota's crop and 81 percent of North Dakota's [in 2004]" (Zent, 2004).

These new seeds allow farmers to spray Roundup (a herbicide) on the fields, killing all plant growth except the crop, or, in the case of another variety of corn—Bt corn—the whole plant is toxic to certain insects and acts as its own insecticide. Brewster Kneen (1999) has criticized this technology, saying that it produces monocultures that survive only by eradicating "their neighbors and co-habitants" (p. 11).

Early in 2004, Monsanto announced plans to release transgenic—Roundup Ready—hard red spring wheat for farmers to plant in the spring. This kind of wheat, grown in northern climates, is used by the baking industry, so there is a clear connection between the wheat in the field and the food on the table.

Originally a chemical company, Monsanto got into the life-sciences business when it saw opportunity to sell its herbicide in tandem with seed genetically modified to be resistant to that herbicide. Monsanto's plan was to gain cooperation from local researchers at land grant universities who had developed local varieties and to then transfer their [Monsanto's] genetics into local varieties. Already, at North Dakota State University (NDSU), a controlled licensing program, named Roughrider Genetics, had been developed by the University Research Foundation to keep track of licensed materials.

According to Dale Zetocha, executive director of the NDSU Research Foundation and director of the NDSU Technology Transfer Office, the process would be to work out an agreement between Roughrider Genetics and Monsanto that would permit NDSU to develop and begin to multiply Roundup-Ready local varieties of hard red wheat. When these varieties were fully developed, they would be released to seedmen, who would multiply them further, developing registered and certified seed to sell to farmers as "Roughrider wheat." In short, the new technology needed to pass from Monsanto to local researchers to local seedmen to local farmers, the actual producers (personal interview, November 22, 2004).

In the past, such technology transfer efforts had been quite successful: the new technology and production methods diffused through the farm economy pretty much as predicted by Everett Rogers' diffusion theory. Just as in the case of hybrid corn a half century earlier, there had been early adopters of transgenic corn and soybeans who had become agents of change by persuading other farmers to adopt the new technology (Rogers, 1995, p. 31 ff.).

When Monsanto approached North Dakota State University about developing transgenic wheat, Duane Hauck, director of NDSU Extension Service, felt pressure to buy into the program because the University of Minnesota and South Dakota State

University had already agreed to do so through unilateral executive decisions at the top. Despite pressures caused by neighboring universities' quick buy-in, Hauck felt that it was important to open dialog with various constituents in North Dakota and to try to gain consensus before entering the agreement (personal communication, December 16, 2004).

A cooperative spring wheat program was formed among North Dakota State University, South Dakota State University, the University of Minnesota, the Western Plant Breeders, and Monsanto. This group set six standards that regulated the release of the wheat: the wheat would not be released until, among other conditions, grain handling protocols for handling the transgenic wheat were established, and agreements about how to manage wheat with the Roundup Ready trait were established. This group eventually brought out an informative brochure titled *Bringing New Technologies to Wheat: Information on the Development of Roundup Ready Wheat* (2003), which details the six standards that needed to be met before the transgenic wheat was released.

Ultimately, this effort failed: Monsanto announced its decision to withdraw its transgenic wheat early in May 2004. They did not give specific reasons for the withdrawal, but people involved with the case speculate about the reasons. For instance, Kenneth Grafton, dean of the College of Agriculture at NDSU, said that Canada and the United States had to agree to simultaneous release of the transgenic wheat; but when Canada withdrew, it altered the market situation (personal communication, November 18, 2004). Brad Brummond, NDSU extension agent for Walsh County, suggested that Monsanto withdrew for economic reasons, recognizing that it had invested a great deal of money on a project that was not being readily accepted. It was probably cutting its losses (personal communication, January 7, 2005). Janet Jacobson, President of the Northern Plains Sustainable Agriculture Society (NPSAS), said that she thinks Monsanto underestimated opposition from conventional farmers, who didn't think the technology was needed and who worried about markets and about yet another Roundup Ready crop making crop rotation difficult (personal communication, January 7, 2005).

Underlying these comments is an unstated acknowledgment that Monsanto withdrew because the standards of release were not met. I am particularly interested, in this chapter, in the failure of efforts to work out agreements between genetically modified organism (GMO) producers and non-GMO producers.

THE FORMATION OF THE COEXISTENCE WORKING GROUP

In an attempt to satisfy local constituents, and in response to organic producers' concerns about genetic contamination of organic seeds and crops, NDSU's Extension Service established a coexistence group, consisting of 18 members drawn from various constituencies. A professor of sociology from NDSU, Gary Goreham, facilitated the group, which was supposed to work together for two years. The working group's original purpose was to explore ways to protect against genetic contamination by identifying issues associated with that possibility, writing best management practice protocols, and voting on the protocols.

Those representing organic farmers pulled out in February 2004 during the voting stage, 18 months into the project (Jacobson et al., 2004). After they withdrew, they concentrated their efforts instead on educating the public and testifying before the state legislature. After Karl Limvere, a longtime food activist and minister in the Congregational Church, published a statement on behalf of the Rural Life Committee of the North Dakota Conference of Churches, organic farmers enlisted his help in a campaign to get a law passed that would give the state agriculture commissioner authority to form an advisory committee, hold public hearings, and decide whether or not genetically modified (GM) wheat could be released in the state (personal communication with Limvere, January 12, 2005).

TECHNICAL COMMUNICATOR AS TRANSLATORS OF KNOWLEDGE

Retrospectively, I see ways that technical communicators with sociopolitical awareness could have entered into the process as negotiators of technology. Traditionally, the practice of technical communication has been defined as the process of "bridging" between higher and lower levels of technical knowledge. Technical communicators, in other words, are translators of technical knowledge, and, traditionally the flow of knowledge has been unidirectional, from the expert producer to the novice user. In this role, the professional communicator who is employed by an agency that produces scientific and technical knowledge and products (as is the case with Monsanto and Roughrider Genetics) is similar to a popularizer of science. Communicators in the extension services usually fill a role of this kind: they are charged with making knowledge accessible in an objective manner (personal communication with Becky Koch, director of Extension agriculture communication, NDSU, December 10, 2004).

When the agency paying the salary is an agency that develops scientific and technological innovations, "making science accessible in an objective manner" has strong public-relations and marketing overtones. The unstated objective is to encourage adoption. Translating complex knowledge into simplified versions and publishing that information in accessible materials is one way to facilitate adoption. This is a legitimate communication function for technical and scientific communicators because it accommodates science to the public (Fahnestock, 1986) and technology to the user (Dobrin, 2004). A good example of a public information brochure that performs a public relations function is *Bringing New Technologies to Wheat.* This brochure spells out the standards for release of GM wheat, as we have already seen, but it also attempts to preempt possible objections by giving reassurance that GM wheat will not become an uncontrollable weed, that market strategies will be developed, that breeding programs will improve competitiveness by working with Monsanto, and that Roundup Ready wheat will bring value to wheat growers. The brochure does not indicate who published it, but because it is available from Monsanto's archive of publications, it apparently is a Monsanto publication.

Also, materials produced by the NDSU Extension Service are good examples of documents that translate scientific knowledge into a simpler, more accessible form and, in so doing, perform public relations and market functions. One of their brochures, *Agriculture Biotechnology: What are the Issues?* (2002), provides answers to several questions: What is biotechnology, and why is it being used in our food supply? How long has genetic engineering been used in agriculture and food production? What are the goals and potential benefits of agricultural bio-technology? The answers impart real information and acknowledge certain concerns, but they are clearly written from a perspective that supports GM development and, combined with images of wholesome food and smiling faces, are intended to have a calming effect.

The technical communicator as translator of knowledge may work as a producer of routine documents, as an in-service worker, or even as a "symbolic-analytic worker." As Johndan Johnson-Eilola (2004) explains, Robert Reich described these as three areas of service work, and they represent a hierarchy of worker responsibility and status. I agree with Johnson-Eilola that technical communicators who work at the level of a symbolic-analyst are doing challenging and important work, integrating "communication into a much broader range of technological contexts" than the typical technical writer (p. 183).

Even so, as translators, they will attempt to preserve meaning when subject matter crosses boundaries (whether those boundaries are associated with language or conceptual complexity) and, in so doing, align themselves with the producers or originators of innovation. As Slack, Miller, and Doak (2004) put it, the effort to translate knowledge is always an attempt to "ensure . . . the preferred meanings are the ones that get fixed" (p. 167). Even when the translator of knowledge attempts to understand fully the context of the reader and to incorporate the new infor-mation within the reader's existing meaning structures, the goal is to fix meanings by offering an interpretation that recontextualizes and integrates preferred mean-ings. We might say that this is exactly what localization does—it recontextualizes knowledge.

TECHNICAL COMMUNICATORS AS FACILITATORS OF CONSENSUS

However, merely working as a symbolic-analyst who translates knowledge and integrates communication into a wide range of contexts is not sufficient when the technology being transferred is controversial, as is the case with transgenic crops. If we broaden the technical communicator's role to include the task of negotiating science and technology, we redefine the goal associated with that role and problem-atize the communicator's allegiance. I am imagining a role for technical communi-cators as negotiators of interpretations, that is, of integrated meanings, a role similar to the one envisioned by Slack et al. (2004) when they suggest that technical com-municators should think of their work as articulation instead of translation. Whereas a translator only "mediates" meaning, one who articulates meaning challenges exist-ing articulations of power among sender, translator, and receiver (p. 171).

Yet I am thinking of more than a writer reconstructing texts to reflect rearticulated power relations; instead, I am thinking of people actively involved in creating forums and facilitating meetings, as well as composing documents. In this role, the technical communicator creates the conditions for new contexts of understanding to emerge and invites those who hold opposing interpretations to enter into the process of creating that new context and meaning. As Robert Johnson (2004) suggests, instead of thinking of the audience as a targeted or invoked reader, we can strive to create an "involved" audience: "the *involved* audience brings the audience literally into the open, making the intended audience a visible, physical, collaborative presence" (p. 93). When technical communicators adopt this role, they are usually consultants, brought in from the outside to facilitate group work and to oversee the writing of documents.

Julie Hile (2001) describes her experience in this role when she worked with several constituents from BNP railroad to rewrite the company's safety manual. Instead of interviewing people and then retreating to rewrite the manual in private, she and her co-workers gathered 80 people from the company for an all-day writing session. These people included safety professionals, leaders from four unions, veteran railroaders, and rookies (p. 95). By encouraging discussion and suggesting an alternative way of looking at the safety rules, a novel perspective that offered space to create common ground, Hile was able to help constituents reach consensus and draft their own revised safety manual.

CONCLUSION

As Hile's experience demonstrates, technical communicators who facilitate negotiation do not align themselves with the originators of innovation, and they do not necessarily reinforce existing power and authority relations. In the case of transgenic wheat in the upper midwest, someone in Hile's position, with her experience and background in technical communication, could have been helpful to the coexistence group discussed earlier. It seems to me that the role Gary Goreham played as facilitator of the group is one that we in the field of technical communication need to explore. If we were to take this role seriously, two basic questions (How might technical communicators equip themselves to be effective in such roles? What set of negotiation skills do we need to teach our students?) seem to call for close studies of cases like the one I have alluded to briefly here. We might call these forensic reports on technology transfer cases. Such research would attempt to isolate the most important ethical, political, and rhetorical factors in the case. Perhaps we will one day include a collection of case studies about controversial technology negotiations in our required reading for advanced studies in technical communication.

REFERENCES

Agriculture Biotechnology: What are the Issues? (2002). Agriculture Biotechnology Communicators. North Dakota State University Extension Service.

Bringing New Technologies to Wheat: Information on the Development of Roundup Ready Wheat. (2003). Cooperative Spring Wheat Programs. Monsanto. Retrieved November 16, 2006 from http://www.monsanto.com/monsanto/content/sci_tech/literature/techpubs/2003/wheat.pdf

Dobrin, D. (2004). What's technical about technical writing? In J. Johnson-Eilola & S. A. Selber (Eds.), *Central works in technical communication* (pp. 108-123). New York: Oxford University Press.

Fahnestock, J. (1986). Accommodating science: The rhetorical life of scientific facts. *Written Communication, 3,* 275-296.

Hart, K. (2002). *Eating in the dark: America's experiment with genetically engineered food.* New York: Pantheon.

Hile, J. S. (2001). I've been working on the railroad: ReVision at BNP railway. In G. J. Savage & D. L. Sullivan (Eds.), *Writing a professional life: Stories of technical communicators on and off the job* (pp. 93-101). New York: Longman.

Jacobson, J. et al. (2004, February). Withdrawal letter submitted by representatives of organic farming.

Johnson, R. R. (2004). Audience involved: Toward a participatory model of writing. In J. Johnson-Eilola & S. A. Selber (Eds.), *Central works in technical communication* (pp. 91-103). New York: Oxford University Press.

Johnson-Eilola, J. (2004). Relocating the value of work: Technical communication in a post-industrial age. In J. Johnson-Eilola & S. A. Selber (Eds.), *Central works in technical communication* (pp. 175-192). New York: Oxford University Press.

Kneen, B. (1999). *Farmageddon: Food and the culture of biotechnology.* Gabriola Island, British Columbia, Canada: New Society Publishers.

Rogers, E. M. (1995). *Diffusion of innovations* (4th ed.). New York: The Free Press.

Slack, J. D., Miller, D. J., & Doak, J. (2004). The technical communicator as author: Meaning, power, authority. In J. Johnson-Eilola & S. A. Selber (Eds.), *Central works in technical communication* (pp. 161-174). New York: Oxford University Press.

Waddell, C. (1990). The role of *pathos* in the decision-making process: A study in the rhetoric of science policy. *The Quarterly Journal of Speech, 76,* 381-400.

Zent, J. (2004, April 1). More GMO plantings expected. *Fargo Forum.* http://presspass.in-forum.com/index.cfm

PART V

Corporate Environment:
Improving Communication

CHAPTER 17

Technical Language: Learning from the *Columbia* and *Challenger* Reports

Paul M. Dombrowski

We all remember vividly images of the disintegration of the shuttle *Columbia* in 2003 and of the shuttle *Challenger* in 1986. The two events have left indelible impressions of the human cost of space exploration and of the courage of the explorers. Space exploration will always be very dangerous, as the governmental investigations of both disasters repeatedly emphasized. Whether we see these events as unforeseen accidents or as potentially avoidable tragedies hinges on how technical knowledge is understood to be constituted in language, and how the use of language is involved in decision making and practical action. Rather than relying on our personal opinions to decide whether to see the disasters as accidents or as tragedies, we can be guided by the reports of the governmental investigations with their numerous experts on space exploration. Through these reports, we can see in detail how language—in writing, speaking, e-mailing, and even thinking—influenced these complex technological endeavors.

The two disasters, wrenching though they are, provide excellent opportunities for learning vitally important lessons about how technical and professional communication occurs in complex and technologically sophisticated organizational contexts. Comparing the reports of these investigations affords us typical and realistic examples, rather than theoretical speculations, of how communication is used in complex organizations. They also illustrate the crucial importance of language in the negotiation of difficult technical and judgment issues. In addition, the report on *Columbia* emphatically made explicit comparisons between the two events and their organizational and communicative causes, showing them to be related in kind and in history. The *Challenger* disaster was investigated by the

Presidential commission (known as the Rogers Commission) and a Congressional committee. The *Columbia* disaster was investigated by the *Columbia* Accident Investigation Board (CAIB).

PURPOSE

The official report of the *Columbia* shuttle disaster shows that though the technical language used to present information was often thought of as definite and incontrovertible by many of those involved, in crucial instances it was actually rather indefinite and questionable. Even in a "hard" technical field dealing with concrete mechanisms, information is not always clear-cut, a phenomenon reflected in and to some extent caused by language, by words referring to things. Though this awareness, under the name social constructionism, is common among technical and professional communicators, it is often news to technical students, practitioners, and managers. Though knowledge socially constituted in language is not a phenomenon peculiar to the space industry, the *Columbia* report shows that oftentimes space technicians and managers seemed surprisingly unaware of it.

Much the same happened in the *Challenger* situation, 17 years before *Columbia*, as the CAIB repeatedly and emphatically states (*Columbia* Accident Investigation Board, 2003). It appears, as the CAIB noted, that in the 17 years between *Challenger* (1986) and *Columbia* (2003), NASA had not changed significantly in how it does business, what the CAIB calls the "NASA culture" (CAIB, 2003).

This was the board's perspective on responsibility and social origination:

> The Board recognized early on that the accident was probably not an anomalous, random event, but rather likely rooted to some degree in NASA's history and the human space flight program's culture. Accordingly, the Board broadened its mandate at the outset to include an investigation of a wide range of historical and organizational issues, including political and budgetary considerations, compromises, and changing priorities over the life of the Space Shuttle Program. The Board's conviction regarding the importance of these factors strengthened as the investigation progressed, with the result that this report, in its findings, conclusions, and recommendations, places as much weight on these causal factors as on the more easily understood and corrected physical cause of the accident (CAIB, 2003, p. 9).

Though NASA apparently did not learn from *Challenger*, clearly investigators from throughout the aerospace industry *did*. The *Columbia* report reveals, happily, the evolving impact of technical communication theory and principles on investigators, who showed keener awareness of the importance of social context—including "NASA culture" and the larger social context of NASA's activities—in understanding engineering events, in contrast to the *Challenger* reports. The CAIB investigators go so far as to state repeatedly that the organizational culture of NASA was as much a "cause" of the *Columbia* accident as the foam debris that damaged the wing.

In our view, the NASA organizational culture had as much to do with this accident as the foam. Organizational culture refers to the basic values, norms, beliefs, and practices that characterize the functioning of an institution. At the most basic level, organizational culture defines the assumptions that employees make as they carry out their work. It is a powerful force that can persist through reorganizations and the change of key personnel (CAIB, 2003, p. 97).

This evolution of perspective is a credit to the scholarship and teaching in technical and professional communication to which we committed ourselves.

INSTANCES

Several instances of the indefiniteness and social contingency of technical language use in the *Columbia* report stand out:

1. *Operational* vs. *experimental*, *research*, and *developmental*
2. *Mandatory need* ·
3. *Anomaly* and *in-family*
4. The general phenomenon known as *the normalization of deviance*

Each of these will be described in the following sections.

Operational vs. Experimental

Important language difficulties involve even the shuttle itself—what it "is." The shuttle was originally designed as an experimental craft for research and development that would lead to a later craft that would be fully operational. The shuttle itself has never reached the "operational" stage, though several U. S. presidents have spoken of it that way, and led the public to think of it that way. "The organizational causes of this accident are rooted in the Space Shuttle Program's history and culture, including the . . . mischaracterization of the Shuttle as operational rather than developmental" (CAIB, 2003, p. 9).

The CAIB pointedly criticized then-President Nixon for saying in 1972 of the shuttle, "*It will revolutionize transportation into near space, by routinizing it*" (CAIB, 2003, p. 22, emphasis added by CAIB). Later, in 1982, after only its fourth flight, the CAIB notes that then-President Reagan declared, "beginning with the next flight, the *Columbia* and her sister ships will be *fully operational*, ready to provide *economical and routine access to space* for scientific exploration, commercial ventures, and for tasks related to the national security" (CAIB, 2003, p. 23 [emphasis added by CAIB]). The CAIB points out, to the contrary, that the shuttle was at that time still in its early flight-test stage, and actually has never matured beyond the developmental stage. Nevertheless, the language of "operational" and "routinizing" generated pressure to fly the shuttle as often as possible, pressure from the executive branch and from the public impressed upon NASA administrators, managers, and engineers.

Mandatory Need

Shortly after the launch of *Columbia*, it was learned from video and photographic records that some debris had struck the left wing of the shuttle as it was flying about 2,000 mph at an altitude of about 120,000 ft. The shuttle wings were specifically designed on the assumption that *nothing* would strike them or the thermal protection system (TPS) during flight. Some engineers and managers were concerned, and established a Debris Assessment Team (DAT) to explore the implications of this debris strike.

The DAT thought there might be significant damage to the TPS but were not sure. They wanted and informally asked for, but did not receive, additional imagery from Department of Defense (DOD) resources on the ground and in orbit. The request was denied because there was no "mandatory need" for such imagery. Recall that the shuttle TPS was, by design, expected never to be struck by any debris; therefore, there were no formal procedures that would have mandated a particular course of action such as requesting DOD imagery. But to establish a mandatory need, the DAT would need hard evidence that damage had occurred, which they could acquire only through the imagery they asked for—a very real and very serious Catch-22. Additional requests encountered similar confusion and were denied.

As the CAIB report recounts:

> Discussion then moved on to whether the Debris Assessment Team had a "mandatory need" for Department of Defense imaging. Most team members, when asked by the Board what "mandatory need" meant, replied with a shrug of their shoulders. They believed the need for imagery was obvious: without better pictures, engineers would be unable to make reliable predictions of the depth and area of damage. . . . However, team members concluded that although their need was important, they could not cite a "mandatory" requirement for the request. *Analysts on the Debris Assessment Team were in the unenviable position of wanting images to more accurately assess damage while simultaneously needing to prove to Program managers, as a result of their assessment, that there was a need for images in the first place* (CAIB, 2003, p. 157).

This is one of the instances noted by CAIB of "organizational barriers that prevented effective communication of critical safety information and stifled professional differences of opinion" (CAIB, 2003, p. 9). A later review of routine imagery of *Columbia* by DOD ground-based assets shows a reasonable likelihood that significant damage to the wing would have been detectable. Additional DOD assets already in orbit might have yielded even sharper images.

Anomaly

Early on in the shuttle program, unexpected damage was occurring to the thermal tiles from foam debris separating from the external tank during the launch, which exposes the tank to violent vibration, wind, and flexing. Almost every flight incurred damage, sometimes as many as 700 "dings." This was a serious anomaly because the tiles were expected *never* to be struck by anything. The term "anomaly" in this case, as in *Challenger*, indicates that something happened that was not expected to happen, was not desirable, and might have significant consequences. Foam shedding and tile strikes happened so often, though, that they came to be perceived as routine.

The CAIB report refers to this phenomenon as "normalization of deviance" (a term borrowed from sociologist D. Vaughan):

> With each successful landing, it appears that NASA engineers and managers increasingly regarded the foam-shedding as inevitable, and as either unlikely to jeopardize safety or simply an acceptable risk. . . . NASA and contractor personnel came to view foam strikes not as a safety of flight issue, but rather a simple maintenance, or "turnaround" issue. . . . What was originally considered a serious threat to the Orbiter came to be treated as "in-family," a reportable problem that was within the known experience base, was believed to be understood, and was not regarded as a safety-of-flight issue (CAIB, 2003, pp. 122-123).

Elsewhere, the CAIB characterized this phenomenon as "reliance on past success as a substitute for sound engineering practices" (CAIB, 2003, p. 9).

Thus, *anomaly* was transmuted into *routine*, practically as though black became white. As Vaughan (1996) explains, this phenomenon is not peculiar to NASA or the aerospace industry, though one of its most dramatic instances was the *Challenger* disaster.

In-Family

Within NASA, an unusual line of reasoning developed about debris strikes. Since mission after mission returned even though suffering many debris strikes, the successful return of each shuttle came to be perceived as representing an allowable amount of damage to the TPS. Each mission added new data to a data set that came to be known as "in-family," meaning that it had been experienced before and seemed *de facto* to be acceptable. Any new data that fell within the boundaries of the in-family set was deemed acceptable. More importantly, however, new data that fell outside the existing in-family boundaries was perceived not as cause for alarm so much as cause to redefine the boundaries of in-family!

The CAIB says that in-family is a strange term with a denotation like a rubber band. New events outside of the earlier "family" of experience are just incorporated in a new "family" by expanding its boundaries. The problem is that in-family also carries connotations of familiarity, acceptability, even safety.

CHALLENGER REDUX

The *Columbia* findings, tragically, resonate with the *Challenger* findings of confused language, social pressures, and ethical lapses reported by scholars such as Winsor (1990), Gross and Walzer (1994), Pace (1988), and Moore (1992). In an earlier article, I traced differences between the reports by the Presidential Commission and the Congressional committee investigating *Challenger* (Dombrowski,

1991). In another article, I examined two *Challenger* terms in detail: anomaly and flightworthiness (Dombrowski, 1992).

Anomaly

Let me review the *Challenger* disaster. The solid rocket motors of the shuttle are so big that they are manufactured in segments, then assembled into a stack. The segments are sealed by two rubber-like O-rings, about the width of a pencil but forming a circle about 38 feet in circumference, and with generous gobs of "special putty." The O-rings were designed never to be contacted by the exhaust gases. From the earliest shuttle missions, however, some charring of the O-rings was noted after recovery of the boosters. Because this was not supposed to happen, it was rightly referred to as an "anomaly." As mission after mission returned successfully with some charring, the charring became accepted as normal and so no longer anomalous. It was as though black became white!

Several scholars have described how this phenomenon played out regarding *Challenger* (Dombrowski, 1991, 1992, 2006; Gross & Walzer, 1994; Moore, 1992; Pace, 1988; Winsor, 1990). For instance, I explain how, after numerous repeated instances in which the orbiter returned without disaster, this anomaly came to be perceived as normal and routine; indeed, the specific amount of charring being used as a numerical measure of the safety factor allowable for charring (Dombrowski, 1992, pp. 78-79).

The reality, of course, was that this was a danger signal that went unheeded and was defused by reconceptualizing it. Richard Feynman, a Nobel laureate in physics and the most renowned scientist on the Rogers commission, wrote a famous dissenting opinion to the Rogers report, titled "Personal Observations on the Reliability of the Space Shuttle" and published as Appendix F of the report (Feynman, 1986). Feynman described the phenomenon in stark imagery, including referring to it as "Russian roulette."

Flightworthiness

Flightworthiness, whether of a spacecraft or of an airliner, is supposedly a definite technical judgment determined by a large number of specific technical criteria. Ordinarily, it has an additional built-in safety factor. Managers meet with engineers to decide whether to launch, and the managers *assume* that the shuttle *is not* flightworthy, and so engineers have the burden of proving instead that it *is* flightworthy. It is like the presumption of innocence in an American criminal trial, in which the prosecution must overcome the presumption. With *Columbia*, however, when managers learned that engineers had grave concerns, they reversed their assumption—they assumed that the shuttle *was* flightworthy and saddled engineers with having to prove that it *was not* flightworthy—a stance they were not prepared for and unable to convincingly demonstrate (Dombrowski, 1991, p. 212). As a result, the managers took their assumption as confirmed and approved the launch. Remember—the engineers came in with the same body of technical information at hand, but that same body yielded different results depending on the argumentative assumptions brought to them. We know the outcome.

A similar, though not identical, reversal of assumptions was operative regarding *Columbia*. The CAIB points out, regarding the denied requests for DOD imagery:

> When managers in the Shuttle Program denied the team's request for imagery, the Debris Assessment Team was put in the untenable position of having to prove that a safety-of-flight issue existed without the very images that would permit such a determination. This is precisely the opposite of how an effective safety culture would act. Organizations that deal with high-risk operations must always have a healthy fear of failure—operations must be proved safe, rather than the other way around. NASA inverted this burden of proof (CAIB, 2003, p. 190).

A FINAL MESSAGE

Perhaps the most tragic instance of misleading language use is the e-mail message from Mission Control to the shuttle commander while it was in orbit a couple days before the fateful reentry (see Figure 1). The e-mail mentions the foam strike quite casually and incidentally as only a public affairs (media) matter, then explicitly characterizes the event as of "absolutely no concern for [re-]entry." The fuller reality, kept from the commander and crew, is that on the ground a good number of engineering and management individuals and groups were quite concerned about possible damage to the TPS and therefore risk to reentry.

Though some *post facto* critics suggest that this misrepresentation was intended to prevent pointless apprehension about an unfixable risk, the reality is that several options for alternative actions were possible, including docking with the International Space Station to await another shuttle flight. It is not known whether the obscurity of the discussion was intentional.

CONCLUSION

We can learn several lessons from these tragic accidents—indeed, we must. Space exploration is an inherently very risky enterprise, and the courageous men and women who undertake it deserve our best efforts toward their success.

1. Data do not equal meaning. Though collecting data is usually a mechanical act, interpreting it into meaning and extending it to application is a very human act, vulnerable to the foibles that define our very nature.
2. Language use—in the terms we choose to use, how we use them, and the concepts they are taken to represent—shapes knowledge as much as empirical facts do.
3. We *are* learning, though, as the CAIB concludes, NASA has not. Throughout technical fields, there is a maturing understanding of technical communication as having both empirical and social contexts and sources.

NOTE: This is private/personal mail and not for release to media.

From: STICH, J. S. (Steve) (JSC-DAB) (NASA)
Sent: Thursday, January 23, 2003 5:13 PM
To: CDR; PLT
CC: BECK, KELLY B. (JSC-DAB) (NASA); ENGELAUF, PHILIP L. (JSC-DAB)
(NASA); CAIN, LEROY E. (JSC-DAB) (NASA); HANLEY, JEFFREY M.
(JEFF) (JSC-DAB) (NASA); AUSTIN, BRYAN P. (JSC-DAB) (NASA)
Subject: INFO: Possible PAO Event Question

Rick and Willie,

You guys are doing a fantastic job staying on the timeline and accomplishing great
science. Keep up the good work and let us know if there is anything that we can do better
from an MCC/POCC standpoint.

There is one item that I would like to make you aware of for the upcoming PAO event on
Blue FD 10 and for future PAO events later in the mission. This item is not even worth
mentioning other than wanting to make sure that you are not surprised by it in a question
from a reporter.

During ascent at approximately 80 seconds, photo analysis shows that some debris from
the area of the −Y ET Bipod Attach Point came loose and subsequently impacted the
orbiter left wing, in the area of transition from Chine to Main Wing, creating a shower of
smaller particles.

The impact appears to be totally on the lower surface and no particles are seen to traverse
over the upper surface of the wing. *Experts have reviewed the high speed photography and
there is no concern for RCC or tile damage. We have seen this same phenomenon on
several other flights and there is absolutely no concern for entry* [emphasis added].

That is all for now. It's a pleasure working with you every day.

Figure 1. E-mail message from Mission Control to shuttle commander.

4. There has also been a maturing of the scope and dimensions of technical
communication—not just formal reports and written texts but verbal and
electronic forms, and informal, unrecorded, "unauthorized" discourse such as
attitudes, expectations, questions and intimations, social pressures, and even
words not spoken.

5. Ethical responsibility is both an individual and social or organizational burden.
The CAIB noted:

Engineers' failed attempts were not just a matter of psychological frames
and interpretations. The obstacles these engineers faced were political and
organizational. They were rooted in NASA history and the decisions of
leaders that had altered NASA culture, structure, and the structures of the
safety system and affected the social context of decision making for both

accidents (CAIB, 2003, p. 200). . . . In neither impending crisis [Challenger or Columbia] did management recognize how structure and hierarchy can silence employees. . . . In perhaps the ultimate example of engineering concerns not making their way upstream, Challenger astronauts were told that the cold temperature was not a problem, and Columbia astronauts were told that the foam strike was not a problem (CAIB, 2003, p. 202).

For further reading, I recommend *Comm Check. . .: The Final Flight of the Shuttle Columbia* by Cabbage and Harwood (2004). For a concise review of the loss of *Columbia*, the investigation of the disaster, and an insightful after-report interview with Gehman, who chaired the CAIB, I recommend W. Langewiesche's "*Columbia*'s Last Flight" (2003) in *The Atlantic Monthly*, a well-researched yet readable source.

REFERENCES

Cabbage, M., & Harwood, W. (2004). *Comm check . . .: The final flight of the shuttle Columbia*. New York: Free Press.

Columbia Accident Investigation Board (CAIB). (2003, August). *Report of the* Columbia *accident investigation board, Volume I*. Washington, DC: GPO and NASA.

Dombrowski, P. M. (1991). The lessons of the *Challenger* investigations. *IEEE Transactions on Professional Communication, 43*(4), 211-216.

Dombrowski, P. M. (1992). *Challenger* and the social contingency of meaning: Two lessons for the technical communication classroom. *Technical Communication Quarterly, 1*(3), 73-86.

Dombrowski, P. M. (2006). The two shuttle accident reports: Context in technical communication. *Journal of Technical Writing and Communication, 36*(3), 231-252.

Feynman, R. P. (1986). Personal observations on the reliability of the Space Shuttle. Appendix F to Vol. 2 of *Report to the President of the Presidential Commission on the Space Shuttle* Challenger *Accident*. http://history.nasa.gov/rogersreport/v2appf.htm

Gross A., & Walzer, A. E. (1994, April). Positivists, post-modernists, Aristotelians, and the *Challenger* disaster. *College English, 56,* 420-433.

Langewiesche, W. (2003, November). *Columbia*'s last flight. *Atlantic Monthly, 58-87.*

Moore, P. (1992). When politeness is fatal: Technical communication and the *Challenger* accident. *Journal of Business and Technical Communication, 6*(3), 269-292.

Pace, R. C. (1988). Technical communication, group differentiation, and the decision to launch the space shuttle *Challenger. Journal of Technical Writing and Communication, 18,* 207-220.

Vaughan, D. (1996). *The* Challenger *launch decision: Risky technology, culture, and deviance at NASA*. Chicago, IL: University of Chicago Press.

Winsor, D. (1990). The construction of knowledge in organizations: Asking the right questions about the shuttle *Challenger. Journal of Business and Technical Communication, 4*(2), 7-20.

CHAPTER 18

The Theoretical Foundations of Service Leadership: A New Paradigm

Judith B. Strother and Svafa Grönfeldt

Leadership theories and customer service concepts have been increasing in importance for many types of organizations around the world. Customer service and customer service communication as research fields are rather new, but the topics have been incorporated as subtopics in some management courses and even taught as a specialized course in some university curricula.

The rate of change in our service-driven economy calls for a new approach to service management. Organizations that used to fear the uncertainty of change are now faced with the even greater uncertainty and dangers associated with staying the same (Cameron & Quinn, 1999). However, even the more flexible organizations have not always had the necessary model to allow them to make the best possible adaptations to change.

Traditional concepts of customer service—usually focused on frontline customer service providers—do not incorporate all the necessary elements to allow a corporation to achieve success in that area. Therefore, through research within the management, leadership, customer service, and communication areas, the authors developed the paradigm of Service Leadership, based on the evolution of a collective leadership mindset of an entire organization.

SERVICE LEADERSHIP DEFINED

Service Leadership is the culture that empowers the organization to strategize its promises, design its processes, and engage its people in a proactive quest for competitive advantage. A service leadership mindset of an entire organization will

197

consider every employee-customer encounter to be an invaluable opportunity to improve customer service and engender customer loyalty. Under these conditions, every individual takes responsibility and pride in creating or protecting the organization's leading position in service quality or in designated markets by carefully observing and communicating customer needs throughout the organization.

Note that the paradigm engenders three key elements. First, strategies are crucial for developing the service promise, which has to be tied to the organization's goals and mission. Second, the service process must deliver in the most efficient manner to enhance profitability. Third, the service providers (people) and the intellectual capital they offer are the key ingredients in making the service unique and therefore difficult to imitate.

The questions for this chapter are: How did we get to that new paradigm? And how can an organization implement a Service Leadership culture if a different organizational culture is already in place?

THE RESEARCH PROCESS

The concept of service leadership is based on a multidisciplinary approach drawing on theories of leadership, corporate culture, customer service, and methods of strategic management, service management, and human resource management, among others.

Service is composed of *intentions, interactions,* and *impacts.* In other words, a service organization *intends* to provide a certain set of services based on the organization's corporate and service strategies. These strategies are carefully formulated to optimize the organization's operational efficiency and to fulfill expected customer needs. The intended services or the service promise is then delivered through *interactions* with the customers. The interactions are regulated by service processes that can be automated, technologically assisted, or totally dependent on human contact. The *impact* of that interaction depends on how well the customers' expectations are met, and how well their expectations are met in turn affects their level of satisfaction. The impact is delivered through people and processes, determining customers' loyalty and thus ultimately the organization's profitability.

To accomplish this service leadership revolution, pervasive changes must be implemented for the service promise, the service design process, and the utilization of human resources embedded in the people of the organization. The traditional idea of a corporate culture must be expanded. Therefore, all of these areas had to be carefully researched, and that research led to the following assumptions for the concept of Service Leadership:

- *Assumption I*: Organizations can achieve competitive advantage in service through a collective leadership mindset based on strategic application of processes and people to design and deliver the service *promise.*
- *Assumption II*: The *process* assures competitive advantage through speed and accuracy and adaptability of the service delivery, and enhances organizational efficiency by maximizing both internal and external resources.

- *Assumption III*: The *people* assure competitive advantage through proactive adaptability to change by employing innovation, flexibility, and motivation to move the organization forward.

The theoretical framework suggests that the leadership mindset of organizational members is powerful and can be a driving force for sustainable competitive advantage. The following sections present a quick overview of key research areas and the ways that the findings helped frame the new service leadership paradigm.

LEADERSHIP THEORIES

The challenges are great for today's service organizations, but the opportunities for those who master the science of leadership in the service sector are also tremendous. The act of leadership must be integrated into both the marketing and operational strategies of any service organization. In fact, in today's service-driven economy, you cannot expect to achieve one without the other if the company is to adapt to the ever-changing marketplace and the diversity of consumers' needs. The common denominator is the focus on assuming a leadership role, either as a company in the marketplace or as an individual within the organization, regardless of formal authority or power. Thus, the first research area is leadership theory.

Theories of leadership have transitioned through a number of different trends over their very lengthy history, an overview of which is given by Grönfeldt and Strother (2005). Recent developments have moved away from the concept of a single powerful individual, labeled a leader, to a broader concept of leadership aimed at achieving a group goal, not just because of the efforts of one skilled person but because of the contributions of group members (Horner, 1997).

Today, leadership is viewed more as a process and is closely associated with corporate culture. In these theories, a particular group or an organization may include a leader, but when everyone is involved and expected to play an active role in moving the organization forward through leadership efforts, no one needs to be motivated and dominated by that leader. In this view, many individuals can exert small degrees of leadership, regardless of their personal power or their position within the organization.

House and Aditya (1997) argue that there is no evidence that supports claims of stable and long-term effects of leaders on followers' self-esteem, motives, desires, preferences, or values. The leaders can, without a doubt, cause changes in followers' psychological states, but these states often do not continue after the separation of the leader and followers. Further, there is little evidence that charismatic, transformational, or visionary leadership does indeed transform individuals, groups, large divisions of organizations, or total organizations, despite claims that they do so.

Scholars have now begun to recognize that we know too much about leaders, but too little about leadership and its collective power. Linsky and Heifetz (2003) suggest that successful individuals, whom we so often tend to label as leaders, cannot automatically attribute their success to leadership. They claim those individuals have mastered the art of monitoring and fulfilling the needs of those around them, causing them to focus all their efforts on performing anticipated or expected acts. Thus, the organization keeps this "leader" safely tucked away within his or her scope of authority. This, according to these Harvard professors, is not leadership. To them, the act of leadership demands courage to go beyond the safe zone of anticipated acts.

Not only do leaders have to dare to be innovative, leadership itself must be distributed throughout the organization and its culture. Therefore, a collective effort is needed in which every individual believes his or her interest is best served by protecting and preserving the organization's interests and takes the initiative within the framework of the organization's goals to do so. Distribution of leadership allows for the possibility that all members of an organization can and may be leaders in some sense and that each employee considers leadership an integral part of the job. In that respect, managers may be leaders but not necessarily by virtue of just holding management positions. In fact, leadership has become a question of influence, not just authority.

Theories of Organizational Culture

Mintzberg and Quinn (1996), leading contemporary scholars in strategic management, have identified various approaches to strategy formulation and application. One of those strategies is the cultivation of a strong organizational culture. The culture centers around strong organizational values and norms, reinforcing certain sets of behaviors needed to give the organization a competitive edge. As Chatman and Cha (2003, p. 23) concur, organizational or corporate culture is "the glue that holds an organization together, or the rock on which it stands." The big question is whether the culture helps or hinders the organization's ability to execute its strategic objectives. An organization cannot ignore its culture and just hope it develops well. It must be proactive about using its culture to fully execute its strategy, inspire creativity and innovation, as well as develop and reinforce a collective mindset.

No organization has one pure culture throughout the entire organization, but all successful organizations are believed to have a core culture, which is fundamental to the way the organization functions. Without it, the focus of resources and organizational operations is lost, and energy is wasted as people, systems, and processes work out of sync with one another. For the organization to succeed, the core culture must be aligned with the organization's strategy and its core leadership practices (Horner, 1997).

For the last decade, strong organizational cultures have been believed to be critical to bottom-line performance in large organizations. In fact, commitment-based organizations packed with people who fit the organization's values perfectly have repeatedly outperformed other organizations. "The major distinguishing feature in these companies, their most important competitive advantage, the most powerful factor they all highlight as a key ingredient in their success, is their organizational culture" (Cameron & Quinn, 1999, p. 4; see also Schneider, 2000).

Empowerment Theories

The debate over how much individual power individuals should have in an organization has been carried out at least since the beginning of the Industrial Revolution. Since 1990 there have been countless empirical and applied research studies dealing with employee empowerment. In fact, the 1990s were labeled the *empowerment era* (Applebaum, Hebert, & Leoux, 1999). What does the term *empowerment* actually mean? How has it been applied, and can it be applied successfully in a service context?

In the new organizational structure wherein employee participation is expected and indeed needed, the term empowerment is typically used to describe managements' efforts to involve employees in decision making. No consensus has been reached regarding the concept of empowerment or how far organizations should take it. Some definitions of empowerment suggest complete and almost uncontrolled power in the hands of employees. Although many managers recognize the importance of fast decision making and flexibility, this is almost a "license to act irresponsibly" and represents one end of the continuum. At the other end is the limited or controlled empowerment, which involves structured teamwork through careful experimental design, structured meetings, and strict goal-setting and measurement.

The new Service Leadership paradigm takes the management practice of empowerment a step further in an attempt to overcome the disadvantages associated with power transfer and to fully capitalize on investments in higher labor and training costs. In service organizations aiming for service excellence, employees must not have just the authority to point out issues or watch and wait for things to happen. They must always desire service excellence and regard it as their responsibility to be proactive in order to collectively shape their working environment and help to achieve organizational success.

While most managers are fully aware of the importance of cultural management, they may be unable to develop the clarity, consistency, and comprehensiveness that are needed to have the desired effect on employees. In fact, organizational cultures have turned out to be more than most managers bargained for, both as an enabler of competitive advantage as well as a stumbling block for organizational efforts to improve processes and performance.

Management Theory

Adopting an atmosphere of empowerment calls for a change in employee and managerial roles. It also calls for a reversal in the traditional relationship between service provider and customer. Instead of the employee just doing what the manager dictates, he or she must do what the customer wants and needs.

As Heifetz and Linsky point out, "in a firm with a leadership culture, leadership means exercising discretion, taking risks and, again in this context, first meeting the customers' needs in ways that might well be beyond standard operating procedures, job descriptions, and formal authorization, asking for forgiveness later rather than approval beforehand" (Heifetz & Linsky, 2005, p. xii).

The manager's role becomes the creation of certain conditions for active employee participation and initiative. Quinn and Spreitzer (1997) suggest that managers must continuously (a) work to clarify the sense of strategic direction for their people to set a clear strategic vision; (b) strive for participation and involvement to foster openness and teamwork; (c) work to clarify expectations regarding the goals, tasks, and lines of authority to provide a sense of discipline and control; and (d) work to resolve the conflicts among their people to give a sense of support and security. Furthermore, research has shown that employees initiate action and participate more actively when they are intrinsically motivated or have internal justifications for their actions. Managers need to help create a working environment where employees' behaviors are governed from within, but guided by a clear, well-defined corporate framework.

If managers at all levels are now faced with changing roles, then human resources (HR) managers are no exception (Godbout, 2000). To support the new service organization, HR managers' perspective on employees must change from viewing people as a part of production or as just another resource to building human capital as a core source of competitive advantage. Those who want to create a competitive advantage are faced with the following issues (Bartlett & Ghoshal, 2002):

- A building challenge—recruitment and selection
- A linking task—knowledge management through social networks
- A bonding process—within the culture, through loyalty, commitment, and a sense of belonging

INITIATING CHANGE

This new service leadership model requires the changes discussed above throughout the entire organizational culture. Just how is this accomplished in an organization that does not have the required elements? Bringing about constructive organizational change is one of the most difficult challenges today's managers face. Organizations must look to the future for answers, not to the past. The thinking must be shifted from action and reaction to anticipatory action—becoming very proactive.

Effective communication is a critical element of successfully implementing change in an organization. Organizations can move effectively toward their goals if communication is accurate, thorough, and timely. However, if communication is hampered, the entire organization suffers. The challenge for managers in organizations facing rapid changes and harsh competition is to use communication to motivate innovation by creating a supportive climate, which will in turn enhance the organizations' ability to adapt to changes. A supportive climate encourages worker participation, the free and open exchange of information, and the constructive conflict resolution that is necessary to foster innovation.

Planning a change strategy for a new communication climate takes both time and effort. While no simple recipe can ensure success, there are some basic principles that have proven successful in a number of organizations (Clampitt, 2002). If the communication climate change is to be carried out successfully, the management must, through the organizational culture and climate

- Plan the phases of the change,
- Take steps to reduce uncertainty associated with the change,
- Tailor change strategies to individual managers' styles,
- Take appropriate action to organizational members' reaction to each change phase,
- Emphasize innovation,
- Enhance the effectiveness of management-employee communication,
- Change the employee perception of the management, and
- Enhance management's interpersonal skills and communication.

The main risk inherent in changing the corporate climate is that the organization may operate less effectively while the new climate is being created, and as managers modify their practices, procedures, and behaviors to foster it. However, the more consistent management messages are about the new priorities, and the better these priorities are backed up by resources, training, employee recruitment, orientation, and effective reward systems, the more successful the organization will be in facing its challenges and effecting the desired change (Shockely-Zalabak, 1994).

EVALUATING CHANGE

Any organization should employ comprehensive measurement and evaluation processes to determine whether the changes being implemented and the training being conducted are achieving the desired result. Because training takes financial resources away from other needs of the organization, the evaluation process helps management determine whether funds are being well spent and can provide a justification for allocating future funds. In addition, measures make the result of the initiative more tangible, thereby enhancing the commitment of managers to use human-resource-development tools and techniques.

All performance-improvement initiatives must be aligned with organizational strategies and values. To accomplish this alignment, a number of objectives have to be put in place before a new training program can be launched. Hodge (2002) has identified the following three objectives important for this task.

- *Business objectives* specify what the participant will accomplish as a consequence of the application of skill and knowledge in measurable business terms.
- *Performance objectives* provide precise, measurable statements of the behaviors that participant will be able to demonstrate on the job.
- *Learning objectives* describe what participants will be able to do at the end of their training or intervention program, matching the performance objectives as closely as possible.

Evaluation is essential to determine how successfully the objectives have been met. Philips and Stone (2002) have presented a framework for evaluating training and educational programs, human resource programs, organizational development or change initiatives, and technology initiatives. Their framework measures (a) the participants' immediate reactions to the training, (b) the amount of learning that has taken place as a result of the training, (c) the extent to which the new skills or knowledge are applied on the job after the training, (d) the business impact of the initiative, and finally (e) the potential return on investment (ROI) in monetary terms.

CONCLUSION

The development of the new paradigm of Service Leadership has been a journey of discovery through mountains of literature in a number of different fields. It has required synthesizing information and creatively looking at new ways of meshing and implementing key theories. However, it has been rewarding, both in initial reactions to the new concept, in discussions resulting from the publication of the paradigm (Grönfeldt & Strother, 2005; Strother & Grönfeldt, 2006), and in the firm belief that the implementation of the concept, while extremely challenging, will be well worth it for the organizations involved.

There is no doubt that, when an entire organization considers each encounter between an employee and a customer to be a rich opportunity to improve customer service and build customer loyalty, a leadership mindset is in place. In this situation, every employee takes responsibility and pride in helping the organization reach a high level of service quality. They do this by carefully observing and communicating customer needs through organizational channels.

Service Leadership brings a new view of roles and relationships and empowers the entire organization to streamline its strategies and processes accurately and in a timely manner. Effective communication is critical at all stages of the process—from facilitating new ideas to providing employees with needed customer or product information, to building an organizational consensus. This new model gives the organization the ability to be proactive in continuous service adaptation, which in turn, gives it a solid competitive advantage in the marketplace.

REFERENCES

Applebaum, S. H., Hebert, D., & Leoux, S. (1999). Empowerment: Power, culture and leadership—A strategy or fad for the millennium? *Journal of Workplace Learning, 11*(7), 234.
Bartlett, C. A., & Ghoshal, S. (2002). Building competitive advantage through people. *MIT Sloan Management Review, 43*(2), 34-41.
Cameron, K. S., & Quinn, R. E. (1999). *Diagnosing and changing organizational culture: Based on the competing values framework.* Reading, MA: Addison-Wesley.
Chatman, J. A., & Cha, S. E. (2003). Leading by leveraging culture. *California Management Review, 45*(4), 20-32.

Clampitt, P. G. (2002). *Communicating for managerial effectiveness* (2nd ed.). Thousand Oaks, CA: Sage Publications.

Godbout, A. J. (2000). Managing core competencies: The impact of knowledge management on human resource practice in leading-edge organizations. *Knowledge and Process Management, 7*(2), 237-247.

Grönfeldt, S., & Strother, J. (2005). *Service leadership: A quest for competitive advantage.* Thousand Oaks, CA: Sage Publications.

Heifetz, R. A., & Linsky, M. (2005). [Preface]. In S. Grönfeldt & J. Strother (Eds.), *Service leadership: A quest for competitive advantage* (p. xii).Thousand Oaks, CA: Sage Publications.

Hodge, T. K. (2002). *Linking learning and performance: A practical guide to measuring learning and on-the-job application.* Boston, MA: Butterworth-Heinemann.

Horner, M. (1997). Leadership theory: Past, present and future. *Team Performance Management, 3*(4), 270-287.

House, R. J., & Aditya, R. N. (1997). The social scientific study of leadership: Quo Vadis? *Journal of Management, 23*(2), 409-473.

Linsky, M., & Heifetz, R. (2003). *Leadership on the line.* Cambridge, MA: Harvard Business School Press.

Mintzberg, H., & Quinn, B. (1996). *The strategy process: Concepts, context, cases.* Upper Saddle River, NJ: Prentice-Hall, Inc.

Phillips, J., & Stone, R. D. (2002). *How to measure training results: A practical guide to tracking the six key indicators.* New York: McGraw-Hill.

Quinn, R. E., & Spreitzer, G. M. (1997). The road to empowerment: Seven questions every leader should consider. *Organizational Dynamics, 26*(2), 37-49.

Shockely-Zalabak, P. (1994). *Understanding organizational communication.* New York: Longman.

Schneider, W. E. (2000). Why good management ideas fail: The neglected power of organizational culture. Strategy and leadership. In S. P. Kotter & J. L. Heskett (Ed.), *Corporate culture and performance* (pp. 24-29). New York: The Free Press. (Reprinted from Corporate Culture, 1992.)

Strother, J. B., & Grönfeldt, S. (2006, December). *Converting knowledge into action through a Service Leadership mindset.* Paper presented at the Fifth International Studying Leadership Conference, UK: Cranfield School of Management.

CHAPTER 19

Managing Collaboration: Adding Communication and Documentation Environment to a Product Development Cycle

Laura Batson and Susan Feinberg

The purpose of this chapter is to describe a repeatable process for managing communication and interaction patterns of multidisciplinary teams during the product development life cycle. Collaboration among discipline specialists is particularly important in the early phases of the product development cycle, and systemic communication throughout the cycle is critical, especially if the discipline specialists change during the cycle. The intent here is not to advocate the following approach as the best means of managing a complex and lengthy product development cycle, but to illustrate the need for the study of processes that include systemic communication.

Designing and documenting e-learning games may seem like any other product development project. However, our projects are unique in that they are spread over the course of several college semesters with a high student turnover rate and 15 to 20 students participating each semester.

The challenges we faced were to

- Keep project management consistent,
- Keep documentation consistent,
- Make sure that documentation was detailed enough to continue development with a new group of students,
- Educate new participants expediently,
- Train new participants about processes they were unfamiliar with,
- Have documentation easy to use and accessible for everyone to view, and
- Produce the product.

Our approach to the challenges, especially the high participant turnover rate, was twofold: to manage the project and to add a systemic process to communication as part of our product development cycle.

NEED FOR SYSTEMIC PROCESSES

This need for communication processes in a multidisciplinary context is being discussed in universities, government organizations, businesses, and other organizations that deal with the challenges of managing projects. For example, at Stanford University, the Center for Design Research (CDR) has been working with the Stanford Learning Laboratory (Learning Lab) to explore design processes. In a Stanford CDR white paper, Milne (2000) examines more closely the critical methods by which designers negotiate the creative process in a multidisciplinary context.

An example within state government is the state of Washington's detailed communication plan within their Project Management Framework, which outlines the roles and responsibilities of project participants in the review, approval, and dissemination of information about key project processes, events, documents, and milestones (Access Washington, n.d.). These guidelines help manage expectations regarding each project for both internal and external stakeholders.

Within the business community, a study conducted in a research and development (R&D) organization showed how technical communication within a laboratory is critical for successful R&D performances. The research also introduces the importance of a "gatekeeper" or project leader who links the organization with the internal and external stakeholders (Allen, 1977). This research suggests that the organization of team members, including their office layout, affects team communication (Allen, 1977). Later research showed that different types of communication depend on the physical location of team members. The results showed that although proximity of team members can increase communication, management has to promote communication or a collaborative approach will not occur (Allen, 2000).

Although close proximity of project members aids in communication, this is not always practical in today's global environment. Many businesses have intercompany communication challenges, especially those with remote business partners and outsourcing partners. One study outlined the issues that arose within multicompany project collaboration. The lack of defined communication methods and intercompany processes caused overreliance on project managers and lack of trust among team members (Paasivaara & Lassenius, 2001). The study does present solutions to the process, focusing on increasing intercompany understanding in the early stages of the project to build trust. Additional solutions included defining common operating procedures and creating an online monitoring system and central repository (Paasivaara & Lassenius, 2001).

Many software companies are addressing these intercompany communication problems by providing software solutions, through which these companies promise successful collaboration at no risk to business information assets. One company, CoCreate Software, provides a solution that supports business-driven partner relationships by creating effective human-to-human communication across businesses and disciplines. It increases partner communication and limits business exposure by extracting only the data for the project (Alpine, 2003).

This chapter describes the systemic communication environment as it relates to a particular type of interdisciplinary product development project, the creation of e-learning games. The challenge from a product development perspective that differentiates us from previous examples is managing a project with a high turnover rate of multidisciplinary specialists.

HOW WE DETERMINED OUR PROJECT METHODOLOGY

The project management of the group evolved from a modified version of the Rational Unified Process (RUP) software, which is an iterative framework, developed by IBM Rational Software, which identifies four phases of any software development project (see Figure 1). Over time, the project goes through Inception, Elaboration, Construction, and Transition phases. Each phase contains one or more iterations in which you produce an executable, but perhaps incomplete system (except possibly in the Inception phase). During each iteration, you perform activities from several disciplines in varying levels of detail (IBM, n.d.).

The important aspects of the RUP process to our project were the creation of a visual model, the iterative development, and the continuous verification of quality. The creation of a visual model early in the process allowed us to perform usability

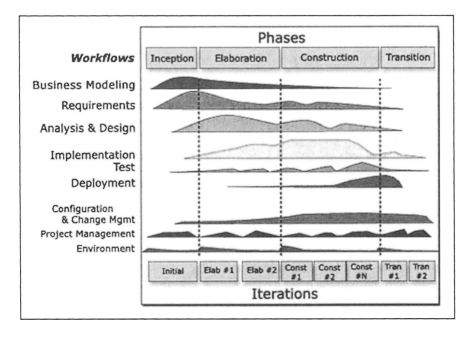

Figure 1. An overview of the RUP.

testing during each phase, but the RUP model did not help us manage a project with a high turnover rate of multidisciplinary specialists (IBM, n.d.).

Usability testing and the storage of data in a repository gave us the idea of using a communication environment as part of the iterative process. This environment diminished the issue of the high turnover rate of multidisciplinary specialists.

Usability testing included a series of tasks given to target individuals to determine how easy a system is to use and what additional problems need to be addressed. It was used throughout our iterative development to ensure the continuous verification of quality, which are best practices of RUP (IBM, n.d.). This approach worked well for us because it allowed for

- Constant testing throughout the development of the game,
- Less impact from requirement or design changes after development had begun, and
- Better management of a class with a high turnover in participants.

The organization of our large group of students evolved to some extent from the RUP workflows, but we added the communication environment as part of the iterative process. The large group reorganized into four subgroups: design, programming, usability testing, and marketing. Working with a large group of 15 to 20 students, who varied from semester to semester, project leaders found it important to maintain consistency of tasks and deliverables throughout the development life cycle, and they stored these documents in a repository for future multidisciplinary specialists.

COMMUNICATION AND DOCUMENTATION ENVIRONMENT (CDE)

To maintain an organized project and the documentation associated with it, project management needed systemic communication. Communication is an important attribute, not mentioned but assumed within the RUP process. "Communication leads to community, that is to understanding, intimacy and mutual valuing" (May, n.d.).

To create this community of better understanding, intimacy, and mutual valuing, we developed a Communication and Document Environment (CDE), which was added to the product life-cycle plan. We determined the following needs for a systemic process of communication in developing a product:

- A repository that is easily accessed by all team members and contains announcements, course information, discussion board, group documentation, and project progress
- A detailed project plan focusing on each team's responsibilities
- Specific tasks for each subgroup
- Regular whole-group meetings and subgroup meetings

A CDE was incorporated in every aspect of the development of CollegePursuit, a CD ROM-based 3-dimensional game intended to teach students and parents the fundamentals of financial aid in a college setting. Figure 2 shows our modified product life-cycle that incorporates CDE.

AN APPLICATION OF THE CDE PROCESS

The CDE process has been used successfully with the roll-out of two e-learning games and a third one under development. The example that we use here is CollegePursuit. This project was carried out under the direction of a professor and research assistant as part of Illinois Institute of Technology's (IIT) Interprofessional Projects Program (IPRO), which brings together students from different disciplines to solve real-world challenges. Figure 3 is a screenshot of the CollegePursuit 3-D e-learning game.

WHAT WE DOCUMENTED:
ORGANIZATION AND TASKS

Initially, detailed tasks were determined for each group throughout the development. With each task, detailed documentation was essential to the success of

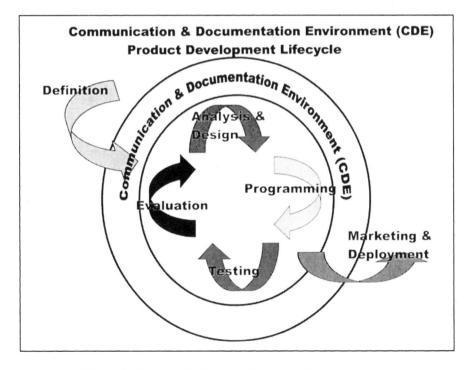

Figure 2. Communication and documentation environment product development cycle.

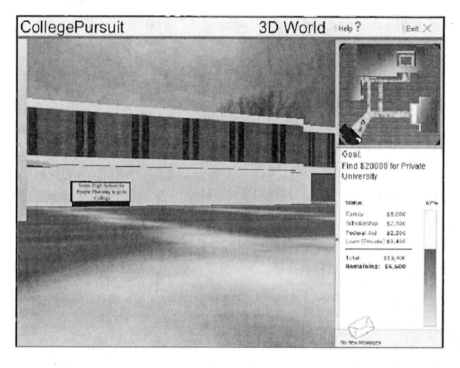

Figure 3. CollegePursuit 3-D game screenshot.
© 2004, The Interprofessional Projects Program at Illinois Institute of Technology.
All rights reserved.

our product development. Below are the subgroups we developed and their primary tasks:

Design: Create "look and feel" of the game, design functionality, document front-end flow of the game, create storyboards and game events, and document scoring for the game.

Programming: Develop beta version of the game; create development documents for easy transition next semester.

Usability Testing: Conduct usability tests throughout development and write up recommendations. Research financial aid information, create user manual, and produce documentation CD.

Marketing: Research content for the game and its feasibility, determine distribution of game software, design marketing materials, and create grant proposal for funding of game.

All participants of the project were assigned to a group, and a detailed project plan was created each semester with weekly assignments. A project timeline is imperative for the success of a project; otherwise, tasks are lost and deadlines are missed. Our project leader's role was to create and maintain the timeline, as well as ensure that all tasks were completed on time or adjust the timeline for any changes.

Creating a timeline can be very easy or very difficult depending on the viabilities needed. Microsoft Word or Excel can easily be used to track tasks, but a more sophisticated tool, such as Microsoft Project, can efficiently organize and track tasks along with resources to keep your projects on time and within budget. Figure 4 is an example of a small part of our project plan completed in Word. The timeline displays tasks by week and then by team responsibilities.

HOW WE DOCUMENTED

Project documentation provides a map to a project: what has been accomplished, what are the results, and what are the next steps. Documentation can be in the form of a word processing document, a spreadsheet, a graphic file, a presentation, system code, and so forth.

Content management applications and publishing software can be used as a content repository and distribution for print, Web, and other types of publishing. These tools can categorize information for easy archiving and retrieval. SharePoint, Intraspect, and Documentum are some content management applications available that are sophisticated in organization and retrieval. Our project did not need the complexity used in these applications. Instead, we had access to an internal tool, Blackboard 5, which is a high-quality and easy-to-use application for content management.

Weekly Tasks		
Week	Tasks and Deliverables	Completion Checklist
Jan 23-Week 1	Meet with team and review last semester	
	➤ Begin project plan	➤ Completed
Jan 30-Week 2	Programming	
	➤ Phase I - determine assignments and development scope	➤ Completed
	➤ Phase I - coding	➤ Completed
	Design	
	➤ Look & Feel - research resource needs	➤ Completed
	➤ Determine assignments and additional tasks	➤ Completed
	➤ Phase II - begin scope and requirements	➤ Completed
	➤ Website - determine assignments	➤ Completed
	Marketing	
	➤ Grant proposal - determine assignments	➤ Completed
	➤ Product Rollout Plan - determine product items (brochure, product packaging, target market for distribution, etc.).	➤ Completed
	Usability	
	➤ User Manual - determine assignments	➤ Deferred to week 3
	➤ Determine test methodology and assignments	➤ Completed

Figure 4. Detailed project plan for weekly tasks.

Using Blackboard 5, a flexible e-Learning software platform from Blackboard Inc., we created archives for each team to post and retrieve documentation, which could be stored for the lifetime of the project. Blackboard technology permitted every member to access all archived documentation. Because we used iterative prototyping for game design and testing, we had numerous versions of documentation, so we had a historical record of our problems, solutions, and changes.

We documented everything from design requirements to the user manual as well as the usability studies and the marketing proposal seeking funding. Because of the high student turnover rate throughout the three-semester product life cycle, students needed a way to "get up to speed" at an expeditious rate, and Blackboard provided this environment.

Blackboard categorized our information in five sections:

- Announcements—allowed project manager to post messages regarding special meetings or other announcements
- Course Information—allowed project manager to post general information regarding the project (that is, project plan, budget, etc.)
- Discussion Board—allowed a chat room for project participants
- Groups—allowed subgroups to post pertinent documentation to be accessed by all group members and authorized outside individuals
- Tools—allowed project manager to post finished tasks, showing the project team the status of all tasks

Figure 5 is a screenshot of Blackboard showing the Announcements page.

Throughout our project, a Communication and Documentation Environment was utilized and the tasks archived in the following screenshot, which tracks the outcomes, as shown in Figure 6.

OUTCOME USING THE NEW MODEL (CDE)

Although the organization of the team and the tools used to document materials for future participants provide the detail, the intent of this chapter is to advocate the need for the study of processes that include systemic communication in a multidisciplinary context. Specifically, our challenge from a product development perspective was to establish a communication model that provides a process for managing a project with a high turnover rate of multidisciplinary specialists. Based on our experience over three years, we have found that merging a product development process with the CDE produces a systemic model for achieving the following goals:

- Systematize project management
- Maintain consistent documentation
- Ensure archival history of the project to prevent repeat of errors
- Educate new participants expediently
- Provide access to all products during the project's life cycle
- Produce the product

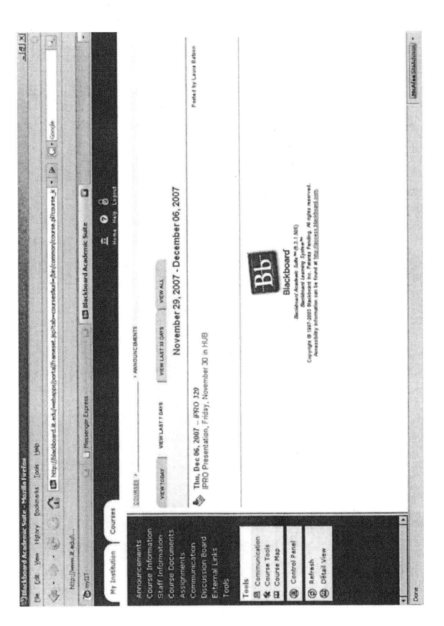

Figure 5. CDE supported by Blackboard.

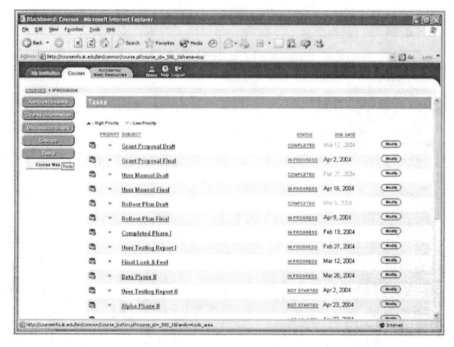

Figure 6. Documentation products archived in a CDE.

Although a stable team of project members aids in communication, this is not always practical in a university environment or today's global environment. Universities, government organizations, and businesses need a more robust communication environment to accommodate a high turnover rate of multidisciplinary experts. Our model advocates such an environment.

REFERENCES

Access Washington. (n.d.). *Communications plan.*
http://www.dis.wa.gov/pmframework/planning/communications.htm

Allen, T. J. (1977). *Managing the flow of technology: Technology transfer and the dissemination of technological information within the R&D organization.* Cambridge, MA: MIT Press.

Allen, T. J. (2000). Architecture and communication among product development engineers. In *Proceedings of the 2000 IEEE Engineering Management Society, EMS—2000* (pp. 153-158). Albuquerque, New Mexico.

Alpine, J. (2003). *Outsourcing product design: Best practices for project team collaboration.* http://www.cocreate.com/docs/IT_Whitepaper.pdf

May, R. (n.d.). *Rollo May Quotes. ThinkExist.com*
http://thinkexist.com/quotation/communication_leads_to_community-that_is-to/339274.html

IBM. (n.d.). *Rational unified process.* http://www-306.ibm.com/software/awdtools/rup/

Milne, A. J. (2000). Analyzing the activity of multidisciplinary teams in the early stages of conceptual design: Method and measures. In S. Scrivener et al. (Eds.), *Proceedings of Co-Designing 2000 Conference.* Coventry, UK: Springer, London.

Paasivaara, M., & Lassenius, C. (2001). Communication in new product development networks—A case study. In *Proceedings of 8th International Product Development Management Conference.* Enschede, The Netherlands.

CHAPTER 20

Virtual Office Communication Protocols: A System for Managing International Virtual Teams

Kirk St.Amant

Online media have expanded the concept of the "office" to virtual environments in which individuals regularly interact with co-workers from other nations. Factors of access and labor cost, moreover, indicate technical communicators will become increasingly involved in international virtual offices (IVOs). Yet the same technologies that overcome traditional barriers of distance can intensify problems related to cultural communication expectations. Technical communicators therefore need to understand how cultural factors can affect online discourse. This chapter examines some of the more problematic areas related to IVOs. It also presents strategies readers can use to avoid miscommunications in IVO settings.

TECHNICAL COMMUNICATION: A FIELD IN TRANSITION

Cyberspace has created a series of new workplace trends. One of the more interesting of these is the use of "virtual offices"—work contexts in which individuals in different locations use online media to interact. The use of such workplaces, moreover, appears to be growing, perhaps due to the perceived benefits of more flexibility, quicker responsiveness, and enhanced knowledge management activities (Burn & Barnett, 1999; Ruppel & Harrington, 2001). Technical communicators, in turn, seem ideally suited for these virtual offices because their job tasks parallel both the tasks for which virtual offices are best suited (creating, modifying, and evaluating information) and the knowledge management activities that can benefit from virtual office models (Belanger, 1999; Ruppel & Harrington, 2001). Thus, technical communicators could increasingly find themselves working in virtual office environments.

Virtual offices will also become more international as the adoption of such workplaces coincides with the growth of international online access. A variety of public- and private-sector programs have allowed India and China to experience rapid growth in online access (When India Wires Up, 2000; Wired China, 2000). Similar programs have helped expand online access in South America and Africa (Kalia, 2001; Tying Latin America Together, 2001). This access brings quick and easy connections to inexpensive yet highly skilled technical workforces in developing nations. For this reason, more online workspaces are becoming IVOs in which employees from different cultures interact (Baily & Farrell, 2004). As IVOs often include subject matter experts (SMEs) (e.g., technicians and engineers) located in other countries, technical communicators will likely find themselves participating in IVOs.

Cultural groups, however, can have different expectations of what constitutes effective and acceptable communication in a professional exchange. On a more general level, different cultures often use different strategies for proving an argument or for persuading an audience. Stephen E. Weiss (1998), for example, explains how individuals from six cultures (Mainland Chinese, French, Japanese, Mexicans, Nigerians, and Saudis) use different methods of organization and persuasion. Other researchers note these cultural variations can also occur at a more microlevel and include expectations of sentence length or implications related to the use of individual words (Li & Koole, 1998; Ulijn & Strother, 1995). Moreover, some research indicates such differences can cause problems in international online exchanges even when all parties are using the same language (Artemeva, 1998; Ma, 1996). Technical communicators will therefore need to understand how cultural factors could affect IVO interactions if they wish to work successfully in such environments.

The remainder of this chapter examines five problematic areas related to culture and IVOs. These areas were selected because they are some of the most common aspects of interacting in IVOs, and they have received relatively little attention in the research literature. The examination of each area includes an explanation of why it is problematic and provides strategies for addressing potential problems in relatively easy but effective ways.

AREA 1: MAKING CONTACT

Making and maintaining contact with others is essential for virtual offices to work. Making contact, however, requires all parties to have a similar understanding of how and when contact should be made; yet cultures can differ markedly on these two points. Such variations can lead to miscommunication and confusion in the virtual workplace.

Expectations related to communication behavior are often linked to the norms of one's culture. (The individual's culture teaches him or her how to behave in various communication situations.) Likewise, cultures teach individuals how to interact via different communication technologies. Many Americans, for example, believe an e-mail merits a quick response. In Ukrainian culture, however, face-to-face communication tends to be preferred, especially in a business setting (Richmond, 1995). Thus, an e-mail to Ukrainian co-workers might not provide as rapid a response as American counterparts might expect. Different cultural assumptions related to e-mail could therefore cause cross-cultural confusion.

One particularly problematic assumption related to IVOs is *when* one should contact international co-workers. Many Americans expect co-workers to be accessible at any time during the work day or work week with the exception of certain holidays (e.g., Christmas day). In France, however, it is not uncommon for offices to close to observe the traditional two-hour lunch period, generally from noon to 2:00 p.m. (Weiss, 1998). Such differences can cause confusion and affect how individuals participating in IVOs interact and perform tasks.

Additionally, international time differences make quick responses to unscheduled messages difficult. These time differences also mean that online messages containing context-sensitive words like *today*, *yesterday*, and *tomorrow* could have different meanings for the sender and the recipient. If, for example, I tell my colleague in Japan I need a report by "tomorrow," do I mean tomorrow according to my time, or do I mean tomorrow according to his time (which could be two days from the time at which I sent the message)?

Therefore, technical communicators must adopt the following communication strategies that account for such cultural and time differences:

- **Agree upon a preferred method for making contact in relation to IVO interactions.** All parties need to agree upon the best means of contacting others when a quick response is essential. They then need to develop a backup plan if this option fails. For example, what does one do if the quick response mode is e-mail, but the electricity fails at a critical time (not uncommon in some eastern European countries)? One solution could be to establish an agreed-upon backup source both parties can easily access (e.g., cell phones).
- **Establish a mutual understanding of when one can contact and be available to receive messages from IVO counterparts.** Technical communicators need to know the time differences as well as vacation and holiday schedules of overseas counterparts. One can use this information to plan for when the earliest response to a message could be received. Such timing information should be provided to all parties from the start of IVO interactions.
- **Establish a single meaning for temporal terms.** Technical communicators should avoid relative date references like "tomorrow" or "yesterday." They should instead provide the day and the date (Monday, October 4) and a chronological context according to the recipient's time frame (e.g., Netherlands time). For example, tell Dutch colleagues data is needed by "Monday, Oct 4, 16:00, Netherlands time," in order to restrict relativistic interpretations.

By following these steps, individuals can increase the chances of making and maintaining contact with co-workers in other nations.

AREA 2: CULTURAL APPRECIATION

The success of virtual offices depends on the ease with which individuals can locate data and exchange information. These disclosure and exchange practices, however, require a degree of trust among all parties. The problem with IVOs is that cultural perceptions of "outsider" can lead to suspicions that affect the levels of trust needed for effective information sharing (Hofstede, 1997; Richmond, 1995). The faceless nature of online exchanges could heighten such suspicions, especially for individuals from cultures that favor face-to-face discussions (St.Amant, 2002). Good working relationships are therefore essential to IVO success, and the more comfortable co-workers are with one another, the more likely they are to exchange information openly.

One way to create effective cross-cultural rapport is to display an understanding of and an appreciation for other cultures. Such displays can create a positive initial impression by revealing that the individual has taken time to research the culture (responsibility and initiative). They also imply that the person is open to working with individuals from other cultures (objectivity). Additionally, displaying knowledge of another culture can indicate interest in forging a long-term relationship, for individuals would not learn specific cultural information if they were not interested in making a relationship work for the long term (Campbell, 1998).

Individuals can use two strategies to display cultural appreciation for international co-workers:

- **Capitalize on geographic information.** If international counterparts mention the name of the region or city in which they are located, learn where that region or city is, and in future communiqués, pose questions that display knowledge of this geographic information. If, for example, a French counterpart says she is from Pau, the individual should learn where that town is and later ask a question such as, "Pau is near Toulouse, isn't it?"
- **Use key phrases in the native language of the overseas counterpart.** Simple opening and closing expressions (e.g., *hello, how are you*, or *thank you*) show an appreciation for another culture and display one's openness to working with other linguistic groups. Additionally, the use of such phrases is an "offensive" strategy, for one does not have to wait for co-workers to provide the geographic or other information needed to make a follow-up comment. These phrases, moreover, do not need to be memorized. Rather, individuals can use a basic foreign language phrase book to locate expressions in other languages. Individuals should, however, stick to the basic phrases, for using phrase books to devise more complex communications could result in awkward and embarrassing messages.

The strategies mentioned here also have the benefit of being rather unobtrusive and can be used regularly and over long periods of time without becoming old. Individuals or organizations that have frequent contact with a particular culture might consider creating a "quick cultural reference guide" containing maps and a list of important phrases in the other language in order to make it easier to locate certain culture-specific information.

AREA 3: STATUS AND COMMUNICATION EXPECTATIONS

Some cultures permit a level of flexibility to circumvent official channels in order to achieve a particular goal. In the United States, for example, individuals with a good idea might be able to present it directly to their division manager rather than having to route it through an immediate supervisor. In other cultures, organizations are more rigid, and employees must use formal channels to interact with superiors. In such systems, attempts to bypass standard processes to contact higher-status individuals are looked upon unfavorably and could be risky to one's career (Hofstede, 1997). Breaching such expectations, moreover, could be something as simple as e-mailing someone at a higher corporate level—a practice rather common in the United States.

In cultures where status is important, formality also tends to be important. In such cultures, one is expected to know when and with whom to be formal and the titles and stylistic conventions used to maintain formality. Americans, however, tend to be quite informal (e.g., many Americans are on a first-name basis with their boss). In IVOs, such factors can become more problematic as research indicates the use of informal tones and styles—even in business exchanges—seems to be exacerbated by online communication technologies (St.Amant, 2002).

To avoid creating turmoil in IVOs, technical communicators should

- **Learn the hierarchy structure present in the cultures with which they interact.** Once this system is identified, the technical communicator should learn how closely individuals must follow the expectations of that system and what repercussions could result from circumventing it. The idea is that individuals who violate the status-communication expectations of a given culture could jeopardize important relationships or erode trust among parties.
- **Determine who one's counterparts are in the context of another culture.** Such information is often needed to ensure that messages go to the correct individual and not to someone of higher status. Technical communicators should also confer with international counterparts before contacting high-status persons from that culture. By transferring information and requests to a counterpart who knows the particular cultural system, individuals can make sure information gets to the correct recipient in the desired manner.
- **Identify high-status individuals in one's own culture to use when sharing information with superiors in other cultures.** Individuals can work with such persons in situations in which it is essential to get information to high-status persons in other cultures. By forming such "preemptive relationships," individuals have someone they can call on to facilitate cross-cultural communication in situations involving high-status individuals in other cultures.

- **Avoid given/first names when addressing someone from another culture.** Rather, use titles such as Mr. or Ms. If the individual has a professional title (e.g., Dr.), use that title when addressing him or her. Ideally, IVO employees should learn the titles of respect used in a given culture and use those titles when communicating with persons from that culture (e.g., Herr Schmit or Madame St. Onge). Using such titles also displays appreciation for the culture of the message's recipient (see previous section on Cultural Appreciation).
- **Learn the naming conventions used by different cultural groups.** Such knowledge can help individuals avoid mishaps related to naming and formality. In the Japanese culture, for example, an individual's family name comes first and is followed by his or her given name. Thus, a name like "John Smith" would become "Smith John." Hence individuals should familiarize themselves with the naming conventions of their cultural partners to make sure the correct degree of formality (e.g., Mr. Smith vs. Mr. John) is used.

Although this advice might seem simplistic, individuals must remember that operating effectively in IVOs is about making and maintaining contact. It is therefore important to recognize status-based expectations to avoid offense and keep communication open.

AREA 4: LANGUAGE OF COMMUNICATION

IVOs often require individuals from different linguistic backgrounds to interact within the same virtual space and through "common tongue." That tongue is often English as it is a main language of international business, science, and technology communication (Eisenberg, 1996).

As technical communication involves interacting with SMEs, it is safe to assume that IVO exchanges will often be in English. This assumption, however, brings with it problems related to fluency. Just because one speaks English does not mean he or she speaks it well or understands the subtle nuances of its use (Varner & Beamer, 1995). Rather, several factors can affect the quality of English-language education in other regions (Rodman, 1996). Additionally, various English dialects exist, and while similar, certain differences could cause communication problems (Crystal, 1995). Individuals who make incorrect assumptions about an international counterpart's fluency in or dialect of English could create messages that confuse that counterpart.

The text-based nature of online exchanges further confounds the issue of language proficiency in IVOs. Individuals generally use nonverbal cues like accents or intonation patterns to determine whether someone is not a native English speaker or is a speaker of a different dialect. Such determinations help individuals use language more carefully to improve listener/recipient comprehension. Yet online media often remove cues that signify language or dialect differences. Without these cues, individuals might forget that an international counterpart is not a native English speaker or forget that a counterpart speaks a different dialect of English.

E-mails, for example, are often brief, and individuals tend to be more tolerant of spelling and grammar errors. The language limitations of an international counterpart might thus be overlooked. This oversight could cause communication problems as English speakers might unknowingly use expressions unfamiliar to speakers of English as a second language (ESL). Strategies technical communicators can use to address these factors include

- **Avoid idiomatic expressions.** Idiomatic expressions are phrases that have a specific cultural meaning different from their literal meaning (e.g., "It is raining cats and dogs" does not mean animals are falling from the sky). ESL speakers, however, have no way of knowing how to interpret the actual (vs. literal) meaning of idioms unless told otherwise (Jones, 1996).
- **Avoid abbreviations.** Abbreviations require a particular background to understand the expressions they represent (Jones, 1996). Understanding the meaning of "IRS," requires one to know that there is an "Internal Revenue Service" and that it is commonly abbreviated using the first letter of each word. If abbreviations are essential, spell out the term upon first use and use some indicator to demonstrate how the abbreviation is formed, such as, "This passage examines the *I*nternal *R*evenue *S*ervice (IRS)."
- **Know the dialect of English spoken by one's counterparts.** Although many English dialects are similar, certain differences can cause comprehension problems. Speakers of various dialects can use different terms for the same object or concept or could have different meanings for the same term. Dialects can also use different idioms or different spellings for the same word. Such differences can cause confusion if individuals in IVOs do not realize international counterparts are using a different dialect of English.

By following these steps, English-speaking technical communicators can improve the chances that co-workers will correctly understand an English-language message.

AREA 5: NUMERIC REPRESENTATIONS

Numbers are central to many business communiqués, yet cultures can use different methods to present numeric information. Failure to recognize such differences can cause confusion or costly mistakes. Of these differences, dates and magnitudes are perhaps the most important to consider.

Dates

In the United States, dates are often written in the order of the month, the day, and then the year, so April 1, 1998 becomes 4-1-98. In other countries, however, the order of the month and the day are often reversed, so 1 April 1998 is represented numerically as 1-4-98. These variations can result in problems if individuals from different cultures associate alternative meaning with the same numbers (e.g., a

French company tells its American suppliers to ship a product on the fourth of January 2006, but used "4-1-06" to present that date).

Magnitudes

Representations of magnitudes help readers understand values and quantities. Many cultures, in turn, have developed punctuation-based markers to help readers recognize magnitude. Such punctuation, however, can result in certain miscommunications in international virtual offices.

The problem is that cultures might assume that certain punctuation marks represent different magnitudes. Many Americans, for example, use commas to indicate large scale (e.g., thousands, millions, billions, etc.) and use periods to indicate fractions such as one half (0.5). The French, however, use periods to indicate large magnitudes (e.g., 1.000 for one thousand) and use commas for fractions or smaller magnitudes (e.g., one half = 0,5). As technical communicators use technical data when creating documents, such differences could cause problems, especially if readers are processing large amounts of data in a hurry.

Technical communicators can take certain steps to address magnitude differences in IVOs:

- **Spell out the month when presenting dates in a document.** Dates written as January 1, 2006 or 1 janvier 2006 prevent assumptions of what number represents the month and what number represents the date.
- **Know the magnitude format used by international counterparts and present magnitude data in that format.** Again, the idea is to make assumptions of sender and receiver match, and catering to the expectations of a given cultural audience is one way to achieve this end.
- **Begin communiqués by stating the magnitude system used.** Doing so helps avoid problems related to different assumptions of what punctuation mark represents a particular scale of magnitude.

These few informative steps can help employees in IVOs improve the chances their international counterparts correctly understand numeric information being presented.

CONCLUSION

Today, widespread use of e-mail and corporate intranets has changed the office from a physical location to a state of mind. It has also opened the office to co-workers from different cultures and countries. This chapter examined five problematic communication areas related to international virtual offices (IVOs) and has presented strategies for working efficiently in this international environment. Readers must now learn more about the cultures with which they will regularly interact, for such understanding is essential to working effectively in an IVO context.

REFERENCES

Artemeva, N. (1998). The writing consultant as cultural interpreter: Bridging cultural perspectives on the genre of the periodic engineering report. *Technical Communication Quarterly, 7,* 285-299.

Baily, M. N., & Farrell, D. (2004, July). Exploding the myths of offshoring. *The McKinsey Quarterly.*
http://www.mckinseyquarterly.com/article_print.aspx?L2=7&L3=10&ar=1453

Belanger, F. (1999). Communication patterns in distributed work groups: A network analysis. *IEEE Transactions on Professional Communication, 42,* 261-275.

Burn, J., & Barnett, M. (1999). Communicating for advantage in the virtual organization. *IEEE Transactions on Professional Communication, 42,* 215-222.

Campbell, C. P. (1998). Rhetorical ethos: A bridge between high-context and low-context cultures? In S. Niemeier, C. P. Campbell, & R. Dirven (Eds.), *The cultural context in business communication* (pp. 31-47). Philadelphia, PA: John Benjamins.

Crystal, D. (1995). *The Cambridge encyclopedia of the English language.* New York: Cambridge University Press.

Eisenberg, A. (1996). Using English as the international language of science. In D. C. Andrews (Ed.), *International dimensions of technical communication* (pp. 1-4). Arlington, VA: Society for Technical Communication.

Hofstede, G. (1997). *Cultures and organizations: Software of the mind.* New York: McGraw-Hill.

Jones, A. R. (1996). Tips on preparing documents for translation. *Global Talk,* 682-693.

Kalia, K. (2001, July/August). Bridging global digital divides. *Silicon Alley Reporter,* 52-54.

Li, X., & Koole, T. (1998). Cultural keywords in Chinese-Dutch business negotiations. In S. Niemeier, C. P. Campbell, & R. Dirven (Eds.), *The cultural context in business communication* (pp. 186-213). Philadelphia, PA: John Benjamins.

Ma, R. (1996). Computer-mediated conversations as a new dimension of intercultural communication between East Asian and North American college students. In S. Herring (Ed.), *Computer-mediated communication: Linguistic, social and cross-cultural perspectives* (pp. 173-186). Philadelphia, PA: John Benjamins.

Richmond, Y. (1995). *From da to yes: Understanding the East Europeans.* Yarmouth, ME: Intercultural Press.

Rodman, L. (1996). Finding new communication paradigms for a new nation: Latvia. In D. C. Andrews (Ed.), *International dimensions of technical communication* (pp. 111-121). Arlington, VA: Society for Technical Communication.

Ruppel, C. P., & Harrington, S. J. (2001). Sharing knowledge through intranets: A study of organizational culture and intranet implementation. *IEEE Transactions on Professional Communication, 44,* 37-52.

St.Amant, K. (2002). When cultures and computers collide. *Journal of Business and Technical Communication, 16,* 196-214.

Tying Latin American together. (2001, Summer). *NYSE Magazine,* 9.

Ulijn, J. M., & Strother, J. B. (1995). *Communicating in business and technology: From psycholinguistic theory to international practice.* Frankfurt, Germany: Peter Lang.

Varner, I., & Beamer, L. (1995) *Intercultural communication in the global workplace.* Boston, MA: Irwin.

Weiss, S. E. (1998). Negotiating with foreign business persons: An introduction for Americans with propositions on six cultures. In S. Niemeier, C. P. Campbell, & R. Dirven (Eds.), *The cultural context in business communication* (pp. 51-118). Philadelphia, PA: John Benjamins.

When India Wires Up. (2000, July 22-28). *The Economist*, 39-40.

Wired China. (2000, July 22-28). *The Economist*, 24-28.

CHAPTER 21

Knowledge Management in the Aerospace Industry

David J. Harvey and Robert Holdsworth

Aerospace is a global industry that employs several million people worldwide. It is a diverse industry, with organizations ranging from multinational aircraft manufacturing companies to companies that manufacture components, to others that manage and operate the vehicles that deliver tools and other supplies. The industry employs a diverse range of workers, from engineers and scientists to general tradesmen, storemen, and baggage handlers.

The industry has two main arms—Civil Aviation and Military Aerospace—both of which represent "big business" to the countries in which aerospace companies reside. The industry is characterized by the following traits:

- Technically diverse and complex systems, dependent on a huge amount of data, information and knowledge, and an increasing need for this to be shared
- Rigid compliance standards governed by design, maintenance, and operating regulations that not only ensure safety requirements are met, but are essential for interface as well as functional and operational compatibility
- Strong downward pressure on prices and margins such that airlines fail or prosper on small changes in aircraft "up time" or availability
- Design solutions and decisions that are critical to airworthiness and personnel safety

The key "drivers" in the aerospace industry's need to embrace knowledge management, and the reason a number of the larger aerospace companies are already doing so, include

- The dispersion of organizations, companies, operations, and suppliers;
- The need for reorganization and change to meet changing customer needs and business environments;

- Demographic issues, particularly the aging of the engineering and scientific population;
- Complexity and interdependencies of systems, requiring access to an incredible range of information and knowledge; and
- Safety and airworthiness assurance across a variety of regulatory environments.

In essence, like any other industry, the aerospace industry expects that any knowledge management initiatives will produce cheaper products more quickly, without compromising product or personnel safety, while maintaining an acceptable level of business risk.

As is the case with many high-technology industries, the aerospace industry has begun identifying the potential of various knowledge management initiatives it could or should pursue; however, a number of barriers are perceived in maximizing the potential benefits.

COMPLIANCE AND SAFETY ISSUES

The aerospace industry is regulated by a variety of agencies across a number of national and regional boundaries. To maximize safety and airworthiness, regulatory authorities place significant demands on the need for consistency and repeatability of process and the rigorous recording and reporting of incidents and accidents. The focus has predominantly been on ensuring that operators, engineers, and maintenance have access to as much accurate information as possible, and that the quality of outcomes (operation, design, and repair) is somehow assured. The intention is that safety be built into the product through the application of accurate data, appropriate tools, and proven processes by trained and authorized people.

Process

Although the process rigor that regulation brings to the industry appears to conflict with the flexibility required of, and sought within, the knowledge management-focused organization, it is potentially through improved knowledge management that regulations can be more flexibly applied. For example, regulations often require a greater number of process steps (e.g., supervisory inspections) when work is to be performed by less qualified or authorized personnel; that is, those less skilled or less knowledgeable. Conversely, work performed by a highly trained workforce would in general require less process definition and hence enable greater flexibility. Thus, improved knowledge management may enable regulatory requirements to be met more efficiently. However, while automation and trusted systems can contribute to the process rigor, the competency of individuals (and hence appropriate authorization) will still have to be assured through objective and subjective assessment.

Information Disclosure

Previously, Taylor and Felton coined the phrase "managing in the void" (Patankar, 2004) to describe the case whereby people are required to make decisions in situations they haven't previously encountered, such as when a maintenance instruction is not specific enough or when an aircraft configuration is different from that which is documented. In today's aerospace maintenance environment, "the void" is becoming larger or more frequent, partially due to a relative decrease in tacit knowledge and partially due to time and cost constraints. Improved knowledge management is fundamental to providing teams and individuals with increased access to others' knowledge, and therefore improving their collective ability to operate successfully in this void. The focus must then shift to assuring the integrity and validating the context of the available knowledge.

One of the paradoxes facing regulators within the aviation industry relates to how much information should be made public. While on face value, the public, and probably the industry in general, would call for full disclosure of information regarding aircraft safety, there is a significant downside.

On the one hand, making known those incidents that have occurred to, or errors made by, one carrier could potentially reduce the likelihood of occurrence to other carriers. However, there is a danger of competitors using such information to discredit another airline or a public perception arising that a particular airline is unsafe, when the majority of its reported incidents had little to do with its own practices or operations. This could then lead to an increased reluctance to report incidents, reduce the level of industry knowledge, and result in reduced safety over time.

The point here is that knowledge management is not simply about providing as much information to as many people as possible and as quickly as possible. It is about information context and optimization of information to maximize knowledge where and when it is required. Providing people (e.g., the flying public) with information that they don't need, can't understand, or may misinterpret is equally as bad as not providing information that they do need; it does not increase "real" knowledge.

Competency and Authority

As previously identified, the competency and authority of individuals is another pillar of airworthiness and safety assurance. Without doubt, improved knowledge management will provide more people access to more information with a consequent increase in security or comfort ("If I have all the information, how can I make a bad decision?").

The inherent danger is in people erroneously equating information with knowledge; believing that they have enough knowledge when all they have is a wealth of information, or perhaps having knowledge that is not applicable in the current context or situation. For example, in Australia I have learned to look right, then left, then right again before I cross the road, but if I applied this knowledge in the United States, without knowing that cars travel on the opposite side of the road there, it could be very dangerous. A person who has learned all his or her relevant knowledge in one environment (or context) may be quite capable of making repair decisions in that particular environment (e.g., 747 aircraft structure), but in a similar environment (e.g., Joint Strike Fighter aircraft structure), his or her knowledge of repair techniques may be invalid. Ultimately, the quality of the decision is a function of wisdom rather than knowledge, that is, the application of knowledge to a particular situation or in a particular context. Thus, there is a need to ensure the validity of the knowledge being applied.

In authorizing people to make decisions, the authority or regulator must (through objective and subjective assessment) assess their knowledge and their competence to apply this knowledge in the correct context. Where the regulator's knowledge base incorporates knowledge of people's competence and the context in which they gained that competence, there is a sounder basis for assessment and a potentially wider scope of authority may be granted.

In the most critical airworthiness situations or designs, independent review or independent verification and validation are often mandated in order to provide a satisfactory level of assuredness. This is largely because, regardless of knowledge and expertise, people are fallible. Knowledge management won't reduce the need for this, but may improve an organization's ability to identify when and by whom the independent review is to be performed. This would ideally be facilitated through having timely access to relevant knowledge of the technical and safety risks associated with the current and previous similar designs.

While at times, as in many other technology-based industries, the regulations and regulators struggle to keep pace with the technologies available, the authors' experience in the Australian military regulatory environment is that regulators can be open to the introduction of automated process, and electronic reporting and information systems, provided a guaranteed level of certainty of compliance can be demonstrated. The onus, however, has been, and should be, on the regulated organization to make the case for change.

Knowledge management should not be considered an alternative to regulation nor a guarantee of safety. Although knowledge management will not replace the fundamental requirements of assured individual competence, controlled delegations of authority, validity of process and data, and independence of review where applicable, it can

- Facilitate rapid identification of alternative decision makers or subject matter experts (potentially in parent organizations or subsidiaries);
- Improve the quality, quantity, and accessibility of the information available to authorities and decision makers (and hence potentially increase their knowledge);
- Provide improved contextual information (e.g., the latest competency assessment and experience of the original designer can be made available to the approver of the design);
- Increase the likelihood that all relevant information has been considered;
- Reduce preparation and review time and in doing so free up key people to be applied to approvals and certification;
- Ensure that the key people are able to spend more time sharing knowledge and wisdom; and
- Facilitate retention of knowledge/skills of key employees.

So, far from being seen as incompatible with stringent regulatory environments, knowledge management should be seen as a means of bringing efficiency to such an environment in terms of content management and distribution, training, and knowledge transfer.

ORGANIZATIONAL ISSUES

Knowledge harvesting—the understanding, collation, dispersion, and exploitation of what the company already knows—offers huge potential gains, particularly to the large aerospace companies. The technical knowledge possessed by the tens of thousands of employees of these companies is incredible, and the ability to identify and access this knowledge globally and in real time would represent a huge competitive advantage. So, what is so difficult today, where the technology appears to be widely available?

For large aerospace companies the problem is not so much the technology but the logistics and costs involved in implementing the technologies and knowledge management processes.

Let's first consider the issues associated with the identification and storage of currently held knowledge that has not previously been "managed." In the case of a military aerospace systems manufacturer with operations in a variety of countries, these issues may include the following:

- Was the knowledge developed for a national government, foreign government, or another contractor, or as part of a self-funded R&D activity?
- Who owns the rights to distribute and use this knowledge and under what circumstances?
- Is the knowledge subject to any security classification or caveats, and therefore, who is allowed to access and exploit this knowledge (according to company rules and government and international laws)?
- Does the International Traffic in Arms Regulation (ITAR) apply?
- What should be done with the huge paper-based information legacy, particularly when aircraft operate for upwards of 30 years?
- Does administrative staff have appropriate knowledge and security clearances to categorize and store the legacy content?

The transition of the entire suite of legacy knowledge, much of which relates to key aircraft and systems documentation such as design specifications and calculations, manufacturing processes and drawings, to new management systems, represents an enormous "one-off" cost to large companies. Unfortunately, the costs of sorting and validating this data prior to transition to improve integrity and reduce future management overheads is also burdensome.

In practice, knowledge that could be advantageous to certain teams or agencies within the company may not be releasable to those people. Situations even arise in which foreign employees who have made considerable contributions to aspects of a company's knowledge are then precluded from accessing their own knowledge "products" once these have been classified and released to the end customer.

The contracting and development of large aerospace projects typically takes place over many years, such that the implementation of a company's intellectual property may take considerable time to materialize. Therefore the protection of information and technology over extended periods is usually given greater importance than the sharing of knowledge.

Further conspiring against knowledge management initiatives is the inherent nature of large companies—large bureaucracies, long-term contracts, and large-scale products that are tied to the current processes and infrastructure, and a wide demography with vastly differing expertise with the required technologies.

Having determined that a knowledge management environment is to be established, and having identified the appropriate technologies, large aerospace organizations, like any large company, will still find the transition to new automated systems difficult because

- The organizations are typically "stove-piped" in terms of the tools and systems they use (these individual tools are often integrated with customer systems);
- Projects often run over many years, and tools and systems may be project- or platform-specific;
- Very large projects may involve multiple companies, each of whom has its own proprietary systems and processes, leading to inherent dispersal of information and knowledge;
- There is a reluctance to change systems that are "working just fine" on individual projects; and
- Budgets for process improvement and training are often held at a program or project level, yet the benefits from the introduction of knowledge management practices are not evenly distributed across the organization (so "who pays?" becomes a significant issue).

The aerospace industry by nature is conservative and bureaucratic, with a significant portion of its personnel being ex-military. In order to "face off" with the customer, the basic organization structure has a strong correlation with the customers' organizational structure. Hence, particularly when the customer is defense or government, the structure is often hierarchical and deep. In such organizations, the improvements brought about by the establishment of knowledge management practices and technology will be limited by these structures and the corresponding delegations and authorities, and the application of knowledge will consequently be suboptimal.

As with all large businesses, the cost of doing business inefficiently is considerably more difficult to track than the cost of upgrading IT systems and conducting training across tens of thousands of staff, hence justifying the cost of large-scale change represents a significant challenge.

Karl-Erik Sveiby, Professor in Knowledge Management at the Swedish Business School, believes that the confusion between knowledge and information has caused managers to invest billions of dollars in information technology for little return (Malhotra, 1998). The aerospace industry would be as guilty as any other in this regard. The implication is that before embarking on knowledge management initiatives, management needs to become more knowledgeable about the existing business environment and what it is the company hopes to achieve through these initiatives.

Overall it can be extremely difficult for multinational defense aerospace companies to identify just what they do know, what competitive advantage may be accrued through managing this knowledge, and what this advantage will be worth. Even having identified that implementation of knowledge management practices and systems will be of benefit to the organization, it is extremely expensive and time-consuming for these companies to identify and implement processes and systems that will ensure the integrity and validity of information and knowledge, and that the security of classified and proprietary knowledge is safeguarded.

PEOPLE ISSUES

As identified by S. M. Suryanarayana, "It's the collaboration and use of the relevant knowledge that presents the issue" (2002). Creating the right environment for interaction of staff represents another challenge to the aerospace industry. Particularly in defense aerospace, there are large costs involved in just making collaboration and communication possible. As previously identified, security and IP safeguards are always a concern, and there is often an underlying fear of a net negative outcome in the information exchange between companies (i.e., "They will learn more from us than we will from them").

Within large aerospace companies, as in most large organizations, employment terms and conditions as well as remuneration systems are generally based on companywide standards; status and remuneration are usually more closely correlated with employees' accountability and responsibility than with their knowledge, innovative potential, or flexibility.

However, in some aerospace companies, there has been a recent awakening to the inherent value of the organization's capability, that is, its people and their knowledge and skills. Training, mentoring, and knowledge sharing are in some instances taking on greater precedence, with an aim to "growing" people faster.

The perceived knowledge management challenges also relate to the types of people found within the industry. Whereas managers may gain their self-esteem from the size of their budget, numbers of staff, or position in the organization chart, the self-esteem and status of scientists and engineers is often a function of what they know. Although there is often an organizational expectation that these people will share their knowledge through goodwill, this could be considered akin to the willingness of an executive to share his personal assistant or his budget. Furthermore, these key technical employees are often not "people persons" and may also require training in communication and mentoring in order to maximize their effectiveness.

Recognition of the knowledge and competencies of technical personnel, and particularly their knowledge-sharing efforts, such as that offered by Boeing's Technical Fellowship, is a positive move toward retaining and leveraging the organization's knowledge base. Such recognition is the first step in establishing a level of trust and mutual commitment between the knowledge seeker (the organization and its young employees) and knowledge providers (the organization's graybeards).

As in any a project-based, schedule-driven industry, it is often difficult to find the time and space to create and share knowledge. This is because it is inherently difficult to place a value on this activity when your current project is behind schedule or there is an aircraft full of passengers awaiting an engineering decision to enable it to take off. In the absence of quantifiable measures that value learning or knowledge-sharing activities, such as metrics on the long-term outcomes and returns, their justification will be difficult and may have to rely on the tacit knowledge of the approving manager (or on a leap of faith).

CONCLUSIONS

The aerospace industry is characterized by a number of factors seen as significant drivers for establishing knowledge management systems within organizations. A number of challenges exist for companies within the industry in implementing knowledge management initiatives. This chapter has identified that while aviation's regulatory environments may not appear ideally suited to a knowledge management environment, the application of knowledge management practices to the implementation of regulations may offer considerable efficiencies and flexibility. Increasing the available knowledge and making it more readily available may reduce process overheads and ensure better use of key people.

The aerospace industry's business and operating environment presents some challenges to the implementation of knowledge management initiatives. These challenges include the organizational size and structure, the vastness of the existing knowledge base and storage, as well as access issues. Because of the considerable investment that will be required by large companies, a key to actually deciding to pursue knowledge management initiatives will be a clear understanding of the cost savings, risk mitigation, and competitive advantage that may accrue were these initiatives adopted.

FUTURE WORK

The authors intend to carry out further work in the following knowledge management areas:

- Achieving management involvement and understanding of the knowledge management needs of technical environments (in the absence of detailed understanding, management will generally only champion implementation of initiatives, when personal risk is low)
- Strategies for specifying and executing large knowledge management projects. (New initiatives in large companies often begin in a blaze of glory but fade away without achieving the desired outcome—the "damp squib" phenomenon.)

- Capturing knowledge /skills as people work, to avoid the "brain drain" when they retire/leave
- Optimizing the knowledge management environment for configuration management

REFERENCES

Malhotra, Y. (1998, July/August). Deciphering the knowledge management hype. *The Journal for Quality & Participation.* http://www.brint.com/km/whatis.htm

Patankar, M. S. (2004). Causal-comparative analysis of self-reported and FAA rule violation datasets among aircraft mechanics. *International Journal of Applied Aviation Studies, 2*(2), 87-100.

Suryanarayana, S. M. (2002). Information management challenges from the aerospace industry. In *Proceedings of the 28th VLDB Conference* (pp. 1006-1007). Hong Kong, China.

CHAPTER 22

Using Their Digital Notes: Three Cases to Make Tacit Knowledge Visible in a Web-Based Surrounding

Liesbeth Rentinck

Knowledge management (KM) is important for many organizations. The National Institute for Health and Environment in the Netherlands is a governmental office that benefits people, society, and the environment, matching their expertise, knowledge, and research with that of colleagues from around the world. In its position as an executive government advisory board, it is obvious that knowledge is the main target of this organization.

This chapter elaborates on the development of a new method of knowledge communication where the work of the scientist is the core of the knowledge that is used in the communication. This method can contribute to the sharing of implicit and tacit knowledge in an organization. By developing applications that make it possible to share the knowledge through an XML database directly extracted from the work of scientists, it is possible to manage this knowledge directly from the source: the work of the scientist. Three cases are presented here in which these applications are used to manage knowledge.

THEORETICAL FRAMEWORK ABOUT KNOWLEDGE MANAGEMENT

No organization can function without information. And when there is information, it needs to be managed. To classify the different processes of KM, Tiwana (1999) introduced the concept of "focus," which deals with management choices about the desired knowledge. This focus contains strategic and operational knowledge.

KNOWLEDGE MAPPING

After establishing a KM strategy, it is very important to investigate the detailed knowledge that is necessary for an organization. This investigation process is called "knowledge mapping" by Boersma (2002). Knowledge maps are important for the strategic operations on knowledge, but an organization needs a structure to recognize and find the knowledge within this organization. It is important to disclose the essential information. Many KM experts such as Weggeman (1997) advise using a KM system.

An organization may consist of "bunches" of knowledge islands. When these islands are spread around the organization and the culture of the organization is very local, it is very difficult to place all the knowledge islands into one structured system. To solve this problem, Weggeman (1997) proposed "yellow pages," a system that tells where information can be found. Regardless of what system is used to store the information or how the information is embedded, these yellow pages can give an overview of the existing information. Davenport and Prusac (1998) also speak of yellow pages. In case three of this chapter, I describe how to use an XML-based yellow pages system as a metastructure to disclose the information islands.

As Miranda and Saunders (2002) described in their article, there is a common ground in the knowledge within an organization. Knowledge is a social construct; knowledge is constructed within the social setting of an organization or group. For example, when two surgeons meet, they can communicate about their profession because they express their thoughts within the schema of their profession.

WHAT IS KNOWLEDGE?

According to Weggeman (1997), knowledge (K) is described as an instrument to fulfill a task. This process depends on the information (I), the experience of the employee (E), the skill (V) of this employee, and his or her values and beliefs (attitude [A]). This scheme can be described in a mathematical formula as $K = I * EVA$. For example, if a man has to paint a house, the knowledge (K) he uses for this job is affected by the fact that he knows implicitly (I) that the house cannot be painted on the outside when it rains. He is quite experienced (E) in painting houses; he has the skill (V) to use a paintbrush. And finally his background beliefs result in an attitude (A) causes him to post notices with the text "wet paint" because he does not want his work to be damaged by touching it before it is dry.

My problem with this elaboration on knowledge is that it presumes a human factor about knowledge that is assigned to a certain task. Knowledge can be seen as a set of instructions that is embedded in an action (such as making cars or painting houses) and that can be used by the target group (mechanics, painters).

Van Engers (2001) has another definition of knowledge (see Figure 1).

In this model, there is a transition from unformalized knowledge toward formalized knowledge. Elicitation, structuring, and formalizing are recognized as elaborations on this transition. This model is more applicable to knowledge for a group

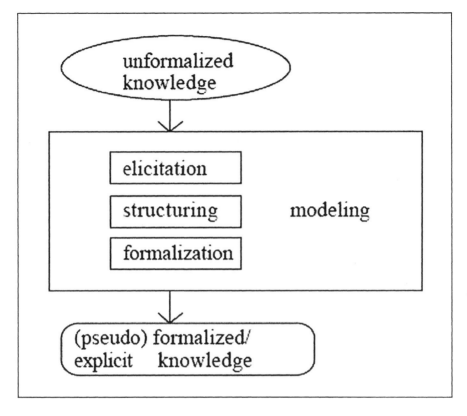

Figure 1. Van Engers's model of knowledge modeling (2001).
Reproduced with the permission of Tom Van Engers.

of employees, but the elaborations are only applicable to knowledge defined in rules. In his thesis, Van Engers (2001) defines KM as an instrument for making decisions. KM contains an implicit boundary for the knowledge: by defining the decision task, we predefine and formalize the knowledge.

Another definition of knowledge is from Davenport and Prusac (1998). They define the following steps for the transition of information into knowledge: categorization, calculation, conceptualization, condensation, correction. These factors are called the five Cs. This definition is very applicable, but only for the functional elaboration of information to transform it into knowledge. It tells nothing about the specific goal of knowledge.

What binds these models is that knowledge is a construct. There is a transition to change data into knowledge, and the domain of the knowledge is restricted. The constructed knowledge is valid only in a certain context. The purpose and the context are important for the kind of transition that is used to construct the knowledge. Therefore, in this chapter, I use the following definition of knowledge:

> Knowledge is a transition of data to construct information that can be interpreted by a target group within a recognizable context.

In this definition, it is clear that there is a difference between information and knowledge. Someone can use this knowledge to change its information into meaning. If we compare this definition to the rules and decisions of Van Engers (2001), the rules might be seen as the transitions of data for the income tax categories of the target group.

In my definition of knowledge, I use *interpreted* because knowledge has its source in the human rational mind. The transitions must fit closely to the target group and must be interpretable within the intended context. The five C's of Davenport and Prusac can be used to construct the knowledge.

Boersma (2002) made a distinction between categories of knowledge: facts, procedures, interpretative knowledge, and background knowledge.

These first two categories of knowledge have already been mentioned here; the last two categories are different. Whereas facts and procedures can be uniform to a large group, interpretative knowledge requires processes in the human mind. The information requires us to infer background knowledge with the new knowledge to interpret this information to execute the task. A transition of facts and procedures results in interpretable knowledge.

Managing implicit or tacit knowledge is not easy. This knowledge is not explicitly defined, so it needs interpretation and inference. Tacit knowledge, which resides mainly in a person's mind, is often called the "human capital" of an organization. A lot of so-called tacit knowledge resides on "sticky notes" and lists on personal computers, which can be made explicit within a KM system. Many employees use a structure within these notes. The human mind strives to structure knowledge (Kintsch, 1998). This structure is important for the inferences of old knowledge with new knowledge.

In this chapter, I will describe a method through which this "hidden" knowledge can be shared with other employees. The knowledge manager's challenge is to use this tacit knowledge for knowledge sharing, which can enlarge the knowledge capital of an organization and make it less vulnerable. This concept is from the point of view of "information deliverers," not the "information users" that York & Studer (2001) described in his report. This approach is chosen because experiences with other projects, in which information systems were designed to store information, failed due to a lack of accessible information. By using the information deliverers' approach, I hope to get convenient information for knowledge sharing. This does not mean that the "circle" of knowledge mapping (determining the available knowledge, determining which knowledge is missing, and suggesting measures to fill the "gap" of missing knowledge) must be denied. Many intranets fail and become simply bulletin boards for documents as Stenmark (2003) describes. He pleads for an open intranet concept to stimulate creative, innovative actions by employees. In this view, a scheme-free approach is a step toward this design.

TRANSFORMING INTO XML AND PUBLISHING

Within the Dutch National Institute for Health and Environment (RIVM), hidden knowledge is translated into XML databases. XML is a free-form translation format that can be used to label pieces of information. Because of this feature, it is very convenient for the different forms of tacit knowledge we want to "catch" in a knowledge system.

Many sticky notes or other examples of hidden knowledge are written by scientists in Excel, and a Visual Basic macro is designed to translate the Excel spreadsheet into an XML database, for which no scheme is used, because this would hinder the creative and free generation of knowledge. JavaScripts and XSL (Extensible Stylesheet Language) functions are designed for the publication of these scheme-free XML databases.

If several scientists want to integrate their scheme-free XML databases, they must all agree about the fieldnames of the integrated information. If, for example, scientists want to publish a table with the standards for substances from two different authorities, they must use the same fieldname for the names of the substances. With this constructed relation (fieldname), the information from these two XML databases can be integrated in one publication.

The final versions of the XML databases are embedded in an intranet and an Internet Web site. Within this setting, the hidden information on standards, abbreviations, group members, and so on is transited into explicit shared knowledge. Generic JavaScript and XSL functions support the publication of integrated information.

A MODEL FOR KM

From this theory about knowledge and the practical application for KM, it is possible to create a KM model (see Figure 2).

For publication on the Internet, a content management system (CMS) is used. All elements are placed in a coherent structure within this CMS. This approach empowers the structure of all published elements and manages the links and changes of the content of an element.

A different solution is chosen for intranet publications for integrated XML information and for tables with links to other documents. The information about the documents or the XML databases is placed in a separate XML database. This database is also transformed from an Excel file into XML. This XML database consists of the metadata about the underlying XML tables or documents in a different format. It is a metastructure to enclose and manage the different databases and documents.

There are two different ways of publishing on the Internet: publication of the metastructure with links to documents (not in XML), and publication of all XML information in the metastructure.

These two publications can be filtered with a search task that retrieves only the documents or information for which the user is searching.

In a schematic model, this metastructure can be described as follows (see Figure 3).

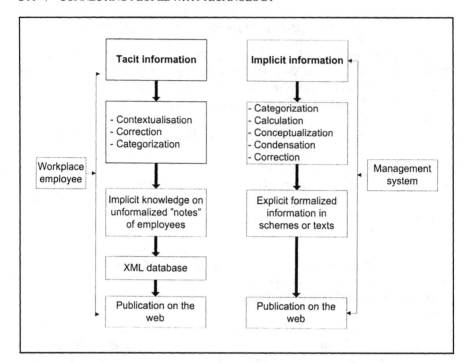

Figure 2. Model for managing implicit and explicit knowledge and publishing on a Web site.

THREE PRACTICAL CASES

At the RIVM, the method for knowledge management described here is practiced in three different situations in which a shared and published knowledge system is necessary. One case is for publishing on a public Internet site (www.stoffen-risico.nl); the other two cases are published on an intranet site in the RIVM organization. These cases are described in the following paragraphs.

Case 1. Information about Standards for Substances

The first case involved implementing a page on the Internet about standards for risks of substances. These risk standards were established by different authorities, and it was very difficult to determine whether a substance was included among these standards. By drawing on the different Excel tables of these authorities prepared by the members, the data remains the responsibility of these members. They can change data, add data, or formulate rules to put the data in a different context. In terms of knowledge from the five important Cs of Davenport and Prusac (1998)—categorization, calculation, conceptualization, condensation, correction— we see that these members add rows to their table to categorize their

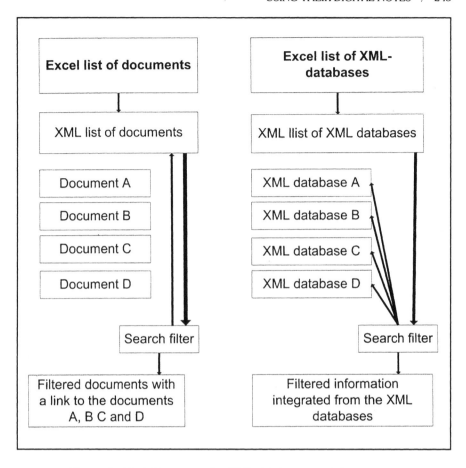

Figure 3. Model for managing XML databases and documents.

substances into groups of risk standards. They add columns with references to reports about the method used to calculate the standard. They add extra columns with names of organizations to establish the authority of these standards and thus create the context of these standards. And finally, they create new rows in the table when a new standard is established to correct the old standard. Because the scientists maintain the data in Excel spreadsheets, they can detect and correct errors very quickly.

This is a way to make the scientists feel involved in the "knowledge process"; it became clear that scientists want to play a role in the transition from information to knowledge. They still see the published knowledge as their own data and that fact is very important. It helps to keep the data up-to-date. The Excel tables of the scientists are enriched with some rules. The names of the columns and a row with directions for publication are added, along with simple assigners to filter out the data or to add a hyperlink or a URL to a document. When these enrichments are made, the data is transferred by the scientists into an XML database with a Visual Basic macro. This XML data is used for an integrated search environment on a Web site.

Shortly after publishing these lists of standards on an Internet site (http://www. stoffen-risico.nl) there was a change in information-seeking behavior by the scientists themselves. Instead of contacting different scientists to ask questions about standards, they discovered that it was much easier to use the Internet site to search for the substances. The base Excel table was no longer a difficult instrument, but a solid base for publishing and searching for different substances.

A point of consideration is the maintenance of this concept. An environment has been created to store the XML databases, and an assistant has been trained to add search queries for the Internet pages.

Case 2. Sharing Knowledge on the Intranet

Since publishing the standards for substances, more Excel tables were found to be suitable for publishing on an intranet site. The secretary's office is mainly responsible for these Excel tables, but other employees also offered tables to publish on the intranet. It was possible to transport these tables in XML with the Visual Basic macro from Case 1. Because there was already a set of JavaScript functions for publishing the results from Case 1, these functions were also suitable for the tables for the intranet site. Figure 4 illustrates an example of an intranet page with buttons to search an XML table.

Importing this information inside an intranet page proved to be a very good start for a knowledge-sharing network. Instead of browsing through directories with possibly suitable Excel tables, now the information is displayed within a usable navigation menu on an intranet site. The first reactions have been positive because of the transparent publication of the information. The Web site also proved to be an instrument to control and correct the information in the Excel sheets.

Considerations on These Two Cases

In both cases, the success of the concept depended on the amount of freedom in implementing the concept. There is no predefined DTD scheme (Document Type Definition) for the Excel tables; the XML is generated from the information in the Excel tables themselves. The owners of the data are responsible for the data and the few rules for their Excel tables. If they want to integrate their information with other XML databases, they can negotiate with other owners about their fieldnames to relate the same information in each other's tables; but this is not always necessary. The search process is free within the fields of the XML table, and this provides freely integrated searches through a list of XML tables. Even the list of tables (the so-called yellow pages of the knowledge maps) can be generated from Excel tables.

An example of such an integrated publication of data from different XML databases is shown in Figure 5.

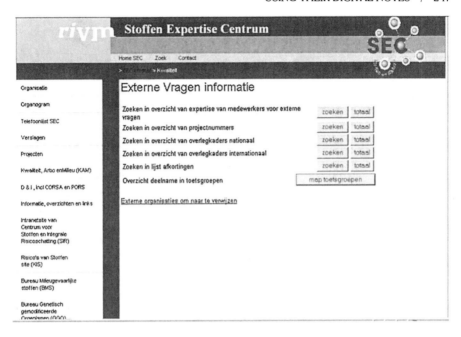

Figure 4. Example of an intranet page with buttons to search an XML table. Reproduced with the permission of the Dutch National Institute for Public Health and the Environment.

Case 3. Yellow Pages for Quality Documents

In the third case, a special solution was devised for the wider distribution of quality documents. For quality purposes, some documents (such as quality handbooks) must be available to all employees. But the documents are stored in a distributed system in different formats (Word, Excel, PDF, etc.). These documents are maintained in different divisions within the organization.

The solution was to create Excel tables with lists of documents available to all employees. These tables are yellow pages that tell where the documents are stored and what information the documents contain. By placing a hyperlink to the defined document in the Excel table, it is possible to open the requested document. Every department has its own Excel table with a list of documents. These tables are transported into XML tables and disclosed in the same way (using JavaScript functions on an intranet) as in Cases 1 and 2. To provide a listing of all documents together, a yellow-page XML is generated.

The difference between this Case and Cases 1 and 2 is that columns of the Excel table are predefined, like a DTD. But there is still the freedom to make more columns in the Excel table. The employees of the different departments are trained to maintain their own Excel tables and to transport them into an XML database. Because of the

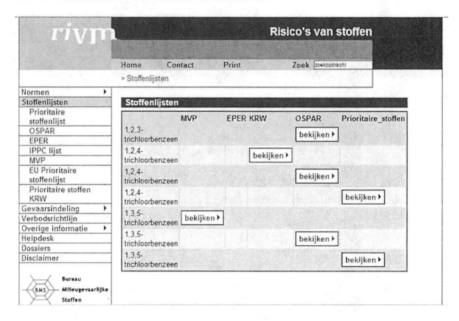

Figure 5. Example of an intranet page with information from
different XML databases on the search term *Benzene*.
Reproduced with the permission of the Dutch National Institute
for Public Health and the Environment.

large number of participants, the Visual Basic macro must contain some predefined
solutions (such as path and name of the XML database, as well as translation of
keywords) and also some predefined column names (which will be translated into
XML fieldnames in the Visual Basic macro) for the final publication in an intranet
site. The Excel template must be more robust to avoid errors and misunderstandings.

CONCLUSIONS AND DISCUSSION OF
THE THREE CASES

All three cases were based on the concept of a free use of XML. But it is very
important to design good Visual Basic functions to transport the Excel tables into an
XML database. A set of JavaScript or XSL functions is needed to publish this XML
database information on a Web site. The corporate network must contain a place to
put the documents. Employees must be trained to use the Excel tables and to
transport the tables into XML databases. By providing the Webmasters with a set of
JavaScript or XSL publishing functions, information can be published without
difficult HTML programming. What is left is an environment in which it is possible
to enable communication about the knowledge of the scientists. Without XML
transformation and publishing of this XML data, every table must be redesigned
when the data changes or the context of justification changes. This would require a
lot of effort by an HTML programmer.

Providing a process in which the scientists can direct their own *a posteriori* constructed knowledge and publish it immediately on a Web site is a step toward knowledge sharing in a manageable way.

GENERAL CONCLUSIONS

In this chapter, I described three cases of knowledge management. It proved to be important to use a system that is very close to the work of the scientists and the managers of documents, who can keep control over their own work and the way the information is published in a defined context. Tacit, implicit knowledge is not only in the head of scientists, but is often captured on their own digital notes. These notes are very important if we want to promote knowledge sharing, and we must encourage them to export them in XML databases so that this information can be published within an organization. Also, yellow pages with metainformation about XML databases and documents can be handled in the same way. This approach results in an environment where not only the information in the scientists' digital notes can be shared, but also the metainformation about these notes, and even other documents can be captured in this system.

The concept described here will contribute to this knowledge sharing. But informing people about the concept and generating enthusiasm for joining the system is very important in making the project successful. This task must not be underestimated.

REFERENCES

Boersma, J. (2002). *Management van Kennis*. Assen: Van Gorkum.

Davenport, T. H., & Prusac, L. (1998). *Working knowledge: How organizations manage what they know*. Boston, MA: Harvard Business School Press.

Kintsch, W. (1998). *Cognition, a paradigm for comprehension*. Cambridge, MA: Cambridge University Press.

Miranda, S. M., & Saunders, C. S. (2002). The social construction of meaning: An alternative perspective on information sharing. *Information Systems Research, 14*(1), 87-106

Nieuwenhuyzen, P., & De Meulder A. (2004). *Informatie Professional, 8*(12), 34-37.

Stenmark, D. (2003). Knowledge creation and the Web: Factors indicating why some intranets succeed where others fail. *Knowledge and Process Management, 10*(3), 207-216.

Tiwana, A. (1999). *Knowledge management toolkit: The practical techniques for building a knowledge management system*. Paramus, NJ: Prentice-Hall.

Van Engers, T. M. (2001). *Knowledge management*, article published by the Dutch Tax Services.

Weggeman, M. C. D. P. (1997). *Kennismanagement*. Schiedam: Scriptum.

York, S., & Studer, R. (2001). *On-to-knowledge methodology*. On-To-Knowledge EU IST-1999-10132 Project Deliverable D16.

Contributors

SUSAN ALLENDER-HAGEDORN has been a science and engineering writer and editor for over 25 years, and she has taught Technical and Business Writing, editing, and literature classes at several U.S. universities (for the last 19 years at Virginia Tech, Blacksburg, Virginia). Although she teaches in an English Department, her doctorate is in Science and Technology Studies, and her major research interests lie in the communication of science to the public, public perceptions of science, and science rhetoric. Currently, as well as teaching, she is founding editor of an international peer-refereed science journal, *The Journal of Environmental Detection,* and she is Webmaster of the award-winning Public Perceptions of Biotechnology Webpage (http://filebox.vt.edu:8080/users/chagedor/fileboxmigration/cals/cses/chagedor/index.html). She also is bibliographer for the Society for Literature, Science, and the Arts.

LAURENCE ANTHONY is Associate Professor in the School of Science and Engineering at Waseda University, Japan, where he teaches technical reading, writing, and presentation skills, and is coordinator of the technical English program. He received the M.A. degree in TESL/TEFL, and the PhD in Applied Linguistics from the University of Birmingham, United Kingdom, and the B.Sc. degree in mathematical physics from the University of Manchester Institute of Science and Technology (UMIST), United Kingdom. His primary research interests are in corpus linguistics, educational technology, genre analysis, and natural language processing.

CAROL BARNUM is Director of The Usability Center and Professor of Information Design and Communication at Southern Polytechnic in Marietta (Atlanta), Georgia. She is the author of *Usability Testing and Research* (Allyn & Bacon/Longman, 2002).

JENNIFER BARRICK is an International Project Engineer working in Microsoft's Windows International division. Her Master's degree in Technical Japanese/Technical Communication and her longtime interests in cross-cultural and computer-mediated communication are in action every day as she helps millions of people across the globe access up-to-date and locally relevant user content on Microsoft Web properties.

ALEXANDRA ("SANDY") BARTELL is a technical communicator and Web designer at The Boeing Company. She is a member of the Administrative Committee and co-chair of the Electronic Information Committee for the IEEE Professional Communication Society (PCS), as well as a senior member of the Society for Technical Communication (STC). Sandy received an MBA from Monmouth University and her Masters in Science in Technical Communication at the University of Washington where she is currently pursuing her PhD studies. Her primary areas of interest information design and usability applied to electronic media.

LAURA BATSON is currently a PhD candidate in Technical Communication at the Illinois Institute of Technology (IIT). She is currently teaching English Composition, Technical Communication, and Inter-Professional Development at the IIT. In addition, she is an accomplished technical communication specialist skilled in usability, instructional design, technical writing, and project management. She has managed projects for over nine years, managing all phases of the product development life cycle.

KIM SYDOW CAMPBELL is Professor and Derrell Thomas Faculty Fellow in the Culverhouse College of Commerce at the University of Alabama. Her most recent work focuses on rapport management within workplace relationships. She collaborated with Alabama Medicaid Agency in creating a multimedia educational product for primary care physicians designed to enhance the physician-patient relationship through a better understanding of health literacy and medical home. Her research has been published in *Business Communication Quarterly, College Composition & Communication, Health Care Management Review, Environmental Professional, Journal of Business Communication, Journal of Business and Technical Communication, Journal of Technical Writing and Communication, Management Communication Quarterly, Technical Communication Quarterly,* and *Technical Communication.* She has served as editor-in-chief of the *IEEE Transactions on Professional Communication* since 1998.

ELISABETH CUDDIHY is a doctoral student in the Department of Technical Communication at the University of Washington. Her primary area of interest is in the development of methodologies and supporting tools that aid user interface designers during the design process. She is also interested in information design, information visualization, and education. Elisabeth holds a Master's degree in Computer Science from the State University of New York at Buffalo and has worked in the software industry designing scientific software applications.

DAVID DAYTON, formerly an associate of The Usability Center at Southern Polytechnic, now teaches technical writing and information design at Towson University in Baltimore County, Maryland.

PAUL M. DOMBROWSKI is Professor of English at the University of Central Florida, specializing in technical communication, ethics, and rhetoric and the doctoral program in Texts and Technology. He has published two books, *Ethics in Technical Communication* (2000) and *Humanistic Aspects of Technical Communication* (1994), and numerous articles on technical communication and ethics, particularly regarding the shuttle *Challenger* and *Columbia.* He has also taught technical communication and writing at Ohio University, Pennsylvania State University, and Rensselaer Polytechnic Institute.

MARGARETHA ERIKSSON, B.Sc., M.Sc.E.E., SMIEEE, works as professional translator, technical writer, and Project Manager at Irbis Konsult AB, Stockholm, Sweden. She began her career as a technical translator at IBM in Stockholm 1989 with OS and software, followed by further translations into Swedish for major brands at Oracle, HP, SAP, Kodak, and Vodafone. As terminology expert she has translated electronic and engineering terms in Eurodicautom and term databases into Swedish. She is actively involved in the creation of IT related terminology in Sweden and a member of STC (Nordic), IEEE PCS, and SFO.

SUSAN FEINBERG is Professor of Communications and Director of the Usability Testing and Evaluation Center at Illinois Institute of Technology. She is a Fellow of STC and recipient of the Jay R. Gould Award for Excellence in Teaching Technical Communication. She and the IIT interdisciplinary teams have won numerous awards for the design and development of e-learning games for adults and students in grades K-12.

MARIE-LOUISE FLACKE has over 15 years experience in international documentation, localization, and usability testing. Maitre de Conferences associee at the Universite de Haute-Bretagne (UHB) since January 2007, she teaches technical communication to multilingual students as part of the university's multimedia Master's program (http://www.master-en-traduction.net/). She also teaches technical writing at the University of Brest (UBO) and the University of Paris 7. A graduate of the Technical Writing Program at the American University of Paris, Marie-Louise has worked for a diverse range of companies in the IT, telecoms, network security, aeronautics, and pharmaceutical industries. In 2003 and 2006, she was appointed Judge to the STC Trans-European Technical Communications Competition. Her professional memberships include the French society for technical communication (CRT), the STC France Chapter, and the UK Association of Proposal Management Professionals (www.ukapmp.org). From 2003 to 2006, she was Vice President of INTECOM (www.intecom.org), the international council of technical communication societies.

KEVIN GILLIS is Vice President of Managed File Transfer Products at Ipswitch in Lexington, Massachusetts. He has managed and shipped to market over 100 commercial product releases for respected properties, including WS_FTP, WhatsUp, *TIME Magazine,* Lotus, and IBM, generating over $200 million in sales.

SVAFA GRÖNFELDT is President of Reykjavik University.

RENU GUPTA has a PhD in language education from Stanford University and is an Assistant Professor at the University of Aizu. She has over 30 years of experience in language education in the United States, Singapore, India, and Iran. Her research interests include bilingual education and the media, writing systems, and teacher beliefs. Her research has been published in the *ESP Journal, British Journal of Educational Technology,* and *Journal of Education for Teaching.*

DAVID HARVEY has 24 years' experience in the Defense Industry including 15 years in the Australian Defence Force and nine years with Boeing Australia. Mr. Harvey has worked in areas of avionics engineering, logistics, and maintenance management. More recently, he has been involved with engineering capability management, including Capability Maturity Model initiatives, process improvement, workforce planning, configuration management, and airworthiness regulations. He is now interested in looking at strategies for defining, undertaking, and measuring organizational improvement, including knowledge management initiatives. Mr. Harvey has completed Master's Degree in Engineering Science, is currently undertaking Environmental Engineering studies and is a keen artist.

MARK HASELKORN is founding chair of the Department of Technical Communication in the College of Engineering at the University of Washington and he also founded and directs the UW's Interdisciplinary Program in Humanitarian Relief, a cross-campus program of research and education that works closely with the international humanitarian sector. Dr. Haselkorn is currently leading an NSF initiative to define and mobilize the research community for the emerging frontier of "Humanitarian Service Science & Engineering." He has worked with the military on a number of projects, including the integration of DoD and VA electronic medical records and the Air Force's strategic management of ICT under the threat of Y2K (a study published by the National Research Council). He has conducted foundational research in the area of intelligent transportation systems and managed a series of projects totaling over $3M, including development of the first Web-based real-time traveler information system (Traffic Report, 1990). Dr. Haselkorn is the incoming President of the IEEE Professional Communication Society.

ROBERT HOLDSWORTH has 30 years' experience in electronics and aerospace, including 17 years in defense-related work. Mr. Holdsworth has predominantly worked in the design of complex systems, including aircraft systems integration, control systems, microprocessors, and communications systems. As Boeing Australia's Chief Engineer for military aircraft, and a Boeing Technical Fellow, he promoted process and system improvement, and mentoring and training initiatives to increase the organization's knowledge levels. He has recently left Boeing to establish his own electronics business. He has a Master's degree and PhD in Electrical Engineering and loves nothing more than spending an afternoon "tinkering" with cars.

CAREL JANSEN is a full professor in Business Communication at the Radboud University Nijmegen in the Netherlands. He is also affiliated as extraordinary processor with Stellenbosch University in South Africa. Carel Jansen published books and articles on professional communication and on research into information and document design. For more information, see http://www.careljansen.nl

JOSEPH JEYARAJ completed his PhD in Technical and Professional Communication at Illinois State University and currently teaches technical and professional writing in the School of Engineering and Computational Sciences at Liberty University. He created the field of postcolonial technical communication and specializes in technical and professional writing, postcolonial rhetoric, and pedagogical theory. He has published in journals such as *The Journal of Business and Communication, Pretexts: Literary and Cultural Studies,* and *The Knowledge Society Journal* and has other publications forthcoming in journals like *College*

Composition and Communication, The Journal of Technical Writing and Communication, and *The Indian Journal of Public Affairs and Policy Research.*

STEVEN B. KATZ is the Roy Pearce Professor of Professional Communication at Clemson University. He is the co-author with Ann Penrose of *Writing in the Sciences: Exploring Conventions of Scientific Discourse,* and *The Epistemic Music of Rhetoric.* Dr. Katz has written several articles on the rhetorical ethics of environmental, medical, and technical communication, and has been the recipient of the National Council of Teacher's of English Award for Best Article on the Theory of Scientific and Technical Communication; some of this work has been reprinted, most recently in *Central Works in Professional Communication* (Oxford University Press, 2004). He also has presented papers on biotechnology communication—at the American Association for the Advancement of Science (subsequently published in AgBioForum), Crop Life Canada—and has consulted internationally with the biotechnology and pesticide industry on communicating ethically with the public.

SETH S. LEOPOLD, MD, is Vice Chair of the Department of Orthopaedics and Sports Medicine at the University of Washington. His clinical specialty is hip and knee replacement surgery, and minimally-invasive joint replacement. His areas of research interest outside the surgical domain include identification and measurement of the influence of unusual sources of bias in the clinical literature, the relationship between confidence and competence in psychomotor skills education, and use of the Internet to promote patient self-education on health-related topics.

ALFONS MAES is a full professor in Communication Sciences at Tilburg University, the Netherlands, and is head of the research program "Communication and Cognition." He published articles on discourse reference, document design, instructive discourse, multimodal and digital communication. For more information, see www.tilburguniversity.nl/faculties/humanities/people/maes/

CHRISTINA MAIERS is a Senior Consultant at MTG Management Consultants, LLC, a technology and management consulting firm that serves local and state government agencies throughout the United States and Canada. Ms. Maiers has a Master of Public Administration (MPA) from the Evans School of Public Affairs at the University of Washington, and a Master's Degree (MA) from Central European University in Budapest, Hungary. While attending the University of Washington, Ms. Maiers was a research assistant for the Interdisciplinary Program on Humanitarian Relief (IPHR), and received a fellowship to analyze humanitarian logistics in East Africa. Ms. Maiers received the 2005 Pealy Prize for the best international degree project for the research conducted during this fellowship. Before attending the Evans School, Ms. Maiers was a part of the democratization effort in Kosovo and monitored parliamentary elections in Central Asia for the Organization for Security and Cooperation in Europe (OSCE), in addition to working with local non-profit organizations in Romania and Serbia.

BRANDON MAUST received a dual degree in English and Biochemistry from the University of Washington. He is currently working under Professor James Mullins in the Department of Microbiology on Viroverse, a project to collect and analyze clinical and laboratory data in infectious disease research. His programming background is in system administration and Web-based applications.

LEO NOORDMAN is a Professor Emeritus of Discourse Studies at Tilburg University in The Netherlands. His research concerns psycholinguistic processes in text comprehension, in particular inference processes.

JOE O'CONNOR is Documentation Manager of File Transfer Products at Ipswitch in Lexington, Massachusetts.

THOMAS ORR, PhD, is Professor at the University of Aizu and Director of the university's Center for Language Research, where he conducts research on professional communication in science and technology with the aim of developing effective educational programs and materials of especial benefit to nonnative speakers of English. He has taught English for more than 20 years to native and nonnative speakers in the United States and Japan, and has had his research published by IEEE, Wiley-InterScience, Halldin, Rodopi, Baywood, TESOL, JALT, JACET, and others.

WHITNEY QUESENBERY is a user researcher and usability expert with a passion for clear communication. She has been in the field since 1989, working with companies from The Open University to the National Cancer Institute. As a member of two U.S. government advisory committees, she is working to create accessibility requirements and to improve the usability and accessibility of voting systems for U.S. elections. Her most recent publication is a chapter on "Storytelling and Narrative" in *The Personas Lifecycle,* by Pruitt and Adlin. She's also proud that one of her articles won an award as a Society for Technical Communication (STC) Outstanding Journal Article, and that her chapter "Dimensions of Usability" in *Content and Complexity* turns up on so many course reading lists. Whitney has served as President of the Usability Professionals' Association (UPA), and manager for the STC Usability SIG. She created a popular usability Web site at http://www.stcsig.org/usability. She helped launch World Usability Day on November 3, 2005, bringing together people at over 100 sites around the world to highlight the need to "make it easy." Before she was seduced by a little beige computer into the world of usability, Whitney was a theatrical lighting designer on and off Broadway. The lessons from the theater stay with her in creating user experiences.

LIESBETH RENTINCK is an information and communication advisor at the National Institute for Public Health and the Environment (RIVM) in The Netherlands. With an education in informatics and communication sciences, she can make a bridge between technical issues and communication challenges. She works in the section Environment and is involved in several (Web-based) projects on communication issues. One of her last projects is an Environment Portal for professionals. Strategic communication plans for corporate branding of the work of the RIVM are one of her specialties. In the past few years, she also worked on a research project on professional writing with new media.

MARGARET REYNOLDS earned a Masters of Public Administration (MPA) student at the Evans School of Public Affairs, University of Washington (UW). Before joining the the Evans School, she worked within the American Chamber of Commerce in Shanghai and the Asian Law Research Center at the UW. During her time in graduate school, she conducted extensive research on humanitarian relief logistics and information systems and led an interdisciplinary student research initiative on the role of GIS in humanitarian relief.

CHERYL WOOD RUGGIERO has taught composition, technical writing, and grammar at Virginia Tech since 1974, has edited science and engineering documents, has edited Virginia Tech's composition textbook, is author of two widely-used Web sites (the Grammar Gym; Plagiarism and Honor), and serves as Virginia Tech English Department Assistant Chair. Her interest in connecting popular culture and science grows from experiences with students preparing for research careers, as well as with their professional mentors: few recognize where their scientific ethics, assumptions, and values come from. She hopes to encourage exploration of the linguistic and social spaces where science lives.

KIRK ST.AMANT is an associate professor of Professional and Technical communication at East Carolina University. His research interests include international online interactions, international e-commerce, and international outsourcing, and he has previoulsy taught courses in international business, business communication, and business ethics for the Consortium of Ukranian Management Education (CEUME) and the Kyiv Mohyla Business School. He has also worked as an ESL tutor and tutor trainer, and has been the Director of Tutoring (and a specialist ESL tutor) for the Online Writing Center at the University of Minnesota.

REINHARD SCHÄLER has been involved in the localization industry in a variety of roles since 1987. He is the founder and director of the Localisation Research Centre (LRC) at the University of Limerick, the editor of *Localisation Focus—The International Journal for Localisation,* a founding editor of the *Journal of Specialised Translation (JosTrans),* a founder and CEO of The Institute of Localisation Professionals (TILP), and a member of the OASIS Technical Committees on the XML-based Localisation Interchange File Format (XLIFF) and Translation Web Services (Trans-WS). He is a lecturer at the Department of Computer Science and Information Systems (CSIS) at the University of Limerick.

CATHERINE F. SMITH is Professor of English/Technical and Professional Communication at East Carolina University and Adjunct Professor of Public Policy at the University of North Carolina-Chapel Hill. She is author of *Writing Public Policy: A Practical Guide to Communicating in the Policy Making Process* (Oxford University Press, 2005). Research interests: risk and hazard communication, public policy communication, professional communication in government, and political discourse analysis.

JAN H. SPYRIDAKIS is a Professor in the Department of Technical Communication at the University of Washington where she teaches courses on style in writing, research methodology, and international and advanced technical communication. Her research focuses on document and screen design variables that affect comprehension and usability, cross-cultural audiences, and the refinement of research methods. She has a special interest in Internet-based research. She has published numerous articles and received many publication and teaching awards; she is a member of IEEE and also a Fellow of the Society for Technical Communication.

MICHAËL STEEHOUDER is the chair of Technical and Professional Communication at the University of Twente, Enschede, The Netherlands. His research interests include the design of procedural instructions, user support, and rhetorical aspects of technical communication. He published over 150 articles in Dutch and international journals, and textbooks on professional communication skills, forms design, and software manuals. Michaël is past president of STIC, the Dutch society for technical communication, member of the Administrative Committee of the IEEE Professional Communication Society, and associate editor of *IEEE Transaction on Professional Communication.* He was awarded with the Ronald S. Blicq Award for Distinction in Technical Communication Education in 2006.

JUDITH STROTHER, an Associate Member of IEEE, is Professor of Applied Linguistics and Chair of the graduate program in Technical and Professional Communication at Florida Institute of Technology.

DALE L. SULLIVAN is Professor of English and Department Head at North Dakota State University. He has been a member of the graduate faculties at Michigan Technological University, The University of Nebraska at Kearney, Northern Illinois University, The University of Minnesota, and North Dakota State University.

FLOOR VAN HOREN is a plain language consultant. She is also a copywriter and a teacher of plain language.

CAROLYN WEI is a user experience researcher at Google where she studies users of social applications. She received her PhD in Technical Communication at the University of Washington in 2007. Her research interests include computer-mediated communication, mobile phones, and emerging markets.

ATSUKO K. YAMAZAKI is Associate Professor at the Institute of Technologists, Japan, where she teaches English and Japanese communication in the fields of science and engineering, teaches computer programming, and conducts research in the areas of professional communication and the simulation of adaptive behavior. She has held leadership positions in JACET, is a member of the Japanese Society for Artificial Intelligence (JSAI), and is Guest Investigator at Woods Hole Oceanographic Institution in the United States. Her work has been published by Elsevier, CRC Press, IEEE, JSAI, JALT, JACET, and others.

Index

For details on these titles from Baywood's Technical Communications Series,
visit http://baywood.com.

ONLINE EDUCATION
Global Questions, Local Answers
Kelli Cargile Cook and Keith Grant-Davie

—— Winner of the 2006 NCTE award for Best Collection of Essays ——
in Technical or Scientific Communication

POWER AND LEGITIMACY IN TECHNICAL COMMUNICATION
Volume I: The Historical and Contemporary Struggle
for Professional Status
Editors: Teresa Kynell-Hunt and Gerald J. Savage

POWER AND LEGITIMACY IN TECHNICAL COMMUNICATION
Volume II: Strategies for Professional Status
Editors: Teresa Kynell-Hunt and Gerald J. Savage

TWISTED RAILS, SUNKEN SHIPS
The Rhetoric of Nineteenth Century Steamboat and Railroad
Accident Investigation Reports, 1833-1879
R. John Brockmann

VISUALIZING TECHNICAL INFORMATION
A Cultural Critique
Lee E. Brasseur

EXPLODING STEAMBOATS, SENATE DEBATES
AND TECHNICAL REPORTS
The Convergence of Technology, Politics and Rhetoric
in the Steamboat Bill of 1838
R. John Brockmann

EXPLORING THE RHETORIC OF INTERNATIONAL
PROFESSIONAL COMMUNICATION
An Agenda for Teachers and Researchers
Editors: Carl R. Lovitt and Dixie Goswami

THE EMERGENCE OF A TRADITION
Technical Writing in the English Renaissance, 1475-1640
Elizabeth Tebeaux

PUBLICATIONS MANAGEMENT
Essays for Professional Communicators
Editors: O. Jane Allen and Lynn H. Deming